THE LIGHT OF COMMON DAY

BORN Lady Diana Manners, the youngest child of the 8th Duke of Rutland, Lady Diana Cooper became famous as a great socialite between the wars and during her marriage to Duff Cooper—the politician, writer and first Viscount Norwich—whose wife she became in 1919.

This is the second part of her three-volume autobiography, in which she dwells on her years as an actress and Duff Cooper's career as a politician. But these are also times which overflow with events of historic significance—the General Strike, the death of King George V in 1936 and the German invasion of Poland—ending in the outbreak of the "dreaded war". *The Light of Common Day* combines a first-hand account of a crucial period of British history alongside events of personal importance—such as the birth of John Julius Norwich in 1929—and offers fascinating insights into the lives of the British aristocracy. For the social whirl continues despite the unholy times and includes literary figures such as Hilaire Belloc and Evelyn Waugh.

Lady Diana Cooper's autobiography consists of a previous and a subsequent volume, *The Common Years* and *Trumpets from the Steep* and is available as a boxed set. The author lives in London in the aristocratic bohemia of Little Venice.

The Light
of Common Day

AUTOBIOGRAPHY

DIANA COOPER

CENTURY PUBLISHING
LONDON

LESTER & ORPEN DENNYS DENEAU
MARKETING SERVICES LTD
TORONTO

© Rupert Hart-Davis, 1959

All rights reserved

First published in Great Britain in 1959 by
Rupert Hart-Davis Ltd

This edition published in 1984 by
Century Publishing Co. Ltd,
Portland House, 12–13 Greek Street, London WIV 5LE

ISBN 0 7126 0956 3

Published in Canada by
Lester & Orpen Dennys Deneau Marketing Services Ltd,
78 Sullivan Street, Ontario, Canada

*The cover shows a detail of Boxing in the
Park from Art-Gout-Beauté*

Reprinted in Great Britain by
Richard Clay (The Chaucer Press) Ltd, Bungay, Suffolk

The Rainbow comes and goes,
And lovely is the Rose . . .

At length the Man perceives it die away,
And fade into the light of common day . . .

The Cataracts blow their trumpets from the steep,
No more shall grief of mine the season wrong . . .

WORDSWORTH
*Ode (Intimations of Immortality from
Recollections of Early Childhood)*

Contents

The Light of Common Day

CHAPTER ONE

The Miracle

IN November 1923, with a high heart, unaccustomed courage, a certain confidence in my new vocation, and the splendid vision of *The Miracle* no longer a mirage, I boarded the pretty dancing *Aquitania* for my first ocean journey. Duff was by my side and in my heart, so everything delighted and excited us—the fine big cabin, the bath with fresh and sea water, the springing decks and space, the interminable menus, the orchestra and the bustle, the cupboard-trunks, bouquets and radiograms, but through the delight and excitement flitted the sinister shade of the *Titanic*. I felt something of a Columbus too. In 1923 not so many of my English friends had crossed the Atlantic, and we were farewelled as though for circumnavigation, with Fortnum & Mason provisions, cases of champagne, prayers, telegrams and a bevy of friends to speed us well at Southampton. On the third day it got rough, the *Titanic* shadow loomed darker and I suffered fearful shame when Duff took me to the ship's kind doctor that he might prescribe some calmative. He handed me bromide with a look of contemptuous pity. "I suppose there are any amount of frightened people like me?" I said hopefully. "Sometimes a few emigrants in the hold," he replied.

Duff was sympathetic, so it did not matter. The bromide did not calm, but the waves did. We threw ourselves into the amusing novelty of life on a big liner—auctions, hat-pools, and horses and camels in the gymnasium. Halfway over, radiograms began fluttering in from friends in America. Less welcome ones arrived from newspapers, and formidable ones from Morris Gest, warning me of the pressmen at Quarantine and suggesting replies that I should give to difficult questions. This made me nervous, as some of the instructions, I saw on reading, I could not obey. To the question: "Who is to be the first to play the Madonna?" I was to answer: "I am," and to the supplementary "How did I know?" "Because I had had a message from God."

I naturally replied, when they asked me, that I had no idea who would be the Madonna. I only knew that I had been engaged first. The cameras clicked away and the "Just one more"'s seemed to have no end, but I did not then mind what I now abhor, and I had confidence in being well dressed by Madame Ospovat (the Russian designer of genius who had become famous in London overnight), though in the photographs of those days I look grotesque. On the quay stood Chaliapin and Morris Gest, who pinched Chaliapin's cheek in greeting. This seemed too familiar to Chaliapin, loud words were said in Russian and a quickly forgotten blow administered. Beloved Kommer was there to pour essential oils on us all, and soon we were installed in our beautiful suite at the Ambassador Hotel, with a Bible each by our beds and the crystal New York sky a background to our high-perched luxury. It was Sunday and as quiet as a trafficless town can be. There were no orchids for me, but for Duff a case of Scotch and another of Bourbon whisky from Cole Porter, and also the key of Carroll Carstairs's liquor-locker at the Knickerbocker Club, with which to fight Prohibition. Duff went down to explore while I unpacked. He came up to say that he had met George Gordon Moore in the lift and that we were supping with him that night.

So much for the pre-war London stories that he could not show his face in New York.

At five o'clock I was to be ready for rehearsal. First we must have lunch, and gape and marvel at the canyons of architecture. We went to a restaurant on Fifth Avenue— Pierre's—shy as bumpkins and feeling lost and foreign. Duff was asked if he would have tea or coffee with his lunch. He all but collapsed. Kommer fetched me for my ordeal. I had made a Nun's rehearsal-dress to give me a little confidence, but I was very frightened. We drove to a vast unheated hall. It was freezing outside, and there was a big brazier of live charcoal, round which cowered some fifty shiverers, while another fifty or so were being rehearsed. Reinhardt strolled in, calm, with cigar-smoke curling round his magnificent brow and light compassionate eyes. I knew only him and Kommer, and it was to take me a little time to learn the rest of them. Luckily no one seemed in the least interested in my arrival. Maria Carmi was not due in New York for another three or four weeks. "Stand here, Miss Manners," said Mr West, a stage-manager. So I stood there on a chair, suddenly very, very happy. I had come back to what I was used to—rehearsals and stage jargon and the palpitating interest of "shop."

The Nun in *The Miracle* is as important a part as the Madonna, and from the day of this production's inception stars and beginners were praying and hustling to be given it. But it was an amateur who won it. Crossing the ocean a few weeks earlier, Reinhardt had noticed a magnificent young girl of eighteen, returning from buying her debutante's trousseau in Paris. She was Rosamond Pinchot, daughter of Amos and niece of Governor Pinchot. She was rich, very beautiful, athletic, with a coltish grace and a strange face belonging to valleys and hills rather than gilded rooms and dance-bands. She had never thought of the stage, but she agreed, encouraged by her parents, to take the part of the Nun. Reinhardt was proud of his choice and became prouder as Rosamond was moulded by him into perfection. She was too busy rehearsing to pay any attention to me. I felt myself lucky in being allowed to stand and wait, learn the music and lose my fears.

Morris Gest knew well what he was doing when he engaged two women to play one part. The production was so enormous, and the turning of the Century Theatre into a cathedral so mighty a conversion, that the rehearsals and building took six weeks longer than anticipated. Publicity had to be kept explosive, and what better way than to build up a story of the Lion and the Unicorn? I found it dreadfully disagreeable, and there were days when the headlines made me threaten and even want to go home. Duff would be leaving me very soon, and Maria Carmi had declared that she would not rehearse in front of me. Advisers and friends seemed to think that to play on the first night was essential to my fame, and they finally persuaded Duff to have a showdown with Morris Gest. It failed completely. Duff asked for a guarantee that I should have the lead and not become the understudy, without which he threatened to take me back to England. What hope had he with these seasoned theatre-sharks? Fobbed off with a "Trust me" and a leering wink from Gest, he sailed away, leaving me, in tears, to my fate. I felt ill with misery and fears, always fears, of immediate peril on the sea, of time and space, and the height of New York. Only the studio made it bearable. Letters tell more truthfully and more keenly the unhappiness than memory does, and mine for six months are an unpardonable jeremiad, a daily Gummidge-whine:

THE LION AND THE UNICORN

New York

I got home at five, having had my poor nut washed. I looked so dejected that the barber said "Poor kid." A lady had a hare-lip. It illustrated how foreign we feel in America and I felt surprised that there should be hare-lips here.

9 December 1923

I slept on my sofa, to be awakened an hour later by very noisy newsboys. I felt that they must be shouting an Atlantic disaster and worked myself up naughtily.

10 December

Your wireless today more to my liking in words than I could have prayed for. Those wretched newsboys I wrote of yesterday were screaming disaster, and darling Wadey on her despised eighteenth floor had the same panic as I had.

I lunched in a funnier, still cheaper place than Child's. You take a long look at all the eggs, meat, fish, veg in appetising concoctions, you pick and carry your dish off to an armchair with one elephantine spatulate arm on which you place your plate, glass and utensils. I chose corned beef hash, a big sugar cake and a glass of milk (20 cents). I'm so sad that I'll go and send you a cable. That sometimes helps.

The radiograms from east, west and mid-ocean flashed daily. So did the letters. We studied departures and arrivals of ships, calculating their knots and hours to know when we might hope for a batch of letters.

I was learning from the master of masters and falling in love with him, gaining confidence and making friends in and out of the theatre. The rehearsals lasted until 4 a.m., but did not begin until the afternoon. The great barrack hall got colder as the Christmas snow blocked the streets, and the brazier glowed less adequately. To see imagination fashion material with nature's prodigality astounded me as might a real miracle. *The Miracle*, having no script and no stage-directions, had to be designed as it grew. The story was a legend, and the gathering of it together was claimed by Karl Vollmöller, but it was Reinhardt who carved it into its Gothic-Freudian shape, selecting and discarding and inventing. Werner Krauss, the famous German actor who played the Spielmann or Power of Evil, built his own part with an ebullience of graven stones and gargoyles and arches that bridged to Good. He was the central pillar. He had the roof to bear and carried it on dancing feet, an unbowed Atlas, for which responsibility he claimed a bottle of spirits and two of wine daily—not an easy assignment in spite of *The Miracle*'s private bootlegger.

11 December

I breathe prayers for you incessantly, even when thinking of other things. "My Mummy" sails today. I shall have to pray for her too. O dear, O damn!

I feel discouraged with my part and think that I have gone back, due to never being rehearsed. They've got into a groove of "She's all right." I'm not. I dread to think of what "my Mummy" will say to the pressmen. She must have said at Southampton that I went on the pictures originally because of "desperate poverty." So all day the reporters have buzzed and shadowed me to discover what we call "poor." Oggie [Lynn] lands tomorrow.

Maria Carmi had arrived. In America she used her married name, Princess Matchabelli. She had been too obedient to the impresario's dictates and had said silly things to her interviewers.

12 December

Carmi refused to meet me. One rehearsal, she says, at which I must not be present, for fear (I suppose) that I might pick up some good business—a disappointment to me, as I had relied on doing so. I'm forbidden the studio in consequence. The cast's account is not favourable. She behaved very *grande dame*, stretched out a left hand to all the principals' mouths and put all their backs up . . .

I sent Oggie to have a look at Carmi. The cast is out to poison her. She looked savage, dressed completely in leopard, old but tall and thin. There are awful interviews in tonight's papers. She is referred to as "Royal" and she tells how God visited her and said "Play My Mother," and a lot about being Reinhardt's choice. Her ex-husband Vollmöller appeared tonight, the Miracle legend's ex-humer. He had travelled over on the same boat and not known that she was aboard. He's a German—specs and *Kultur*. He shocked and adulated me. I don't get his game.

As, on account of the Carmi competition, I was to play on alternate nights, the Pinchot family thought that their young daughter should be equally favoured (*I* considered the cutting down of my performances a disfavour). So the old search for another Nun began. There was a pen (not too near the brazier) where the postulants sat day after day, the discouraged giving place to new hopefuls. Ina Claire had hesitated at the gate, so had Marion Davies. As the opening night drew nearer and the Nun was still not chosen, it became easier for the directors to pick someone who knew the part perfectly, having heard and seen the tireless teaching and application of Reinhardt and Pinchot.

13 December

They worried me today about playing the Nun until I agreed to try it, on the condition that they would say without embarrassment and fear of hurting that I was unsuited. I'm glad I stood out and only gave in to the trial to get them out of their difficulties. I'll do it far better, I know, than the understudies they have tried, yet so much worse than Pinchot.

The parts of the Madonna and Nun lend themselves to doubling, since they are in one way the same.

I never had the potter's thumb to shape me to this part. I

came out cast from a mould and saved them all a lot of trouble, and there was plenty of trouble. The cathedral and stained-glass windows, the organ, the choir and the cloisters would not materialise on promised dates, and while the creators waited, better ideas crowded, jostled and fought with one another. Norman Bel Geddes, the scene-designer, Werner Krauss and Reinhardt were all three too rich in invention to tolerate satisfaction. Scenes, costumes, music and crowd-dispersals were made, unmade and remade. My attendant black shade these days took the shape of myself alone on the stage with the enemy audience in front. The thought of standing as a statue of the Madonna, motionless for an hour, held no fear, with nuns and crowds within moral reach, but to break my stony cerements *alone* and take upon myself life and movement, to walk down my niche's steps that wound through candles and reliquaries and votive offerings, my eyes raised to the high gothic arches, *alone*: this I could not contemplate without panic.

The under-stage-manager said today, staring at our cathedral set: "We got a cathedral in New York. I had a look at it. Fine it was. Did you ever see a cathedral, ma'am?" He also said about the ballet of nymphs which nearly ruins *The Miracle*: "I don't think it fits in. Lesbianism don't fit in. Fokine can't get away from Lesbianism." How staggering if these words had come from an English stage-hand!

Take care—if anything happens to you it happens to me.

It is natural for someone who has created a part to fight innovation. This Maria Carmi did tooth and nail. At Olympia she had been a sitting waxen figure, brocaded and jewelled. The new statue was a standing fourteenth-century Virgin, with Child held high in one hand. Maria Carmi was a beautiful Italian, taller than me, experienced and seductive and elegantly

dressed. She was allowed to have her way at her own performance, spoiling our primitive atmosphere by baroque
flamboyance.

16 December

I've been to see my stone coat. Rather wonderful, the ghost
breaking through the slab and cerements rather than the laden
graceful Lady of Lourdes. I can't of course stoop to pick up the
foundling Christ, which destroys the part, so Vollmöller may veto
unyielding folds. The idea is to have the prisms streaming through
the stained-glass windows round the theatre onto all the statues but
me, so that when the moment of incarnation comes there will be
true astonishment.

My mother had arrived for several months, perhaps never in
her life so happy, beloved by the entire cast, eating prawns and
rice pudding with me at drugstores, up all night, and for ever
drawing in the darkened studio, with an electric flash-pencil,
the groupings and gestures of the actors.

To the studio at 8. I did nothing until 11.30 when Otto Kahn
and Paul Cravath arrived, so the last act was turned on and I did
it so abominably that I dared not talk to anybody after it was
over. My nerves were pouring icy sweat and tripping me over
my long skirt, my knees jelly. I have been dejected since. What
will the first night rouse in me if Otto Kahn can so much damage
my faint heart? Mother had "high strikes" at rehearsal this morning over her daughter's "art and beauty." Very embarrassing it
was.

Reinhardt, Gest, Krauss, old Schildkraut and Kommer came to
me for a definite answer as to whether I would play the Nun. I've
said that I'll *try*, so tomorrow I start with Richard Boleslawsky
of the Moscow Art Theatre. I'm over-excited, over-tired and very
frightened, but I must venture. It's good for me—anti-lethargy,
anti-phat. I hope you will be pleased and not think I'm making a
fool of myself.

THE MIRACLE

I read these letters with surprise. Why was I not overjoyed and glowing with hope and thankfulness?

22 December

Third week over. I was so happy this morning. The *Leviathan* choked up its mail without delay and from its belly came the loveliest, longest, most satisfying letter from you, full of adventure and love, and a poem. My head was aching with apprehension. The relief numbed it for an hour when I trudged off to the Russian's studio. I plodded for three hours pouring with sweat, as black as a sweep, trying to master the last scene where the Nun returns from the storm with her dead baby. The Crawling Order. Master it I did, but Lord knows how an amateur feels! One moment of certainty to ten of bewilderment. At two we sat down to a real Russian lunch—one Boleslawsky, one German pianist and four stray Russians. No plates, two saucers, a huge semi-carved cold turkey, a samovar, lemon, a loaf of bread, a knife, no other utensils, no excuses. My migraine was worsening, so I walked to the hotel for medicine and brought them back a bottle of gin. They were mad with joy. I should never have drunk it. My rich visitors can do without.

Another three hours' work, thinking every time I stopped that I was going to die—heart and head throbbing wrong. (I believe it's lack of stimulant that is killing me.) I staggered back to the main rehearsal and reported to Reinhardt that I had mastered a scene in base but accurate imitation of Pinchot. He was horrified and said that I mustn't be in the least like Rosamond. Ecstatic I must be, not animal. (How am I to be ecstatic, I wonder?) So all today will have been wasted. Everybody was worn out and peevish, so a pause was called until tomorrow. Make everyone who can pray for me. Tell Maurice, Belloc, Polly Cotton, Katharine and all the Mariolaters to burn me candles and entrust me to Our Blessed Lady.

Christmas in 1923 was already commercialised, ablaze with electric trees, pretty green window-wreaths, obscene Santas and deafening carols in the shops. I had my mother and Olga Lynn as symbols of home.

KNEE-CAPS FOR PRAYING

Olga hung a stuffed stocking on my bed that held a diamond guard ring, a bottle of rare scent, a cigarette-case and shagreen box, silk stockings and chiffon handkerchiefs. In return I had nothing for her. It's terrible. . . . I've hated Christmas—my occupation gone. I long for tomorrow when rehearsals are resumed. They alone are strenuous enough to numb my achings for you.

I never tired at rehearsals, and they grew to last almost the clock round. A new and dear friend, Bertram Cruger, became my nurse and playmate. He would bring me sandwiches and hot coffee in cardboard containers at 3 a.m. and be sympathetic with my panics and self-dissatisfaction. He believed in the play and had no fears, but I knew him already for an incurable optimist.

I got up early and went to a smart sports shop to buy knee-caps so that I may now do "praying, much praying" and falling on my joints without so much pain.

We cannot get into the theatre yet. They have forbidden fires in the studio and altogether things are so unsatisfactory and stale that they gave me my freedom for twenty-four hours or more. I dashed home to bed. My Mummy also in bed with what Holbrook calls "potmaine" poisoning.

Letters tell of perpetual postponement, and every day lost was added to our separation, since the contract was for sixteen weeks of performance. The cathedral-theatre had to be made in such a way that the public, before and after the performance, could walk about as they do at Chartres. The proscenium arch was scrapped; there was no curtain, and chancel-steps led to the high altar; the pillars were not merely façades; the stalls were turned into pews. There were aisles and side-aisles, a resounding organ and, round the whole, gothic stained-glass windows. It could not be ready in time. The days dragged leadenly for us. Only the public were kept on the alert for news of the two stars fighting to win the lead. As the dread night drew nearer Maria Carmi, who sensed that she was to play second, suggested to Kommer an arrangement that would save her face. A reconciliation was to take place before the press and photographers. Our names were to be put into a hat and a little child should draw lots. The first name would be the first Madonna's. To me it sounded a common solution, and Kommer made it less savoury by telling me that the draw was to be cooked and that I was the winner designate.

3 January 1924

I'm battered and bruised as the pulp of an old medlar from Nun rehearsals. At 4 the telephone rang rudely and a peremptory message told me to be at the studio by 5. I rang up Kommer for an explanation. He admitted that it was to meet Carmi and draw the contemptible lots. I said that nothing would drag me out of bed. I disapproved anyway. K. oiled me down and said that Reinhardt minded as much as I did and yet was bowing to the circumstances. So I fetched up at a very disgraceful séance. For our first meeting no one was present but Gest, Reinhardt, de Weerth and Kommer, twenty-four photographers and pressmen. Carmi arrived, terribly flash in black and diamonds, with a left hand's languid greeting. I felt my Cinderellaism overdone and was horrified by her youth and beauty, height and elegance. She was the woman of the world to my shabby and awkward bumpkin. Her first words were *"Ora la commedia è finita."* Mine was *"Spero,"* which I hope she took wrong. We were then photographed. My spirit was fainting and flaring up alternately. The little child was looked for. We waited and waited. No little child and no time to waste, so Kommer must draw the lot instead, Kommer so much lighter-fingered to pick the prize for me. Just at the moment of drawing Carmi said: "Stop! Before we draw I would like to say that if you *want* the first night so badly I will give it to you. I protested because I created the part, but I will give it to you." I was speechless and forgetful that she was guarding herself against certain failure, and it seemed to me for a moment generously fine. The cameras clicked, and a great lump gathered in my throat,

so I couldn't answer anything except "I don't want the first night."
Kommer's sensitive hand drew out my name. I felt debased by the
beastliness of it all, and raged that I should have to suffer the embarrassment and humiliation of cheating in this country that can't
paint a good production without framing it in glistening mud.
They all made it worse still by congratulating me, including Carmi,
the tears coursed down my silly old cheeks, and to cap it all Gest
said: "You're so 'uman, dear." I felt that I wanted to behave dra-
matically like the Nun and cover my ears and face with my hands
and arms, so I found a screened-off corner and sobbed and sulked
until Reinhardt and Kommer came and soothed me, both a little
ashamed of the proceedings.

4 January

First day of the theatre. Its scaffolding is down. Carmi was
there with her axe buried. She put Reinhardt in a rage (my docility
has spoilt him) and he told me and Pinchot not to act, but only to
mark time before her. The stone coat will be stunning. Pinchot's
father says that my performance of the Nun is "bully."

5 January

Tonight five terrible days of dress rehearsals began. Worse than
I thought. The clothes, I fear, may ruin all. Bel Geddes doesn't
know about movement. His cathedral is sublime, but his clothes
(like my stone coat) are carapaces, cancelling movement and grace.
Krauss lost his temper about his costume. Pinchot and the designer quarrelled permanently, I think because she is too young and
rude to forgive the rude, tired and anxious. Schildkraut raged
round because his dressing-room isn't on the stage. Mine isn't fit
to trap a rat in, but I keep my trap shut. Kommer went further
than I've ever heard him in uncalm when he said that he couldn't
be in two places at once. Reinhardt said: "*Weiter, weiter, de Weerth,
weiter, weiter*" with infinitely weary rage in his lovely voice. Bel
Geddes took to not answering to his name and leaving the building.
Pinchot cried unceasingly. I had a very bad cold but enjoyed every
minute of it until 4 a.m.

Now I'm in bed with a newly-opened telegram of congratulation and wishes for personal success from unknown Lyn Harding! The English on alien soil cling pathetically close. I'm tired, tired. I've put some stinking embrocation all over my chest, and onto that I've clapped Thermogene smouldering wool, and I'm burning like a crater. I do need you here to laugh at me.

7 January

Cold worse. Nothing but drugs, sweat, dope and poultice. Mother just as bad. Got up for rehearsal. Carmi so difficult that she has been banished for this week. Pinchot's nose bled at 4, so she left (dressed) for home and with great courage re-dressed when it stopped and took her place until 5.30 a.m. Bertram Cruger is my buckler and staff. He never fails in tender services—coffee in cartons, waiting until all hours. I'm lucky he loves me.

Great depression follows last rehearsals, known no doubt to all actors. Clothes have spoilt everything, so has the set with its unnecessary steps and stairs, pillars and properties, all so much better in the studio. After all, simplicity is of the first importance. No props, no pretence. There is only one prop that matters and that is the Holy Child. I can't get one made that doesn't look like a foetus, and no one listens to me because I don't have to work in with the others and therefore need not be reckoned with. All these contorting nervous fears and fatigue breed terrors of other kinds, never properly under restraint.

5 a.m. I'm just in. I had a miserable bowel-aching day because of no answer to my cable to you. I know myself foolish and tried not to let my fears flame, but they did. So I sent another wire asking Holbrook how you fared.

12 January

Nauseated with misery. *Miracle* worse than ever. Everything wrong, me included, and nothing ready. Now they've "braced" my stone coat with steel, and I can't get in or out. I'm just home, having had my back broken by Krauss's straw. He caught me in my dressing-room looking utterly woebegone. We groaned together in pidgin German, and he told me how ten years ago a German novelist had written a book with Reinhardt as the hero. It told of his rise to fame, and in the end this artist-producer goes to a *fremdes Land* and there he creates what is to be the crown of his genius—a super-colossal production. The night comes and gradually the audience starts hissing and whistling. I felt faint and had to sit down. He then told me that he thought of taking flight tomorrow. He couldn't face it, he said. He must escape. He is so sadistic that he may have done all this to watch me writhe. He certainly succeeded and I hope felt better. My desperation is in the best theatre tradition and a better augury than satisfaction. Bertram has managed, against all precedents, to get admittance to the rehearsals, so he is always there to any hour. He runs out and buys me milk, and telephones and gets Mother a doctor, and once he even produced a bottle of champagne because Oggie told him to.

15 January

Two lines to take you my love and tell you that it's all over and successful. I dread tomorrow's papers. A few contretemps ruined my hopes. I say: "He'll be proud of me" when the ordeal of immobility seems unbearable.

The press was very good to me. I was not then or ever very anxious to read reviews, and when I did steel myself to the task, however glowing the praise, I felt it insufficient.

16 January

All day I tried to get a rehearsal with the finished stone coat, a necessity that I had never managed. I got it one hour before the bells clanged, summoning New Yorkers to church. The bells are tremendous and ring for half an hour. The coat needs a week's practice to perfect the carrying round of it (me enclosed) in the finale. This scurrying didn't add to my peace.

I got on to the stage ten minutes before the play was advertised to begin—already an improvement. As originally planned and rehearsed I was to be in place when the doors opened. Now, with locomotor ataxy legs I merge in (black-cloaked) among a knot of nuns and glide behind the church banner that conceals the holy statue. Behind it I wriggle into my carapace and put on my crown and am handed the Holy Child. What was my horror when they handed me (surreptitiously as rehearsed) a new impossible baby made of snow-white unpainted papier-mâché, a three-year-old, huge and unholdable. I whispered my rage to the praying nuns and in time got the property Child I was accustomed to, with no hole in its poor side to hold it by. The rest went well enough until the last touching moment when I break for a minute out of the stone into the animate to gather up the Nun's brat, miraculously transfigured by death into the infant Christ. There again lay, in Death's skeleton hand, the enormous obscene repudiated abortion, glowing with inner electricity connected by a white umbilical cord. I managed somehow to grasp it and was surprised that my stone folds held my rage in bounds. Once "off" I lost my temper as no temperamental prima donna has ever done. It was a vile surprise and ruined the end from an artistic point of view. I was too cross to enjoy the fifteen minutes' applause and the chancel banked up with flowers and felt outraged at being forced to take calls. A Madonna should not. Geddes threw a faint in the wings and remained for an hour unconscious. Reinhardt cried.

Today I think that I hate the profession. Rehearsing is heaven, but acting too painful. Tomorrow I rehearse the Nun with Carmi. Next day I act it, so fears are without end. So are the dangers, since they've jammed all the exits with extra chairs.

Duff received the following telegram from C. B. Cochran:

WIFE'S PERFORMANCE EXQUISITELY BEAUTIFUL UNQUESTIONABLE WORK OF SENSITIVE ARTIST WITH MANY INDIVIDUAL SUBTLETIES THE RESULT OF THOUGHT AND COMPLETE MASTERY OF RARE RESOURCES.

Our friend Valentine Castlerosse wrote:

I am really writing to you about Diana. My dear Duff, she's too magnificent. I can't describe how superb she is. There are only a certain number of superlatives. . . . I saw her as the Nun. I was really overcome.

I went with Charles B. Cochran (of London). You remember that he was the first man to produce *The Miracle*. He told me before we started that he didn't think he'd enjoy it as he was prejudiced:

(1) against anything but dyed-in-the-wool professionals;
(2) because he had seen Miss Pinchot and thought the show anyway well inferior to his own production.

We arrived late and that's all wrong. Before I'd been there three minutes I was gasping—really minding what was happening. Forgot the theatre, forgot New York, women, cards and Prohibition, the market, forgot everything but was rivetted (how many ts are there?). There was no nonsense. I have never been so carried away and you know that *The Miracle* is Diana. It is ridiculous for me to try and describe the effect that Diana has on this enormous crowd. She holds them tight, tortures them, frightens them. The audience groan and writhe. One very soon forgets it's a play.

I dripped with emotion. Cochran did the same. I was delighted. His voice shook. He said that Diana was the finest actress he had ever seen. Diana is bored to death and very homesick, but there— her performance puts her in the class of the immortals. I can't describe everything in detail. I thought it wonderful. I fancy though that without Diana one's rather cynical subconscious self would assert itself. She lifts the whole thing into the sublime.

I wrote to Duff on 25 January:

Again all over. I must be a pretty good actress. It was frightening and flurrying because of the quick changes. One feels like "Any more Dickens characters?" and the man who dives into a mirror and comes up with Pickwick's bald head or Fagin's nose. Reinhardt thought *"Unser Vater"* very good—*"eine so süsse Stimme."* For my part, like past childbirth's pain, I cannot remember how it came, except that I used the American "as we forgive those" as Pinchot does. We never thought that my rasp would be a *"süsse Stimme."*

26 January

My last excitement and last hope is over and successful. Now no more fright, and the acute longing for you and home is overpowering, yet only two weeks of the sixteen gone. It's sad that I should have my life's triumph without you, and you had yours in the war. Our real triumph is our happiness together after so many years ($4\frac{1}{2}$!).

The letters drone on. My mother weighed on me. She had had pneumonia and still coughed, and she could not rest or eat. The late theatre hours were her rest from everything disagreeable and, seeing me economising in the luxurious Ambassador Hotel and eating in drugstores, she overdid thrift and could not order an egg. She became desperately weak and her mind was on *The Miracle* only.

I went to a boot-shop, Mother with me. She lay in motionless coma while I tried on a hundred pairs. The owner of the business said he had heard that *The Miracle* was wonderful and that he was going one night. The word roused Mother from her coma (due to malnutrition) and she shouted "Not Mondays or Fridays" (Carmi's days) and relapsed again.

I've bought a glorious fur coat made of honey-coloured lamb or pony or maybe foxhound.

16 February

Had tea with good Schuyler Parsons. He promised me a coat for my old old Russian Volotskoy, once a Lord Chief Justice or a Sir Thomas Lipton or something of that kidney, who makes sixteen dollars a week in the crowd and speaks Academy French. When I asked him whether he had no better coat than the cotton one he wears, he said "*Pas précisément.*" Schuyler had pink-eye, so I didn't go in—just grabbed the coat and ran for it.

I went to a charity ball and was cheered to the echo. Then I sat in a box and was cheered again, and the limelight was thrown on me and I had to stand and bow. I thought I should die, yet I *should* have been so pleased. Many would have loved it.

Hoytie Wyborg, who with her sisters had taken London by storm in 1914, guided me gently through the New York mazes. Home and love sickness grew upon me with the weeks, though I had a lot to support me—a few new friends who would be lifelong and some old English ones. Valentine Castlerosse, a constant comfort and chuckle, lived in the same hotel. My mother was there for three months. She would not go home in spite of petitions. She was giving exhibitions of her pictures, and was happy day and night. Olga Lynn, a rip-roaring success in New York, was giving concerts in candle-lit drawing-rooms. Artur Rubinstein, already famous, was there, and Augustus John to paint Joe Widener. Sert was painting gloriously ebullient frescoes of Sinbad the Sailor for the Cosden house in Palm Beach. Kommer was ever near, trying to teach me German by reading Schnitzler's *Grüne Kakadu* while my mother drew us. Snow and rain fell, and fire-alarm sirens at night kept me awake. Central Park looked as dank as a prison-yard. I teased my poor friend Bertram about his country's shortcomings, his accent and his ice-creams, and he laughed at my English failings. We went a lot to silent films, in enormous sofa-stalls, and I would cry when I saw the King in his coach and tell Bertram that it was made of pure gold. He was patient and told me to wait for the spring to bring magnolias to Central Park and dogwood to the country.

In New York the streets were paved with gold. Everyone I knew of every class was flourishing, moving further west, getting a new radio set, buying a fur coat or a better car. I was used to our country "going to the dogs" and was incredulous and then fascinated to watch a story of success unfolding.

I love walking the streets. I passed a shop dedicated to dressing the very fat. "Stylish Stout Inc" it was called.
I thought I'd go and see Bob Chandler * in his big wandering

---

* Famous figure and inventor of art mediums. He married the beautiful Lina Cavalieri and on his wedding day received a telegram from his brother-in-law in a mental home which read " Who's loony now?"

house-workshop. Terrible smells, enough to anaesthetise one. Chandler still his old entertaining inaudible self, gay and alive. In his attic studio we found two old crony topers drinking neat whisky (a cat in a separate chair drawn up to the grog-tray), both boon companions fresh from inebriate homes, one for dropsy, the other for d.t.'s Bob asked a lot about you and kept repeating: "To think of you two bums marrying."

The nest-egg was being laid. After a struggle where I showed, to my surprise, an iron strength, I got another 150 dollars a week, and every extra matinée, of which there were many (one for Eleanora Duse, two or three for the profession—any excuse was jumped at) brought me fifty dollars more. Reprints of my old articles written by Duff, a testimonial for Pond's products and austere economy would lay a bigger egg. Besides, tours were already being planned, a silent film was to be made and a season in London was contemplated. The future was secure, but I refused to rejoice.

I have such fearful nights. It has to do with separation, of course. Odd, and I'm rather glad that it should get no better. I wake with a long anguished coming-to and a feeling of sinking death merged with nightmare dread, and a muddled recollection of anguish that makes my sleep-confused brain think that an omen of disaster to you has been sent me. This I can't throw off. It happens often.

Duff's daily letters were the opposite of mine, always cheerful, packed with affection, social life, quips and quotations from books that he was reading, poems, jokes, waiting for ships with letters, looking for constituencies, hoping for one at Melton Mowbray (soon snapped up by another candidate) and asking whether he would be wrong to leave the Foreign Office. Anyhow he was going to. Did I think he was right? I wrote:

What of your life's plans? You know that I've always been for throwing up the F.O. and now I suppose I can always make money should anything go wrong. We cannot spoil a magnificent ship for £1000 p.a. (taxed at that). Mr Strasburger says he'd gladly pay all your election expenses. Bear that in mind. Why should he?

Duff's determination hardened as several constituencies appeared and disappeared. There was no hurry. A General Election was not expected until the autumn. Meanwhile he could work and play and come to fetch me away when my contract ended. He sounded on admirable terms with my family, and wrote in reply to a suggestion that my mother should be sent for, as her happy life in New York was killing her:

I think your father is having a riotous time. He is putting down new pile carpet all over Arlington Street and re-covering the chairs. He has bought a Rolls Royce and is having the Duchess's car entirely remade. He has a luncheon party every day. It might also be thought that Sister Malony, who comes in at the end of every luncheon party looking quite pretty, very painted and beautifully dressed, is his mistress. Any outside observer would say that she was. Perhaps he will leave her everything.

I could not tell my mother this alarming news, so she stayed until her wife's conscience smote her in late April. Then Oggie developed chicken-pox (of course I thought that it was smallpox) and quarantine gave my mother an extra three weeks. Duff wrote in March:

There is the faintest shade of a breath of a ghost of a touch of spring in the air. How can I face the reality without you? From you I *cannot* be absent in the spring.

We were indeed both idolisers of spring. Already new plans and sailings were being studied. With half the term still to go a further shadow came to darken the gloom. The theatre asked for another month. The nest-egg would grow larger by 1800 pounds, but could I endure? Spring comes like a bounding hound in New York. Park Avenue wears a transfigured look. The sky is a glimmering crown. A few of my letters cheer up and see the funny side, and Duff writes scoldingly of my ingratitude to God, my fears, and above all my doubt of his fidelity. I must have taunted him with a familiar name used too often or, worse, an oft-repeated new Christian name. I doubted too his remaining staid as he had become since marriage, and feared a return to reckless living. He reproved me by a sonnet which, with the help of spring, strengthened me for a spell:

> Doubt not, brave heart, oh never dare to doubt,
>   Lest care and calumny should breed distrust,
>   Lest the fine steel of faith should gather rust,
> And we should lose what we were lost without.
> Our castle of delight is girt about
>   By envious allies, Jealousy, Disgust,
>   Weariness, Separation, Age and Lust,
> And still the traitor at the gate is Doubt.
>
> Mount guard with me, beloved; you and I
>   Will baffle our besiegers with disdain.
> The royal standard of our troth flies high
>   As e'er it flew, and shall not dip again;
> So all assaults shall only serve to prove
> Our faith impregnable, our changeless love.

and later:

17 March

I think your criticism of "allies" is right. All that line is bad. "Disgust" is nonsense. You might sometimes irritate but could never disgust me. Suppose we substitute:

PRAISE FROM STANISLAVSKY

Our citadel of light is girt about
With swords of darkness, allies of the dust,
Jealousy, Separation, Lies and Lust.

New York

Imagine my surprise when the manicurist of Jolies Mains gave me a rich man's card and told me that he had suggested that if I want any fun I should telephone him. "I know as you're acting the Madonna you have to behave circumspectly, but when you want to break out, just collect a bunch of girls and go round to his place. He'll give you a good time."

Yesterday I sat next Stanislavsky and Douglas Fairbanks. S. needed the French tongue and it wore me out. He told me his stage theories. They are so different to my practice that I got depressed.

Next day

Stanislavsky says that I'm a great artist. Tell Maurice to put that in his pipe and smoke it.

Jo Davidson the sculptor made a bust of me as the Madonna. I remember spring mornings (the magnolias out in a night) walking across Central Park in the electric air to his studio, Valentine Castlerosse sometimes with me. I would take my Bedlington terrier (looking more like a lamb than a dog) without the obligatory muzzle, and Irish Valentine would blanch and whimper with fear of the police arresting him as accomplice to this contempt of by-laws. Jo and I would cook hamburgers in the studio after the sittings, and we would laugh and I would forget to moan. Harrington Mann painted a lovely picture of my statue, and it stood in a Fifth Avenue window. In 1931 it was on an easel in the Drury Lane foyer, and I have never seen it since, any more than I have seen Jo's statue, or an ample baroque bust by the Belgian Rousseau, a life-size portrait by Sir John Lavery and several McEvoys. And then one is surprised at losing spectacles and railway tickets!

So long ago, but freshly remembered now, are the people and the houses of Long Island that used to spoil me, the bowers of dogwood, the green golf-courses (on which I never played), holding on to rails under leaning sails on the dashing Sound, and the natural hospitality that became dearer to me as their spring and my departure met. Gone were my glooms.

I think so much of your returning to me. I lie for hours making little arrangements of how I will go to Cunard's or the White Star and get a permit for Quarantine, and how I'll sneak up the gangway with the camera-men, and of what I'll wear (it will be May, warm and sunny). It makes me forget all my woes.

From now until Duff's arrival the letters throb with anticipation. There is no other theme. It might be war-leave over again. I was always happiest with the theatre people. I knew that I should have pangs when the cast broke up, but then *The Miracle* was born to be a phoenix, with no language to stamp out its fires. Already its pyres were built in two continents, and we all knew that we should be together again.

25 Apri

Such an affecting last evening at the theatre. They all took a long goodbye of Mother, and she cried and I felt a beast to let her go. I've just looked at her ticket. It's on F Deck and it will be some bolting-hutch of beastliness among the lower barnacles. My heart breaks for her leaving her last real fun in life and going back to monotony.

It's a blindingly radiant morning. Does that make it better or worse? Better, as it stimulates physically. Mother sat up until five, I hope not crying. Once she gets to Nantucket she'll start thinking of John's rheumatism and Caroline's glands and feel better.

Duff wrote from Brighton:

27 Apri

I came down here yesterday for Maurice [Baring]'s fiftieth birthday. There were fifty-two people to dinner—Hilary, Chesterton,

E. V. Lucas, Harry Preston, Bluey Baker, Squire, lots of sailors and airmen. Maurice made a speech in rhyme, Chesterton, Harry Preston and I in prose. Hilary says that he has written you six sonnets and sent them to Katharine to forward to you.

This letter is necessarily disjointed as it is being written in the smoking-room of the Royal York on the morning after. Everyone is sitting round drinking shandygaff, and fresh people keep coming in, and everyone says "What happened to you last night?" and "Do you remember when, etc." A hurricane is blowing. After dinner Maurice insisted on bathing. They all tried to stop him and there was a free fight on the beach. I said that he ought to be allowed to bathe if he wanted to and I fought on his side. He finally got into the water and an energetic sailor stripped stark naked and plunged in after him. He didn't stay in long. I brought him back and gave him a hot bath.

I see in *The Times* this morning that the Duchess of Rutland and Viscount Castlerosse have sailed on the *Majestic*. O to think that I shall be sailing on it next week! It seems too good to be true.

Suddenly time gallops. A ticket is bought for the *Majestic* (not the coveted and saucy *Aquitania*) and the radios crackle:

"GLAD NEWS ARRIVED. OVEREXCITED."

"BUSTLE UP I'M LONELY"

"FAIR WINDS SPEED YOU TO ME"

"O O THE WIND AND THE RAIN. I'M FRIGHTENED"

"I'M TOO IMPATIENT TO SLEEP"

It was now that Duff first saw me act. He was always, I think, a little afraid and embarrassed when watching me. I can understand the reason, but I find it impossible to define.

Belloc's six sonnets he brought with him, reluctantly sent by Katharine Asquith, who had inadvertently told me that Hilary was unhappy about my playing the Madonna. I could not blame him, and delighted in his explanation: "Lady Diana playing the part of Our Lady in America, the Poet gravely wished her another rôle, but hearing that Mrs Asquith had made him out rougher than he had in truth been, he wrote these ensuing." Five of the sonnets have been published; here is one of them:

Do not believe when lovely lips report
That I lost anchor in rough seas of jest,
Or turned, in false confusion manifest,
To pleading folly in high beauty's court;
Or said of that you do (which in the doing
You maim yourself) what things I could not say,
For dread of unassuaged remorse ensuing
On one light word which haunts us all our way.

That I grow sour, who only lack delight;
That I descend to sneer, who only grieve:
That from my depth I should contemn your height;
That with my blame my mockery you receive—
Huntress and splendour of the woodland night,
Diana of this world, do not believe.

In June we came back to Gower Street, and to Bognor and summer holidays with Juliet Duff and Venetia and the neighbouring Holdens. Duff burnt his boats and sent in his resignation to the Foreign Office. It seemed to him a terrible step to give up a profession that he had worked at for ten years, but he left without a pang of regret.

CHAPTER TWO

Dolls in Exile

IN July Oldham adopted Duff as a candidate. "The Plan" was no longer a blueprint. The elevation was rising. Together we returned to New York for *The Miracle*'s second opening. We crossed with the Prince of Wales and enjoyed the fêtes and follies of the polo season on Long Island. I must again suffer separation, but not for long, and I think of those autumn weeks of bright dyes in Long Island and New Jersey with calm and grateful remembrance. It was short-lived, for the election of 1924 was upon us, and Duff telegraphed from Oldham, where he was nursing the constituency, getting to know and be known, for me to join him. Morris Gest had agreed to liberate me in such a case, so I took the next boat and sailed with faithful Wade for English hustings.

When, in early October, I met Duff at Oldham the fight had begun, a three-cornered fight with two seats to be won. Duff was in great heart. My inner self (that has my shape, colour and features and is mercifully invisible) was bowed double with certainty of defeat and was making plans how best to comfort him. It was my first election, and that bent self was weighed down still further by its inadequacy and inability to speak on a platform. All Members' wives could speak fearlessly and glibly, and Joan Grigg, known to me since nursery days and now wife of Edward Grigg, the Liberal candidate, spoke without inhibition. Why should I be the exception? My family, quickening with admiration of Duff (now become the young Disraeli), had rallied in full force. My mother was there with my two sisters, a stray uncle, cousins and friends, Juliet Duff, Rosemary Ednam, Diana Westmorland, and Maurice Baring to take care of the Catholic vote—a good fighting force, all living at the Midland Hotel in Manchester. Oldham is some miles away, and at an early hour we reported daily to the Party's headquarters and were given our canvassing orders for the day. There was a luncheon break when we all met to exchange our morning's experiences. Though I did a good bit of canvassing, my place was more often by Duff's side touring the cotton-mills, visiting clubs and sitting tortured on the platform for three or four meetings every evening.

The first time that I heard Duff address his audience I thought that I must be dreaming or that he had learnt his speech by heart. The sensible sentences rolled out without hesitation. There was nothing flustered about his calm stance and clear delivery, his hands clasping the lapels of his coat in a classical nineteenth-century way. He carried no notes and did not fidget. The speech was colourful and when necessary passionate, the applause uproarious. The chairman, the councillors, even the over-anxious agent, were completely satisfied. I had never believed in Duff's powers of oratory. I knew him as a first-class actor of charades; dressed up as a judge with a white fox for a wig, he could deliver a summing-up to make a gay party cry with laughter. But this was different, and here he was as serious as a real judge and bound (I immediately felt certain) to gain every vote in the constituency. I saw too the reason for my mother's different tone towards the Family's new Pride. The situation shone like noontide.

Elections are detestable when the candidate is one's all. It is interesting and amusing to work for a stranger or a friend in whose principles one believes, but canvassing at all times I find miserably disagreeable—the knock on the door and the housewife's unpredictable mood, influenced by whether she has the dinner or the high tea in the making, is wringing linen or having a nap. Her head is poked out of the door, and if she recognises the Party she favours she will open it wider, dry her hands and say: "Come forward." She may be ready to talk about politics and wages, or she may say: "We've always voted Blue and always shall." She may ask questions showing an unmade-up mind or she may (this I found more often with Liberal and Labour people) take refuge behind the secrecy of the ballot. I marvelled when they did not bang the door in our silly, smirking, out-to-please faces. Some did (the militant Labourites naturally, since the fight was joined), for indeed canvassing is an uncivilised intrusion into any man's house and into the privacy of his views. I think that perhaps I am wrong to be so sensitive. Lancashire people are almost alone in their directness, their disinterested loyalty and uprightness. They have pride in these qualities and much warmth and humour. The warmth is real; they never dissemble. They take this canvassing intrusion as normal to election time. They have said to me with hurt regret: "No one's been down our street. We're neglected. I've opened door to no one." Behind their uniform lace curtains they would press me to "a cup of tea, luv?" and offer "ornaments" (whisky or rum) to improve it.

Lancashire girls are very pretty. The damp climate and the damper mills, kept hot and humid for the cotton-yarn, give their complexions an unusual pink-and-white clarity. In those days they all wore gay clattering clogs and thick grey woollen shawls that protected them from crown to knees from the foggy cold. I loved the mills because the girls mobbed me and kissed me and thought me funny. I promised them a clog dance if they put my husband in, which I later performed as best I could. Duff summed it all up in *Old Men Forget*:

The combination of anxiety and tedium is very trying. The solitary subject of conversation, to which, however hard one may try to avoid it, one always returns, the good ideas which suddenly strike one's supporters, their hopes and fears and petty quarrels, the rumours of one's opponents' successes, the one thing that should have been done and has been forgotten, the great mistake that has been made and that it is too late to rectify, the vast accumulation of daily annoyances culminating in the evening's speeches, which are followed by sleepless nights of pondering over possibly unwise utterances, all these build up an atmosphere of nightmare through which the distant polling day shines with promise of deliverance.

While the tellers tell nothing and impassively count the votes from the secret boxes, one can but be idle for several hours and watch the opponents' piles of voting-cards grow higher than one's own. One must practise changing one's glower to a forced grin, and pray for enough grace to shake the enemy's hated hand and tell him that the best man had to win. But at last the count was declared and announced to the seething crowd outside the Town Hall, and the laurels were for Duff, head of the poll, a few hundred votes ahead of Edward Grigg, the Liberal, and with a majority of 13,000 over Labour.

The next shining morning we motored to my old homes in the Midlands, first to Haddon Hall, now inhabited by my brother John and his wife, where joy was unrestrained, and then on to Belvoir, where my father was waiting at the door to congratulate the first man of the family since his own father's day who was to devote his life to the country's government. Surprise of surprises, we were lodged in the King's Rooms, with our private drawing-room. It was a proud day for me.

There were few weeks in which to relish Duff's fruits of

triumph. *The Miracle* called me for its opening in Cleveland, Ohio. It had drawn peacefully to its New York close, and Reinhardt himself was to re-create it in Cleveland's gigantic Hall. I found it good to be back. The cast had not changed noticeably, but the great Krauss had returned to Germany. Though I loved and admired him dearly, it was restful not to have to overcome daily and nightly the double ordeal of acting with heart and conscience for the public and fighting waves of rage and barely suppressed laughter at his twists and pranks, his baitings and relentless determination to unbalance me. Tiredness unbalanced me too.

13 December 1924

I was exhausted yesterday as I got onto what Morris Gest calls my "pillow." I thought how dreadful it would be to faint. It was upon me already. Followed a ghastly struggle not to collapse. It lasted perhaps twenty minutes—first sick, then that livid sensation of wet cold quicksilver running slowly over one. I prayed desperately to the Virgin. I bit the inside of my cheek and tasted the blood. I made ventriloquist noises, but only the Spielmann came near and said "*Was?*" I couldn't explain, not in German. Then the stage cleared—only Pinchot running like a stag to her music. She heard but could do nothing, and I thought of you in the Great War and my knees buckled under me. I clung on by my neck in the stiff coat and thought wildly what would be best to do—walk out of my stone and ruin the play or wait for loss of consciousness and fall, breaking my neck or skull and certainly spiking my eyes on the hundred electric candle-spikes. The audience swayed and receded, and I found myself in inky darkness on the floor with Pinchot trying to drag me off. The Virgin must have guided my collapse to one side of her candles and softened my fall. The lights had been put out. A dramatic critic had rushed to the office and told them that I was dead. One of the black-garbed invisible stage-hands carried me off. Mr West gave me a whack of whisky and in three minutes I was propped back into my niche. I finished the part and did the Nun that night. All right today, and I've played the Nun again this afternoon. The amusing side is that the audience had no idea that anything was out of order. They are totally bewildered and (blackouts being used as a curtain) hours in total darkness don't surprise them. They are buying seats from each other at fabulous prices. There's not breathing room for ten thousand.

The drugstore I patronise has suddenly produced a most obnoxious drink, slightly clouded bottles, lemonade-colour, with a stench of turps. They call it a highball. It has an effect more powerful and more delightful than anything I've tasted. It made an Ariel out of my Caliban mood. It must be alchemy, as it can't be alcohol.

I was sad to have left Duff, the gallant Member, to climb his ladder alone, and to bear alone the death of his mother in early January. She died in the South of France, too suddenly for him to reach her. I felt thankful that he had not joined me for Christmas but had been exclusively hers at Cimiez for ten days. Only two weeks before her death he had taken her to a circus, and she had enjoyed it with a child's enthusiasm although she was over seventy. She was utterly selfless and handed down to Duff her great charity of heart. Her innocence pitied us all and prayed for us without intruding. Duff loved her deeply and mourned her death with dark grief. I felt myself an absentee. I took comfort in gladness that she lived to know he would be famous.

Just before the Christmas recess he had made a brilliant maiden speech. His letters tell of anxious waiting, fevered excitement, postponement and final delivery. It was acclaimed by the high and the low, and I had showers of congratulations.

Cleveland   *17 December*

So many letters and telegrams about the speech. Tell Nancy Astor more than once how touched I was. Kommer says that you represent him in the House. It's the success that makes missing it heartbreaking, but one couldn't foretell. It would have been foolish to forfeit a fortune for a frost.

Lady Horner said: "Much better than Haldane."

Soon it was Christmas. I wrote from Cleveland:

24 December

At Belvoir now they are filling stockings and breaking glass baubles as they decorate the tree in the guardroom and fit candles onto green-black branches. How many times have I seen my mother, in some long gallery set out with trestle tables groaning with Christmas presents, sorting and culling gifts for the servants and employees. Each must have the individual touch in what they received. Housemaids got automatically two lengths of "print" with which to make their working dresses, but to these must be added something gay and touching—a brooch, a red purse, a lace scarf. The cowmen would inevitably be cold milking in winter hours, and must have wool mufflers and waistcoats and perhaps a photograph in a frame. "He won't want a photograph of Marjorie, Mother!" "He can always take it out and put his children in." This Christmas distribution was a nightmarish balancing puzzle and took days to solve. She loved it. We helped, hated the effort, despised it all and said that they would rather have money. I am sure that we were wrong.

Three weeks in Cleveland were followed, now that my pockets were jingling, by a journey to Nassau, where Viola and Alan Parsons had been sent for Alan's health. He wrote an enchanting book which describes, with his subtle humour, a *Winter in Paradise*. Nassau in 1925 was quite unhurt. For years no hurricane had blown to molest it. There were avenues of royal palms, and on the almost-deserted Hog Island were murmurations and prisms of humming-birds. The peacock sea cannot be altered by fluorescence and Coca-cola, but Bay Street can and has been. We lived in one of the many houses painted palest blue, green, pink or yellow, with cool screened balconies, built by Loyalist refugees after the American War of Independence. We sailed in glass-bottomed boats, watching the rainbow fish darting through the gardens of the sea. We landed on Robinson Crusoe islands with no Friday's footprints, and we gathered, in fantastic clothes, one night at Old Fort, where I danced the bacchante to Viola's piebald faun ("the god pursuing, the maiden hid") on a natural stage that sloped down to the silver-moon-pathed Caribbean Sea.

We are living very native on our verandah. The chairs rock. I tease Alan about his squalor and the ice broken with a boot, food teeming with ants, sucked-dry oranges and blackened knives, and he gets back on me when I pour water over my mosquito-bitten feet because it's less trouble than scratching.

Nothing to buy in the markets, yet I can't keep away. It's the prettiest village one could see in an old Colonial aquarelle. The market sells fruit and poor veg and occasionally a cast turtle disorientated. All the negresses wear white boots and organdie for their black to lower through, and spotted kerchiefs topped by rakish-angled hats. The seas are shark-infested. I hope I choke them if they get me.

On my return to England sadness fell from the air one bright day in May. The Gower Street telephone rang to tell me, and my mother with me, that my father, slightly ailing and in bed, had been seized with a heart attack. We got home as quick as could be, but it was too late. The good old man (he was over seventy) was dead. He had been a loving and wise father. What hot tempers he had started with had long since abated into serenity. His bier lay in the guardroom at Belvoir, upon the long coffin my mother's bay-leaves and her thanks for a happy life. I took her to his funeral, the last and almost the only one I have ever been to.

Then came the ordering of his tomb. My mother seemed at

all times to have a tomb in the making. The base of her son's monument preoccupied her for thirty years. Her portfolios fluttered with tracings of Greek, Roman, Gothic and Renaissance detail, with notes, quotations and surprising sequences of words for epitaphs.

Tombs had a revered, a collector's place in our upbringing. Until my great-grandmother, the creative Duchess, built the Mausoleum to guide her descendants on a flight of angels to Heaven, Bottesford, a few miles from Belvoir, had sepulchred our ancestors. The parish church is indeed packed with family effigies. Templars and other knights, later Earls with one wife (and often two) and their children born and stillborn, in ruffs and doublets and sad little shrouds, lie there beneath painted alabaster. The collection ended in the early eighteenth century, when their black-and-white marble skeletons and tearful cherubs clutching skulls became too numerous and cumbersome for the little church. Goodness knows where the intermediary inheritors lie. Where is Sir Joshua Reynolds's Duke, whose wife Mary Isabella was known as "the beautiful Duchess"? He is commemorated as Viceroy of Ireland by the Rutland Memorial in Dublin's Merrion Square. Where, O where lies the popular Marquess of Granby, Commander-in-Chief of the British Army at Dettingen, whose name and bald pate still give welcome from his pubs? My mother had designed my grandfather's stone figure and struggled for years with his epitaph, and now my dead father must be sculpted by an obedient artist and laid recumbent in his rightful place.

I returned to *The Miracle* to act in the Festspielhaus at the Salzburg Festival of 1925. I had an American friend, Ethel Russell, to whom I was devoted. She glowed with life and zest, infected you with her fun and gusto and then loved you for these qualities. Together with her, Iris Tree and Kommer,

I motored across Bavaria to Salzburg. Kommer was known to his friends the world over by the sweet name of Kaetchen. This is a lady's maid's name, and he earned it by looking after me with the tenderness of one. At Augsburg we joined Emerald Cunard, Gerald Berners, Bertie Abdy and others. At Leopoldskron, Ethel, Iris and I were put in a dormitory at the top of the house which came to be known as *Das Lady's Zimmer* and was lacking in all essentials. Three beds there were, but no looking-glass, basin, rugs or cupboards, hangers or hooks, but so many larks and jokes and secrets and whispers furnished that room that I liked it better than any other.

Festival performances are notoriously unprepared, and Salzburg seemed to me chaos. Duff went to Venice to cure a skin illness with sun concentration, and I wrote to him there:

Salzburg   *14 August*

Emerald has been stung by a wasp on her lip, and it has made her dreadfully fractious. I was at rehearsal until 3 a.m. and am all in with tiredness and despair—nothing ready, not even the Festspielhaus or décor. I had a good cry and got much pampered and spoilt by Iris and Ethel, but at night when I should be thinking and writing to you there is a riot of laughter and talk and wrestling. Kaetchen sleeps opposite and at ten a beastly breakfast is brought in on a big table by four rosy girls and K. joins us. It looks pretty with wide-open windows on the sunny lake and mist-hidden mountains.

15 August

Emerald, still cross, says that the wasps won't leave her alone. I expect it's Dr Oreste's disgusting unguents she puts on her face (as I do). They must be made of wasps' vomit. They smart enough and the rascals return to it. Gerald Berners will shriek: "O, I've been stung!" Then he sticks his finger in his mouth, and she falls for it and believes.

The pandemonium where I write in the stalls is appalling. Hammering deafens. Frau Mildenburg, the famous old singer, is practising chest-notes. The rehearsal was called for nine. It's now twelve and they are still gathering up the débris of last night's *Welt Theater*. Three hours it took on wooden seats, and no entr'acte.

17 August

We were rehearsing on the stage last night at 8.30 with *The Miracle* announced for seven. I've never been so upset. I was sick in the morning with nerves and impotency to get anything done. My coat was soaking wet because I had had to gild and paint it the day before, with the result that I've got a cold today. There's always trouble about my stone baby and the language traps. I shouted to the whole rehearsal, being empty-handed: "*Will niemand mich ein Kind machen?*" Uproar! The only bright moment in the black chaos.

Letty, Aunt Mildred and Betty Manners have arrived *en pèlerinage*.

My sister Letty had married Guy Benson in 1921. We felt her to be safe and happy, and she was to have three more sons to join the two who had been my wedding pages.

It was at Leopoldskron that we persuaded Iris to act the Nun in the *Miracle* tour in America called for October. She fought the idea but lost. It made the difference of night and day to me. The thought of five or six months' touring alone was gloomy, but with Iris constantly with me (that perpetual renewer of spirits, that dearest romantic in clown's clothes that ever jogged me along) I could feel less apprehension. I wrote to Duff:

Salzburg   *18 August*

Such a cold! Suppose I dribble and cough on the pillar tonight? The last performance was a disgrace. I despise Reinhardt for displaying such a cobble and let him know it. Result: we are in all day for rehearsal and outside it's "*wie am ersten Tag.*" We have dressed Iris up as the Nun and she is to be tried out by Reinhardt to see if talent lurks. She is shaking, poor child, and must shake for four more hours.

Later. It's impossible. I'm halfway through the performance, and this is the first moment free from fussing to keep the different groups of friends mellow. There's Gladys, Oggie and Ronnie, there's Letty, Mildred and Betty, there's Iris, Ethel and Kaetchen, Berners and me, and a frightful Gest group.

The picture in the *Tatler* of you asleep, entitled "M.P. in Dreamland," is shaming, though I like to see you sleeping, not spooning. I like to think of you in a motorless town (Venice) where you can't be run over.

Iris has said the Lord's Prayer to Reinhardt, who was delighted and has telegraphed to Gest that she can certainly play the part. So now she'll go with me to America and that makes the whole and entire difference. Kaetchen will take us. "My Mummy" arrives today. She'll be furious at my having a cold.

At the festival I met for the first time Hugo von Hofmannsthal, a name already meaning much in the world and one that was to mean much more to me and my family. He thought me good as the Madonna, and was enthusiastic about writing a new pantomime. He told me the story of his libretto for Strauss's new opera, *Die Ägyptische Helena*, with Scheherazade's art, and begged me to cherish his two sons if one day they were sent with Kaetchen to seek their fortunes in America.

Kaetchen took us across the Atlantic on the *Olympic.* The new Spielmann was in the Second Class, and I had plans of rehearsing Iris in the Nun's part on board. There was no piano that we might use, and if there had been Iris was invincible in resolve not to co-operate. The whole thing (including the salary) embarrassed her. Long-suffering Kaetchen had a cruel time between her obstinacy and my self-pity.

On the Olympic

We work K. cruel hard, making him brush our hair, fetch and carry, tuck us up. In return he gets only scoldings. We give him "treats." They always take him in and turn out to be what most he hates, like lunch on deck or hide-and-seek on A and B deck. Only one laugh today, when K. said to the waiter: "Let me have a halibut."

Kaetchen took us to the Hotel Sinton, Cincinnati, and introduced us to servidors, incinerators and coffee-shops and there left us, the reluctant Nun and her anxious task-mistress. Iris had a ringing success and enjoyed her laudatory notices. The stage manager said that she was like a Holbein statue, whatever that was. She lost her embarrassment and (*always*) her weekly salary. She wore a grey red-lined regimental coat with brass buttons, and the cheques or dollar-bills floated out of its wide pocket as she fumbled for cents to give to beggars. We were warm and comfortable and shown a good time by everyone. It was our first stage-stop, and homesickness was not yet the spectre that for me it was to become.

Kaetchen came to and fro from New York for "treats." He was unhappy by temperament and would pace up and down the room like Felix the Cat, sulky and silent. "What's wrong, Kaetchen?" "Nothing I mean—I mean nothing." Jealousy walked with him, but he had nothing yet to be jealous of. He was suspicious of the space and air that he had to leave, and of the innocent breathers whom he left behind. Perhaps the relentless teasing was warping his nature. I do not think so— he needed it and became an addict.

Kaetchen's treat today was being read aloud to. Iris and I read chapters alternately of two books to confuse him. Hers is *Hunger* by Knut Hamsun, mine the new H. G. Wells. For three hours he endured it. In return he brought us hampers, chocolates and new books, scandal and good financial news.

Clever and godfatherly Otto Kahn was coping with my savings to some jingling tune. "The Boss has made you a thousand dollars" seemed to be often told me—an unwearying repetition.

The *Miracle* train chugged its way to many of the big cities carrying the five-hundred-strong cast (two to a bed), and local students made up the crowd-scenes. They loved the revelry and the thirty dollars a week. Iris and I kept clear of it. So cumbersome is a mobile cathedral that to build and unbuild it left us generally with ten days or a fortnight between cities, during which we returned to the rigours of New York.

New York   *24 October. 1925*

So it's to Boston we go tomorrow. Walking yesterday I dropped in at an animal shop and found an ideal monkey, tame and handleable. This morning I felt an imperative desire for it, stimulated by thinking what a "treat" it would be for Kaetchen. Forty dollars was a wicked extravagance. Iris leads me to folly. It's here and has just made two varied and far-spreading messes. I've called it Jacko. He's an entertaining and decorative goblin and does the classic tricks of grimacing in the glass, smelling bottles, putting the tiny nose in the face-powder, destroying the puff. Wade is furious.

Boston is receiving us as Potentates, Dominions and Powers. The reception committee is headed by the Governor of Massachusetts and leading citizens. The whole cast has been ordered on to the station platform. Kaetchen will be in charge of Jacko and the huge medicine ball (both unpackable).

Boston (Hotel Lenox)   *25 October*

We've fallen on our feet this time—half Beauty's tour in the Beast's castle, half Sarah Bernhardt's triumphant progress. Gest says that the rooms were "built" for us. He means decorated. Drawing-room with grand piano, Spanish *Miracle* style, bells, candles, missals, lampshades of plainsong. Iron gates lead us into the dining-room, heaped with choice fruits, and in the credence stand one dozen champagne, four Château Yquem 1911, two whisky, two gin, one brandy, one vermouth, six Bordeaux, twelve liqueurs (various), a dozen Bass and cigarettes. The bedroom is vast, hung with citron brocade, beds painted lacquer-red, lace sheets, satin covers, flowers actually growing out of everything. The reporters dealt with, Iris, Gest, Kaetchen and I sat down to tenderest lobsters, steaks, alligator pears and pastries washed down with Château Yquem and served by an old retainer.

Next day. It's as sensational outside as in. Shop-windows full of life-sized photographs of us. Some sport gothic arches, stained illuminated glass and wax dummies of the Madonna and Nun. The famous Boston Library, a Temple of Art (Sargent, Abbey etc.) has a room dedicated to photographs and relics of *The Miracle*, photographs of Morris Gest at the age of four, ten and nineteen, and some of Kaetchen, all labelled "From the private collection of Morris Gest."

Five letters from you today. Iris says "I'm glad he loves you so much. I didn't know he did." Don't ever read my letters to Maurice. I'm apt to write him similar descriptions and I hate to be shown up.

I've sent Jacko back. He tried to light matches, unstoppered every bottle he could and threw drinking-glasses about because he found them heavy and inconvenient. The last outrage was when he took up a wide position on the dressing-table among the gold and turquoise, and was sick and sick and sick. A whole bunch of grapes returned in deep purple fluid. As he retched he shook his little head from side to side so as to cover a wider area.

It's midnight, and over our delicate supper Iris and I discuss the change of conditions and desires in ten years. What would we not have given for a privacy like this, unhaunted by mothers and maidenheads? Here we have time, space, a cellar and fullest freedom, and we discuss it before retiring early.

28 October

Huge success, mad applause, Gest sobbing on the chancel steps, Kahn and Jo Davidson and Ziegler from the Metropolitan and Bertram from New York arrived at six to return at midnight. One old actor fell head-first down the steps and badly hurt a woman in the front row. When I pulled the bell it didn't ring. Flowers all the way to a party wonderfully staged with real yew-hedges lit by thick church-candles.

Keep me loved in England. I get so fearful of loss. The *Leviathan* leaves England on the 15th. If I left on 6th I'd have 2½ to 3 days of you. Write what you think. Are Dover cliffs still white?

P.S. I feel like a mandrake torn out of the earth—English earth.

My mother joined me, radiant to be back. She was the happiest of the cast. She had left her golden drawing-rooms overlooking the Green Park and installed herself in the Arlington Street lodge, a great come-down much to her liking. The house had been denuded by a sale and was in the market waiting for some modern Croesus.

In spite of success and interesting expeditions to Salem and houses belonging to Mr Sleeper and John Hayes Hammond, in spite of making a new, dear and lasting friend, Charlie Codman, my nostalgia was gnawing at me. We had midnight matinées, making often eleven performances a week, and tiredness probably accounted for my sad listlessness. Christmas we spent at St Louis. The city was interred in thick-ribbed ice, but *The Miracle* won and the house filled to brimming. There were radio talks, over which we always broke down. Alone we should have been all right, but when we were together and asked serious questions about "our art" we suffered fearful *fou rire*. I can find only one joke in my letters from St Louis:

The last straw was when an apparently intelligent critic came to interview me. He asked me what English authors I knew. I said "George Moore" and added (not wishing to swank) "At least I can't really say I *know* him." This he wrote up as my position forbidding association with writers "Of course I could not *know* him—you understand."

On 20 January 1926 I sent Duff the only poem I ever wrote:

MY ONLY POEM

"It's not a good pome" but mine own and drawn from the well of truth:

> I want to go home.
> I'm feeling alone.
> Groan, groan, hollow groan,
> I want to go home.
>
> I want to go home.
> No one comforts my moan,
> No hope on the 'phone.
> I want to go home.
>
> She wants to go home,
> She hates foreign loam,
> She hates even Rome,
> She wants to go home.
>
> She wants to go home,
> All theatre-thrills flown.
> As the Nun she gets blown.
> The Madonna's lost tone—
> She *does* want to go home.
>
> She wants to go home.
> It's not a good pome,
> But she's only a gnome,
> A poor deformed gnome,
> And she wants to go home.
>
> She wants to go home.
> She's lying alone,
> Her body's like stone.
> O! Duffy, atone!
> Turn her salt tears to foam.
> O dear Mr Gnome!
> I *do* want to go home.

I thought Chicago beautiful. The white steam from the railway-engines (now sunk underground) and from the central heating wreathed in lovely clouds and garlands among the skyscrapers. Sky and lake were crystalline and blue, but we were not very happy there, although successful theatrically. The press was mischievous, and Elinor Patterson, daughter of Joe Patterson of the *Chicago Tribune*, had been engaged to play the Nun. This made Iris rage. I had no choice but to play the Madonna nine or ten times weekly.

Chicago   *2 February 1926*

Gest's first-night speech beat all previous shames. He collapsed onto the Madonna's altar in a state of bogus exhaustion while the applause lasted, and then staggering to his feet, tears gushing, thanked the stage-hands by Christian names, thanked me (tactlessly) for staying in America *six months*, thanked Mother for coming to the U.S., thanked the box-office man's little wife for sitting up with him o' nights, thanked Mrs Patterson (the playing Nun's mother) and the Duchess for giving us birth.

In our apartment house we found Noel Coward and his mother. He was acting in *The Vortex* and (our hours synchronising) we cooked each other's meals in our kitchenettes, buying our provisions at "Piggly-wiggly." We read his new play *Semi-Monde* and even went to a riding academy with him. Iris was bold and ambitious and to the manner trained. Noel and I were definitely no good with horses. Noel said that the brute they gave him would look round and say with savagery: "Bet you can't!" Out of duty I went to the slaughter-houses with Sally Carpenter, a figure of Chicago, and could not eat meat for a month.

We were invited to the house of a famous architect, whose car picked us up from the theatre at midnight and drove into a candle-lit room that had busts of ladies in marble hats and veils, where he received us, dressed as Rodolfo in *La Bohème*. At the piano a negro was banging away. He had his eight fingers (not his thumbs) bound tightly with adhesive plaster, so that long playing would not split them. We drank cocktails in a claustrophobic nautical cabin. The sea, painted on a drop-cloth and dotted with mermaids, rose and fell outside the portholes. Dinner was in Palm Beach (so high and wide a conservatory that we could not see the glass for the bananas). A swimming-pool, lit from below, called for nudes or anyway wilder guests than Iris and me. At coffee-time a man offered us tickets for a hanging next morning: we refused them. Afterwards we toured the house, feeling ashamed of our weary, frumpish reactions. In an Egyptian Room overhanging the lake was a Bed of Ware for ten. We sat gingerly on its edge and watched with nausea a table, laden with ruby caviare, rise from the floor. The Turkish bath had a transparent floor with a secret room beneath, and the Love Nest was a large room carpeted entirely with a black satin mattress. Shoes were left at the door, and we tiptoed in all-but-darkness to the illuminated tank, inset into the middle of the mattress, where albino goldfish were gasping their last. There was a Chinese bed standing on the mattress. We could think of nothing better to say, over and over again, than "How amusing" with less and less conviction. The evening, which we had utterly failed to animate, ended at last. Haunted for days by our lack-lustre, we proposed ourselves again and took Noel Coward for effervescence. A new Apache Room had been decorated especially for the evening, but even Noel's spirit was extinguished.

Iris was my great solace. She was more lively and enterprising than I was, and what sad brooding she shared with me she could string into verses, while I could but mope inertly. Kaetchen came and went, weaving himself ever more faithfully into our lives. The more we loved, the more we teased and baited him.

Iris looked like an eccentric puppet doll, and we had imperceptibly fallen into the way of referring to ourselves as "the Dolls." So we made two dolls of rag, and my mother painted their faces realistically. Wade dressed them in the same material cut like the clothes we always wore. "Iris" had pink Joan of Arc hair and "I" (as in life) looked from beneath a concealing cloche hat. Some demon possessed us to confide this wanton couple to the guard of the Twentieth Century train, and Kaetchen received a telegram in verse to meet "the Dolls" at dawn on the following day. He was due to go to Palm Beach to stay with his devoted friend Otto Kahn. Hearing of our arrival, he gave up his rarer-than-rubies reservation and was on the morning platform with all smiles prepared. A coloured porter handed him the puppets. Disappointment and humiliation must have been difficult to bear, but he had his amusing revenge. He took the dolls two days later to the millionaire's playground, and from Oheka Villa they wrote us daily an account of their sunlit days and wilder nights, of their clothes, presents, jewels, their prowess at games and love. It all but destroyed us, deathly tired in the grey cold of Chicago. They had a costly morocco leather box made for their rest and travel, and Kaetchen did not part with them until his death, when they disappeared, no doubt disintegrated with grief. He also travelled with my mask in wax, cast from the mould of Jo Davidson's bust. That also has vanished. His temperament was so changeable that we could tell at once if our dearest and necessary Kat were black or white of mood. Rex Whistler drew me a picture to order, reversible as a medal. One side showed the purring white sleekness of our pet, with a touch of black warning at his tail's tip. On the other side was a rampant hell-cat with a hopeful flash of white at the end of his lashing tail. That treasure too has gone. It played its part in fore-casting and sometimes checking Kaetchen's temper as he watched us reverse it. I gave him too a reversible dressing-gown, a magpie turncoat.

We were in Chicago many weeks. I had influenza and for the first and only time missed four performances. This lowered me. I wrote to Duff:

To save myself from breakdown I evolved a philosophic com-fort on these lines. I enjoy anticipation more than I am able to savour the present. When I am with you and happy in all and every way, my apprehension of the slightest change, even the trivial imperfections of the moment, can wreck my pleasure. When I am exiled and starved of happiness I have the tremendous anticipation of betterment. It works well enough if I can keep the fear of realising the certainty of life being short, and these days the best, from creeping in. But it always does. What is to be done with me? What am I losing to gain this miserable triumph and these few dollars?

I was appalled too by my appearance, and Iris remembers my looking in the cruel looking-glass and murmuring: "That's over. Now it's nap on personality."

Gest urges and urges me to stay with bribery and blackmail. I can't do it. Do settle. I'm so tired. I want to be treated as a child and not like an executive woman. I want to obey. Photographs of me are like the Fat Woman of Brentford, with the head of Rameses II on top. If I had more guts I'd stay for the extra £2000, but I can't wash out a holiday with you. There are not enough of them in the summer of life. I feel sad days will never cease. I'm tired, tired ... I ... I ... I ... I wonder why I worry to put words between the Is.

Meanwhile Duff in England was working and playing for all he was worth, constituency hard labour, lectures, stumping the country, writing articles tirelessly about the League of Nations. Again his daily letters are mellow bells to my scrannel pipes. They tell of politics and fun, interests, sport, scandals and side-splitting jokes. There is plenty of genuine distress at my absence, but they are still bright with life's colour. Everything goes well. "It started foggy, but by the time I arrived the day was sparkling." He travelled (as we all did, however poor) with his servant, the pompous scoundrel Holbrook. All doors were open to him—my sisters', the Montagus', Ancasters', Wimbornes', Wallaces' and Ednams', Belvoir and Wilton, and Cliveden on political Sundays. He shot over moors and in high pheasant-woods, and at Drummond he had one shot at his stalked stag and killed it dead.

A happy death, his does nearby, having just eaten a delicious meal of fresh grass.

Holbrook is more exasperating out shooting than at any time. I shall end by shooting him. When it pours with rain and he is obviously half-frozen and out of breath, carrying both my guns and a shooting-stick, he does a hypocritical Mark Tapley that makes me see red. He will also use the wrong technical terms and after all these years he fails to distinguish between a hare and a rabbit. Today when an enormous hare was lolloping slowly towards me in the centre of a perfectly open space, he hissed into my ear in a tone of tense excitement: "Very large rabbit coming up in front, sir." He never marks a bird and today put the crown on everything by allowing a wounded bird which he had picked up to fly straight out of his hands and get clean away.

Did I tell you about the nice taxi-driver who took me to the station? " 'Ow's 'er Ladyship?" he asked. I said that you were in America. "I know that," he replied. "Is she 'aving a great time there? Going great guns?" I said you were. "That's right," he said.

In London when he wasn't at the House of Commons he was at delightful dinners of wealth and luxury, in Bohemia or in the clubs (White's, Buck's or the Garrick). The boon companions were Maurice Baring, Hilaire Belloc, Tommy Bouch, Michael Herbert and his brother Sidney, now a Member of Parliament and Secretary to the Prime Minister, Mr Baldwin.

Sat with them at Buck's round the fire talking nonsense and roaring with laughter until five.

My turned-down mouth watered, not for his doings but for his nature and outlook. The only note of disappointment in all these months of letters was when the *Manchester Guardian* tipped him as Under-Secretary to the Foreign Office, and another man was given the post. Who but Duff would have dared to hope for so fine an appointment after one year in the House? He wrote: "The choice of Locker-Lampson is a wise one."

I was back for Easter. Duff met me unexpectedly at Cherbourg. It was dawn, and he was cold and wet with spray from the tender, and for a moment in the half-light I thought that he was a seal. Winter's rains and ruins were over. He took me to Madrid, Seville and Granada on a honeymoon as flawless as the first.

The General Strike was brewing, and in May it broke upon us. At Breccles, after an English spring Sunday of young green and broken sun and cloud, we heard the menacing news. The same sun and green mocked us next day as we motored to London. My heart was deep down in my boots, and I could hardly speak. Duff admitted later to a feeling of sick anxiety, but he did not show it at the time, leaving me to feel myself the yellow streak of the party. I could hear the tumbrils rolling and heads sneezing into the baskets, and yet and yet, the English could not be like that. Then where would it end? The buses were out, so there were jobs to be done driving workers home to Dalston or Hackney. I remember depressed huddled little lunches at Gower Street, with Maurice unnaturally despondent and the normally robust plunged in gloom. Belloc alone seemed totally unmoved and in the highest spirits. The wireless for the first time became to us a necessity. The sky in memory seems dark, pitch-dark at noon. Every day increased the vast hordes of strikers, but, as always in full crisis, the sinews stiffened. All despondency evaporated. Maurice was again A.D.C. to Trenchard. The club boys became special constables. My brother was on night duty from nine to six a.m. Some foolhardies were driving buses and trains. I was a free-lance, driving Duff, taking stranded workers home in my car, telephoning Max Beaverbrook for news and being connected to him by Edwina Mountbatten and Jean Norton, who were operating the *Daily Express* switchboard.

Winston, in full spate, was bringing out a Government news-sheet. Mr Baldwin was keeping our equilibrium by wise speeches on the radio. The papers must have been brought back to life, for I remember distributing *Sunday Expresses* and Duff folded *The Times* after the House rose. He forbade me to join these volunteers, I can't remember why (for fear of picketing perhaps), but join them I did and folded papers back to back with him all through the nights. He never knew until we both received the silver matchbox, engraved with a joke about "Strike," given by *The Times* to all helpers.

The 13th of May was a lucky day (perils past, as we thought), so Venetia and I took ship for France. The porters at Dover were all undergraduates, and never was there a more hilarious crowd of relieved passengers and trolley-happy porters. The boat was loaded in a flash. Women and children were the first to fall before the onrush of laughing students. Feet were crushed by wheels, hats were flying, as the suitcases on running shoulders shot their way through. The cheers could be heard at Calais as we moved out of port. We did not know until next day that the 13th had been a day of renewed fear, as the strikers were said to be still out, but by the evening triumph was assured, thanks to our splendid Mr Baldwin.

Duff was hard-worked that summer, but in August the magic of Venice wrapped us round. Leaving it, we stumbled upon a gleaming milestone. We felt rich, and seeing (of all things) a small Fiat motor-car in a Venetian shop-window, we bought it and once again took to the delights and hazards of the road. We drove to Garda, the unspoilt lake, along the little untrafficked road that led through cypress and myrtle, lemons and oleanders, to Riva. As usual we settled to live there, a decision taken for the twentieth time. We stopped a stranger and asked him whether an unfinished pillared villa was for sale. He did not know, he said, nor care, but he would show us what he himself had just taken. We went down a cypress-sentinelled hill to a point of land silver with olives, and there was his inn, once no doubt a cloistered house, with room in its stone port to hold one fishing-boat with its lemon Venetian sail. We could not stay then, but from that day until 1953 hardly a year of peacetime passed without a week or more of heart's content at San Vigilio. It is for me a shrine of felicity.

CHAPTER THREE

The Reinhardt Circus

In October Iris and I set off, well-advertised missionaries, for the second tour of *The Miracle* in the United States. Duff was to come for our three or four weeks in Philadelphia, and Kaetchen arranged for him to give a few lectures within easy reach. I loved Philadelphia for its blazon of October and for having Duff to cook for, as well as Iris's eleven-year-old son, Ivan Moffat. Duff's lectures I never heard, but they helped me one tormented evening on my pillar when a bug from the property-room found a home in the felt that lined my crown, and tried to eat its way out through my forehead. Ignorant of the cause of the unendurable irritation and fertile at finding panaceas for the hopeless, I arranged that the more uneasy my crowned head the more feathered Duff's cap. He told me (perhaps in thanks) that he never gave a better lecture than that night. Too soon he left us, and our cathedral moved to Kansas City, the heart of America. From the train I wrote to Duff:

I love the negro porters, though I've just been humiliated by one. I was intolerant with him earlier in the day, so now every time he comes in he asks me if I'm still angry and says he doesn't mind men being cross but can't stand it from ladies. He looks at Iris and says: "You're ma friend." I hope that he'll forgive me soon.

We are in a big saloon that turns into an observation car. Each seat had a cuspidor but as we got in early I kicked them all under the individual chairs. Now I can see all the old hicks looking for them mouth-full.

DESERTS DIVIDE US

Kansas City

The Mayor and Chamber of Commerce were on the platform with the whole *Miracle* cast and bouquets to suffocate, fireworks and flares, moving pictures and two Rolls Royces to take us to the Ambassador Hotel, where Mr Tipple the manager and all the staff received us, bowing low and putting a lot of "Your Ladyships" in. This silent, subservient, furtive man had filled our kitchen with groceries and fruit and our two sitting-rooms with flowers, and he had supper prepared for us. The reporters were let in, and we were interviewed acting languidly as tired temperamentals should, but alas! what an awakening disillusion to them all and to the waiters and neighbours when in rushed the bright young things of *The Miracle* all a bit tight, Fritzie, the new Spielmann, telephoning to all his new acquaintances for hootch. Mr Tipple finally produced a bottle of Bourbon (his tipple) and a ukulele was found and the victrola wound up, and a beastly baby doll was produced and jokes made about "changing" the baby, and bath towels brought, and common laughs rang out. But it served to divert me from my distance-phobia in the heart of America and the growing trouble of "deserts divide us, and the waste of seas."

The little Fiat bought in Venice sat sadly in a London garage. One night on the pillar I had a winged thought, quickly flown to England and followed by this letter:

23 November 1926

It's about giving a motor to Mother. I've thought of a wonderful plan. It's to be a great surprise. You must call her up a few days before Christmas and say "Diana has sent you a present. Will you be in if I send it round?" Then send it. Please, Duffy, get up early one morning and go to the Fiat people and effect an exchange. Get a sedan or limousine, one with the driver sitting outside, but compact, small and smart, if there is time painted her own middle-greenish-blue with peacock and coronet on the door, and then get a chauffeur found by Holbrook, a non-drunk from some country repair-shop preferably, nice appearance, all there, neat chauffeur's coat and cap. I can well afford this and I cannot have "my Mummy"

63

walking and denying herself taxis, which she does for my sake through the cold wet weather. It must be kept a secret or she will obstruct the plan. I feel ashamed that I have not done it before. The chauffeur must have willingness for unusual jobs. The readiness is all. For advice ask brother John. Don't let him deter you by saying that she has a car at Belvoir. She'll never use that Renault. I know her too well. It's too big and too expensive in tax and up-keep. I am to pay the man's salary. See to the inside—she likes light-coloured lining and pulleys at the side-windows and some-where for a looking-glass and pencils and paper. I hope that this letter won't worry you. I'm enjoying the idea so much myself. My ordeal on the pillar this afternoon went in a flash thinking about it.

It's snowing hard. I went out riding on Sunshine. I never met a horse as nice as Sunshine. She is tall and chestnut and five-gaited, which is new to me. It's like bicycling. You need not rise to the occasion. She brewed more of that shaving-foam than it took to smother me.

I'm eating a lot to keep the wolf from the face. Thanksgiving Day feast up here tomorrow (Mr Tipple's treat). We've asked four or five of the cast and young von Hofmannsthal. Thank God Kaetchen won't have arrived to act the skeleton black cat at the feast.

Next day

Raimund [von Hofmannsthal] doesn't know about riding yet and it isn't too safe. He has thought of the clever expedient of tying the snaffle round his horse's neck and grabbing the curb in which he puts a knot that he may get more purchase. He is becoming a *bel ami* to these Dolls.

Kaetchen has returned fatter and in good temper. He has been brushing Iris's hair (an hour's "treat") cigarette in mouth, holding her down with one weak hand and brushing up with the other. He is filling the hotwater bottles now.

Kansas City

We're properly launched into the social set of Kansas City. Kaetchen came to call us this morning with one of his worst and most repellent colds that make him intolerable and morbid. A party had been arranged for us after the two performances and I could see that he had been brooding and brooding on "the feast that leads to so much more." He's leaving tonight, poor Kaetchen, and all the cast's and the new friends' faces are wreathed in smiles. Is it not horrid? I really adore Kaetchen. I am undeserving of good things, ungrateful, cold and spoilt, and the wanton waste of true affection will assuredly lead to woeful want of it. Still he does keep us too imprisoned and fearful of his humours, and now he pays for it.

I fuss a lot about "my Mummy" and the pain in her back. She is like me, of course. If it's not one thing it's another.

Almost-daily telegrams in verse were exchanged with Kaetchen, set to the tune of the Weeping Willow Tree. Iris was the best lyricist. Kaetchen's rhymes were shaky in metre but imaginative. I have volumes of them bound in Kaetchen's all-covering morocco, and sometimes I croon them and feel like my mother's maid Barbara singing a song of Willow. The jokes have faded from obscurity into meaninglessness, but one can trace the cruel "treats" broken to the jealous Kat in verse.

Raimund von Hofmannsthal had since Philadephia been an apple of discord. Kaetchen had brought him to *The Miracle* as a means for him to work his passage to California, where he was to forge his fortune. He was nineteen, spoke no word of English, and the Kat could not miaow in French. He was Austrian, intelligent and made in our mould, unlike the other supernumeraries. He was shy and strange and clearly needed protection and affection. We revered and loved his father. It was natural therefore that we should first invite him to drug-store snacks, and then to share kitchenette meals in our flat. Raimund played a pilgrim (not a strenuous part) and a wounded soldier with a blood-stained cloth round his head.

He had to kneel and pray before the miraculous statue, and at other times to run about the church in the dream-world with the rest of the surging crowd. Kaetchen disapproved of favouritising one of a vast cast. He was jealous, so the drugstore snacks were criticised, and pot-luck at home could cause bad sulks. Raimund standing nightly at the stage-door as we came out and silently and very shyly offering me a cigarette would be enough to blanch Kaetchen like an almond. I fear that this attempted embargo upon him only sharpened our wish for Raimund's protection and company. He earned thirty dollars a week on tour, and had to travel (two men to a bed) on the special *Miracle* train. As we had promised Kaetchen not to pay for his snacks, the poor thing was reduced to quelling his hunger-pains with the cheapest thing on the menu, a cheese sandwich at twenty-five cents. The growing boy often had to watch Iris savouring a juicy steak and me gobbling prawns and Russian dressing. In Kansas City, Kaetchen's supervision gone, he was with us at all times.

As the end of the season drew near, the plans for our ten days of freedom crystallised themselves into taking the train to Santa Fé, where Iris knew a Russian horseman. One night on returning to our flat, we found a letter from Raimund to Iris asking her to meet him alone in the coffee-shop of the hotel. I fevered myself to sickness, imagining that he had come on Kaetchen's instructions to break, via her to me, the news of Duff's death. It was relieving and exhilarating to be told that Raimund had only begged to join us on our liberty-trip. He had telegraphed to his father for money, he said, but if it did not come in time he could beg, borrow or steal it. He knew that in duty to himself nothing must obstruct this glamorous and educational adventure. Jailer Kaetchen's place was with Reinhardt in New York. They were both to join us ten days

later in San Francisco. The truth must be told, so the verse
was sent by the telegram that was to put Kaetchen in torment:

> For fear of hold-ups on the road and birds of prey
> Two Dolls who are so grave and gay
> Took a cavalier
> Not unrelated to a foreign bard,
> But if our Cat is black, why then
> All pleasure's marred.

I remember hesitating to administer so cruel a hurt, but once it
was in Western Union's clutch we put repentance behind us
and, like bad children, were off without remorse to the
Western outfitter of Kansas City for an orgy of "dude" buying. We stuck at "chaps," but our boots were best-quality
black kangaroo (stitched and square-toed as for the Armada),
the shirts were checked and the belts coin-studded. Raimund
came in for some equipment too and for a reservation on the
train, and away we steamed with a great platform send-off
from local "flames" and "sparks," who overwhelmed us with
drinks and "glossies," flowers and chocolates, maps and mas-
cots. My spirits had risen tremendously since arrival at Kansas
City unencumbered, with a gay Austrian playmate, and with
California, man's traditional Promised Land, ahead.

Our plan with our Rai is to entrain early, get to Santa Fe thirty
hours later at noon, stay four days and join the train at Albuquerque
on Friday. A few hours in the Grand Canyon, then we pick up the
train for San Francisco. Are we not adventurous? We are calling
on D. H. Lawrence at Taos and on Brett, Lord Esher's daughter,
an old Slade School chum.

All that I had hoped for was fulfilled by adobe-built Santa
Fe and motoring with kind strangers eighty miles to Taos, still
uncontaminated by petrol-pumps and cameras, with "white

lightning" in a gigantic flask, brought by our leader Randal Davey and opened every half-hour to keep the great cold out.

I'm in transports about the swathed Indians and the two buildings looking exactly like the whole of Bethlehem (which town I never saw) and the colour of a Jersey cow. We drove to see Miss Dodge. Lawrence wasn't there, no matter, but Brett was, and so happy in her isolation, and so was Miss D's husband, a blanket Injun, with no conversation but "Ugh!" His recreation is playing pool. The house was full of local art plus Louis XV furniture and good Impressionist paintings. Brett I used to see at the Slade. Deaf now with a trumpet, living twenty miles away without a servant, she had come down to Taos, for the snow threatened to cut her off from milk and bread. She never wishes to leave her hill and nearly collapsed when she heard that Iris and I were on the stage.

We went five-strong to Tex Austin's ranch, a stone's throw of forty miles away. Ivanenko the Olympic champion, Iris's friend, has been found and has joined our throng. We're changing our tomorrow's train-reservations because Davey has real horse-branding to offer at another Tex Austin ranch a hundred miles away. "Tex" isn't there but "Butch" is.

Next day

The horse-branding did not disappoint, with pistols being shot off indoors to stir the sluggish, and "mule's foot" (called so for its kick) being passed round with the roast horse in a loving-panikin to the noise of yelps and whoops. Outside are herds of dear little horses untethered, with one dragging rein that you can grab, and then you clamber into those nice secure saddles that grip you like a vice, with a pommel to hold on to and stirrups like sabots, and no pigskin slipperiness or fiddling with snaffles. I cantered round in an ecstasy that I can still feel. The blue-birds I can still see, and the wild prancings and branding-antics. Ivanenko did everything a bit better than the cowboys did, which was a mistake, and he had to be checked. Iris jumped from a corral-post onto a wild horse's back and stuck its bucking.

PHOENIX FOR DUMPS

The Grand Canyon next day seems not to have been up to hopes. I watched the clouds gathering through the night from the open Pullman. I could not bear the hotel blotting that formidable escutcheon. The cleft was very big, yellow-and-red verdigrised, utterly lifeless and silent, not a bird or animal. Tourists become invisible immediately. I blush to remember the relief of no descents being allowed that day for icy reasons. After three hours' riding round the brink, we threw ourselves on hotel beds in the *désœuvré* fatigue that much-vaunted wonders of the world often encourage. "Phoenix for dumps," we said, and sped on to Chandler, where all was confident morning again.

The expense is ghastly (eight dollars a day *tout compris*) and no haggling allowed. We shall sleep out on our porch and therefore not sleep. Warm as May, birds (rare in America) singing loudly, lambs already born, eagles and big red flowers that I'm sorry to tell you turn out to be castor oil, and this heavenly roadless limitless glimmering desert that with the grey-green scrub makes one's horse feather-hoofed. Queer cactuses in obscene phallic shapes and canary-green in colour erect themselves every few hundred yards. I never enjoyed a ride so much. A horse like Pegasus, stirrups right. We could be happy here if one of us gets consumption.

Lovely sleep. The Boy swung our swingbeds into it. We rode and rode through the desert and rough hills and cactus and sand and sun, and the guide told of Indians and birds and legends while he cooked us steaks on a fire of mosquito-wood. He's very keen for me to come back with you in the autumn and camp in the mountains, and hunt lions and turkeys and coyotes. Next stop San Francisco. I'm fearful of bad news in payment for this happy week, and I dread Kaetchen's face of doom.

San Francisco

Just as I feared—a frightful row and no delectable supper arranged for us, even though Raimund was smuggled away to some "digs."

69

But there were letters from home to compensate. My mother had been mysteriously and gravely ill. As her only reaction to the pain and anxiety was that I should not be told, so determined was she to put no cloud in my sky, I heard of it only when danger was already past. Years before, when threatened with a severe operation, she had denied its imminence and sent Duff and me on a carefree Easter holiday. She had written her last wishes, forbidden the news of her predicament to reach my sister Letty (who was expecting a child), said goodbye alone and secretly to Belvoir and the gardens and avenues that she had made, and only when her recovery was sure did a gay telegram of convalescence reach us in Italy. Such saint-like selflessness I shall never find again. This new scare passed, and she was just able to get to Belvoir for Christmas. On the 24th the gift car and the chauffeur in livery, rug on arm, arrived. Duff wrote on Christmas Day:

I spent a very happy morning yesterday at Hamley's and bought some transfers for Ursula which she wanted, a toy circus for Isobel, the King and Queen going to open Parliament in the State Coach for Charles, and a military band, with musical-box soldiers and a conductor beating time, for Johnnie.

This morning after church the Hillman car came round to the door. It really is a great success and reflects lasting credit on Holbrook and me. I sent a note early to your Mummy saying: "Diana has sent you a present from America which I have to give to you, so let me know at what time you will receive it, and wrap up warm because it has to be given you out of doors." She said that she would come down at one o'clock and swears that she never guessed what it was and feared that it might be an animal, or possibly a fur coat that looked better out of doors. At one o'clock everyone was assembled to see her receive it. She walked out with me through the porter's lodge and when she realised what it was she was quite overcome and could only press my arm very tight and bow her head to hide her tears. She was so delighted. Everything in it is perfect, I think. John suggested that we should go for a turn round the terrace, which eased the situation.

I had a letter from Hilary [Belloc] this morning asking me to send you a telegram and enclosing ten shillings for it. Did I tell you that I dined with Eloise Ancaster and went to a play? The Duke and Duchess of York were there. They are such a sweet little couple and so fond of one another. They reminded me of us, sitting together in the box having private jokes, and in the interval when we were all sitting in the room behind the box they slipped out, and I found them standing together in a dark corner of the passage talking happily as we might. She affects no shadow of airs or graces.

San Francisco delighted us, but relations were strained. I wrote:

Reinhardt in doldrums, the rehearsals a shambles. Noel Coward is on the edge of a nervous breakdown which he proposes to have in China. Catastrophic rows and misery over Kaetchen's sulky ire. Reinhardt says: *"Ich glaube dass es gefährlich ist."* He can't mean suicide! After rudeness and scenes and the pandemonium of the rehearsals he says: *"Ganz hoffnungslos!"* You see that I'm paying for those happy Wild West days.

Later (*4 a.m.*). The Kat row is over. It took from midnight until 3.30. Now at last Kaetchen has gone, broken with shame and repentance. He says that blood gushes to his brain and he doesn't know what he is doing or saying when jealousy grips. He says that we both hate him subconsciously (Freud). I know that I love him dearly and consciously and always will.

Iris and I bought Reinhardt the Chinese gong that he could not afford. He wants it reverberating for five minutes to open his plays at Salzburg. Kaetchen and Iris and I pooled and Mr Gumps (the merchant) took off 100 dollars if we would include his name. The Master was childishly pleased and said *"fabelhaft"* and *"herrlich"* and *"grossartig"* a thousand times.

The letters show that my mood had veered right round. With Raimund as a companion, no relations to carry, competing with Iris for Reinhardt's favours, together with the

glorious State of California, the large-waved Pacific and its
seal-covered rocks, my glooms were dissipated, leaving me
only my fears for Duff's life to pray against. George Moore
had come back like a good genie. Boss of all he surveyed, he
sent Reinhardt and Kaetchen off to Del Monte, and got to
work on launching us socially. His magic lamp lit us and our
way to adventures and parties of fabulous beauty. One dinner I remember at Burlingame, where a clubroom had been
converted by two old ladies (whose profession it was) into a
fairy orchard in Persia at dawn. The walls, seemingly of transparent ice flushed pink, held silver espalier trees bearing golden
apples. On the table for 120 guests were tall staves on which
white peacocks perched, with garlands of flowers linking
them. At the corners were white china elephants as big as
genuine newborns, with white peacock-tails spreading in pride
from their howdahs. Moore produced delightful companions,
Chinatown revels and a nerve-destroying equestrian paper-
chase, where Iris was tossed high into the air and I arrived an
hour after the others, having spoilt a kind man's sport; and best
he invited us to spend our interim at his ranch. We dared not
take our child-friend Raimund.

San Francisco   *5 January 1927*

Goodbye, Frisco! It's over and the last night was a frenzy of
excitement and joyous farewells and tears. It's been one of our best
successes—matinées every day. Crowds at the theatre pay eight
dollars to be allowed to squat on their haunches in crannies from
which the stage is invisible. They get paralysed by cramp and ask
the ushers to "pull" them. Many faint, I suppose, from standing up
and looking down too long. I get a kick out of it but not as much
as anyone else would. The densest jamming is on the statue side of
the stage, and they come in swarms to the dressing-rooms to have
a look. Through last night's swarm swam Elinor Glyn (looking
twenty-five and talking rubbish), fans, photographers, lunatics and

lovers. It would drive another crazy but I rather like it, and I like best dear faithful Sister Chinese White of the Rutland Hospital, who arrives nightly with a delicious hot supper for me.

I acted the Nun marvellously and I really thought when it finished that the audience would surge in one tidal wave over the stage in a paroxysm of emotion. I even formulated a trifling "few words" to deliver through tears of joy and vanity. Wrong! Nothing unusual happened; just the usual "good hand." Other times, when I think that a turnip could have done as well, they "never better" me.

The poor child-friend, his day is over. We opened a bottle of champagne to keep him from tears and because it was the tenth anniversary of Wade's coming to me.

Del Monte

Here for the night, of all places. The most beautiful cedars with old fantastic roots winding into the slow Pacific. Rocks and seals abound. Pinchot arrived. Iris and she are crazy competitors for Reinhardt's heart. I think Iris wins, but low in my consciousness I feel myself Cordelia.

We rode with Pinchot into the breaking waves. She looked like a centaur (no, like the Elgin frieze) stirrup-less. Moore has got the Kat and Reinhardt and Vollmöller into saddles. They are not born to be horsemen. They wear stiff collars and can't look about for "riding."

12 January

I woke with dread upon me, as always before starting something new. We kissed the Kat and the Master goodbye and parted, we for the ranches and isolation, they for filmland. We drove eight miles to the edge of Moore's ranch and rode fifteen to his house, the loveliest thing in nature. No other dwelling in its fifty square miles. Not unlike England, quite as green, no rocks, all grass. Sometimes it's Tuscany, with ilexes springing from the swards. They look like olives grown in proportion to this large country. Hills (not mountains) and a feeling of cultivated friendliness like an orchard, though it's really as wild as on Creation Day. The house was finished today, packed with luxury, scrumptious food and too much champagne. I had a tireless polo-pony that frightened me not at all.

Youngster was its name. Fifteen miles is a long ride for the weak, but the last five, planted with redwood trees so utterly unlike anything seen before, gave me a new lease through wonder. We must be here together. I shall sleep on the balcony tonight.

13 January

Already at 8 a.m. there was a nice noise of polo-balls being tapped and curses and directions. George had bought me fine "chaps" in Frisco, piebald cowskin heavy with doubloons and silver pieces-of-eight. Off we rode again through other hills and redwoods. I wanted an early bed, being bruised and longing to feel at my wellest. No such luck. The champagne and Bourbon flowed until 3 a.m. in such quantities that Iris and I were driven to pouring it into the grate's ashes, the flower-vases, under the sofa, anywhere, because George will not stand for anything abstemious. He sent for his negroes five who run the house, and made them sing in perfect harmony for two hours. If they faltered for a break he would yell: "Get on, boys, do your stuff! I say, do your stuff!" They would answer: "Yes, Masser Moore" and keep at it.

19 January

George was of course feeling terrible today, not admitting it but drinking vile anti-hangover concoctions. "The climate looks after you," he says. It doesn't! Pouring the hootch surreptitiously into flower-vases (during Prohibition) does.

It's difficult to believe in the old life in England and in Emerald and Aunt Mildred and "the Boys" even, and Arlington Street and the Garrick Club. I am ashamed of this blurring, ashamed too that pity fills my heart for them all—all but you. Pride is what fills my heart when I think of you, and an enthusiasm to return to jail if you were in it. So don't fear. I'm always a little restless the first month home. That's due to cessation of the false occupation of travelling and to no work. This nigger likes her work.

A horsy mute arrived today with ten polo-ponies from Texas. He's an uneducated dreary little fourth to Iris, me and George, so we talked only of anthropology and R. L. Stevenson.

THE GARDEN OF ALLAH

All night in the train dread and melancholy grew upon me. Sad to leave, and I know so well how bad things will be. At dawn I brought my conscientious head to the window in duty to the new country. I knew they couldn't keep it up. It's hideous. A cultivated plain with hard rocky hills like a drop-scene. Gest and the Kat were at the station. After a full hour's drive we came to the Garden of Allah, our lodging-to-be. I admit it's entrancing—a tiny white-washed village of two- or three-roomed Spanishish houses, fountains and a swimming pool, arcades and white out-of-doors stairs. Iris and I share one, Kaetchen and Gest and others are in two, and Elinor Patterson in a fourth.

Bertram Cruger had arrived. He and I went to see the sea and found it at Venice, Calif. We went to call on Marion Davies at the M.G.M. studios. Surprising. A place like a dockyard or lunatic asylum with "abandon hope" gates only opened for the bosses and holders of red-tape permits that need to be signed repeatedly. Marion Davies's dressing-room is built in the middle of the sets and is as big as a church in W. R. Hearst's unfailing Spanish-Gothic taste.

Gest wants a longer season here until March 15th. How can I bear it? He's all togged up this evening and has just been in to ask rather sweetly if I think he'll "do." He's wearing a big Lavallière tie and an extremely high-waisted velvet jacket tied tightly above the stomach with a black tape. He says: "We all wear this in Russia, Di dear." He also said: "I joined your school, Di dear, mad on de horses. It's de phenomenalist thing. I took ma feet out of de spurs, let go de reins and went like hell."

Going to dine now in the sitting-room. Twenty Chinese in jade-green silk have brought in the entire dinner from soup to nuts on one tray, so it will be bitterly cold from the second course on.

The child-friend we don't see until Kaetchen goes next week. He sleeps in corners and shadows of the Garden and knows all our comings and goings. Other inhabitants must think that the Garden is haunted. He whistles different tunes and signals at his likes and dislikes as they pass.

31 January

All afternoon I laboured at my stone coat in the theatre, stitching and swearing. Poor bee, that dies young of its own industry. They have given me an enormous car the size of a *wagon-restaurant*. I drive it with trepidation. It takes an hour to get to the theatre and naturally an hour back.

The first night was cruelly alarming and altogether rude and miserable, and the house was packed with screen celebrities. In my unblinking gaze I saw Pickford, Fairbanks, Norma Shearer, Marion Davies, W. R. Hearst, Jannings, Elinor Glyn. To my surprise no one did anything in honour of Reinhardt or any of us—no party, no flowers, no telegrams, no visits to congratulate. Hollywood is unlike any other American city. It would be impossible for say the Fairbanks or Guitrys or Stanislavsky to have a first night in London and not be fêted by the profession at the Savoy or at a private house, wouldn't it? I'm outraged.

Flowers there were in plenty from our own—Ali Mackintosh and Lady Beaverbrook. So it ended with Reinhardt and Kaetchen coming home with us to complain. I could hear the Boy whistling in the Garden, and was frozen with terror of Kaetchen finding him as he walked out. I hate this town, hate it, hate it! I believe that they despise us for being "legitimate" stage.

1 February

One day much like another except that it's Brief February today and I can say "Next month I'll be with my dear." Poor poor bee, she's in a self-pity rhythm and has very little cause in her beautiful hive with three hard-working drones around. Kaetchen has got Raimund out of *The Miracle*, so now the poor boy's *désœuvré* and destitute. He shall be our paid chauffeur and get enough for his cheese sandwiches.

In the new *King of Kings* picture, Schildkraut tells me, the betrayal of Christ is explained as due to a wave of jealousy for Mary Magdalen. No comment.

They don't mind their "p's" here. A newspaper said Miss Constance Talmadge had got a separation from her "Scottish souse Mr Ali Mackintosh."

Three days before the beneficent *Miracle* faded into American memories, Iris and I went together to see Elinor Glyn. She had a cluster of beautiful young men in attendance, one of whom transcended the others in height and wild originality of countenance. He was called Friedrich Ledebur. When we returned to our Garden Iris broke to me the hard news that she would not be travelling back to the East nor yet to England with me. I felt deserted for a whim, lonely and deceived in her affection. It was not, however, a whim, for she married this paragon. *The Miracle* had been a blessed mother to us both. To no other Madonna or Nun had it brought good, but it had answered all our prayers. I was sad to leave alone, and sad to leave our dear Raimund to fend for himself. He looked so woebegone, with empty pockets and only a foreign tongue with which to thrust and parry and find a livelihood. He would have lovesick Iris as a prop for a little longer, and that must console me.

So I went back to England to the pretty Gower Street house, with more dollars in hand for new curtains and for Rex Whistler (of his generation my most loved) to paint us *trompe-l'œil* on the wall. The same delightful life continued, always improving, with plenty of work and play, outings and country Sundays. In spite of this liberty *The Miracle* was my liege lord, and I followed where it led me, faithfully and willingly.

It led me in 1927 to Dortmund in Germany to a gigantic exhibition-hall that dwarfed Olympia. Rosamond Pinchot rallied loyally. The Professor himself was directing it. So big was the hall that the Nun and the crowds used motor-cars in the outer corridors to arrive at the several entrances. Running the length of this huge cathedral at the dress rehearsal, Rosamond sprained her ankle. Consternation! No understudies, no written part! For the first night her foot was bound and injected, and somehow she limped her way gracefully enough through the exacting part, made doubly exhausting by the ground that must be covered, but it was clear at the end that she would be out of the cast for the week's run. There was no one but me to fill the bill. I must take both parts simultaneously. Some girl must be stuck into the niche while I first mimed, then danced, then rampaged round the aisles in an hysterical desire to batter my way out of the prison-church. When the Knight appeared and carried me away to pomps and vanities, the sudden and total darkness allowed me to slip into the niche, panting and trembling from exertion, and to assume with what calm I could the slow-motion of the statue's gradual incarnation. In the second act of six episodes the unfortunate Nun made quick changes in the motor that carried her through different entrances to meet Love, Abduction, Rape, Satanism, Revolution, Crucifixion, Prostitution and Childbirth, while through this pandemonium the Devil stalked and Death danced. In the third act, once more the serene Madonna, I regained the holy niche, returned to stone and, as the light darkened, my place was taken by the static understudy while I, derelict and broken in spirit, crawled back to Mother Church clutching my dying baby. It was a *tour de force* and one that cost me dear in health. At every performance, before going on and after it was over, a doctor would inject me with a glassful of camphor. It made a lump that could be seen through my clinging habit. I played the two parts twice a day. My legs got ill and cramped with running, and I had to be carried into my hotel.

Maurice Baring came to the play, and Henry Bernstein and a

few others who could get to Germany but not to America, and
I regretted that for them I could not do my best in either part,
and some fond friend found Maurice Baring's review of *The
Miracle* cold:

I think the Major [Baring] only says fair about you as the
Madonna. You know I don't much admire *The Miracle* and it gives
me no emotion at all. But when you come off your perch it makes
me catch my breath—"Hats off, gentlemen, here's genius." A
doe * moving gracefully on the stage may not be the noblest thing
in life. All I say is that millions would give their eyes to do it well.
With effortless ease you surpass them all—*quantum lenta solent inter
viburna cupressi*. Sarah Bernhardt was an ugly old bitch but the
terrible gift of beauty is yours. Maurice doesn't mention that.

Reinhardt's message was my reward:

Diana, geliebte Freundin, wunderbare seelensgute tapfere Frau,
zartester nobelster Künstler, bester Kamerad, ich umarme Sie
und bin Ihnen für dieses Leben verbunden. R.†

Duff met me at Annecy and we had a week's rest that did me
no good. I was worn out and fell into a low fever that kept me
in bed in London, treating myself with potions and spells to
enable me by May to join *The Miracle* in Prague, Budapest
and Vienna. I went but I went ill. The whole chapter was
unpropitious. I coughed until the pillar shook. I went to a
doctor who would cocaine my throat before each performance,
but it was no cure. I wanted to enjoy, but could not, the baroque bridges and palaces of Prague, its music and Counts and
peasants. In Budapest things were no better, and there (or was
it in Vienna?) a new doctor who had treated Alfonso XIII

* A dated synonym for a female.
† Diana, beloved friend, wonderful, good, brave woman, most sensitive and noble artist, best companion, I embrace you and am grateful to
you for life. R.

brought me my grandmother's bronchitis-kettle. It had two compartments, one for plain and one for Vichy water. It soaked me with sizzling spittings out of its long spout and the doctor said: "*Sie müssen einen Gummimantel kaufen,*" so I would sit by the hour over the spout in my mackintosh being spat at. To make matters worse I had invited, in a fit of *parvenu* generosity, Viola and Alan Parsons, Hutchie and Mary Hutchinson and Curtis Moffat to be my guests in Vienna at Sacher's Hotel. We were all fractious and Viola and I often in tears. We all pulled different ways, a tug o' war on a cat o' nine tails. I knew that they were seeing me act for the first time, and I was at my very worst. Sacher's was all that it was painted, but with a hidden squalor and spartanism that no one had drawn. Frau Sacher, famous throughout Europe for despotic treatment of emperors and clowns, who cuffed her waiters in public for any laxity in their subservience, or for not knowing the correct *Gotha* appellation of the *Hochgeboren*, would favouritise me, bringing me *bonnes bouches* of foie gras or wild strawberries, with her little bulldogs yapping round her button-boots, and a cigar in her mouth. The only private bath was mine, and from all over the hotel my friends came to use it. Beds of iron, and a service of another century that caused one to wonder, did not soothe our frayed and fluffy nerves. I was glad when it was over.

With *The Miracle* buried (as I thought, never to be exhumed) I could return to a happy convalescence in London with Duff and my friends. They said: "What are you going to do next?" but I was not looking for drama of any sort. The stage never drew me back. I knew that *The Miracle* had taught me nothing. Such art as I had practised was inborn. Least of all had I learnt diction, since the play was silent. Urged by Kaetchen, I had been in New York to see Mrs Carrington, a rich lady who as a hobby tuned raucous voices into music of the spheres. She had taught John Barrymore to speak Hamlet better far than anyone I had ever heard. In London he had vaguely suggested that I should play Princess Anne to his Richard III and, probably buoyed up by this hollow hope, I asked Mrs Carrington's help. She was willing, and we started on a system that bewildered me utterly, but with which I blindly persevered until my voice cracked temporarily and I returned to England.

There was talk of another pantomime written by Hugo von Hofmannsthal, and it seems that I went to America the following winter to hustle and sharpen the organisers, unnecessarily as the piece was never written, but I had got into the habit of an ocean journey once a year. I have the letters that this one brought forth—Duff's unchanging letters of devotion and goodness and zest and remorse for petty sins. One night he made a fool of himself at a casino. I do not remember the occasion, let alone the loss, but the reformed gambler wrote like a shamefaced child:

I cannot forgive myself for my two mad nights at Cannes. I go on and on regretting and building castles based on how differently I should have behaved. I meant so firmly to do nothing of the kind and seem to have done it so insanely without giving a thought to my resolutions. I feel it humiliating and vile to you who are so good and wise about money. At thirty-eight one really ought to know better, and what makes it more maddening is that I was sure I did. My only consolation is in the theory of the even distribution of fortune. I have so much, so much—love, health, work. Money certainly matters least. This loss which has worried me more perhaps than it ought to have, and has spoilt my holiday, has made me realise more than ever, if it were possible, how much I love you and depend on you, and how in any trouble I turn to you.

Bobbety [Cranborne] and I shared a double berth coming home.

Knowing that it was impossible to find out from him which he liked best and that if I insisted on his choosing he would take the one he liked least, I took the one I liked best which is the upper. Come home soon but not sooner than you want to, and know that I am utterly yours so long as this machine etc.

Impossible even to reprove, it was (I think) his swan's flutter. My heart was Highland-Scotch and in this year, with *The Miracle* salary lacking, I was still trying to build a bulwark against want and the workhouse, and for ever enjoining poor Duff to "scrape and save" while I looked for opportunities.

CHAPTER FOUR

St George and the Dragons

THERE was a child called Rosemary, daughter of the famously beautiful Duchess of Sutherland. Her father's Stafford House gave on to Green Park as our house did, and there with our nannies we used to meet. She had lank primrose-coloured hair, a raucous voice, a laugh that quickened the sad to gaiety, a wide mouth and a general look of bedraggled apple-blossom. Her appearance never changed in her short lifetime. She and Eric Ednam married the same year as we did. They lived in great happiness in Worcestershire, blessed with three boys. Duff and I were often at Himley and, like everyone her beams lit, we loved and admired Rosemary. In January 1928 she and Eric invited us to go for a few weeks to Biskra. It was a winter heyday with laughter all the way—laughter smoking a hubble-bubble in Algiers with the very beautiful Countess Charles de Polignac and her husband, both dressed native with veil and scimitar; laughter to find impassable floods in the Sahara; less laughter (from all but Rosemary) when the miscalculating doctor decimally plugged Eric with ten times the injection dose of streptococci. (Eric had no reaction at all, and I was sorry, since he had refused my Guy's-trained ministrations.) There was laughter too as we rode in the desert and ate on eiderdowns under palms with Clare Sheridan and sheikhs and bushagas.

When there was still a week to go in this second Garden of

Allah a telegram arrived offering Duff the post of Financial Secretary to the War Office. It might, for all we knew, have become outdated, as it followed us from stage to stage in Africa, but hope was high and we packed him off cheering in the good ship *Timgad* while we went south to Timgad too. All was well and never too late. Sir Laming Worthington-Evans was the cheerful Secretary of State, and our boy was already on a stout conspicuous rung of the fearful ladder. Duff loved "Worthy," who was one to delegate responsibility gladly. Duff wrote:

He would sometimes hand me a formidable file and say, "This seems to be a complicated question. I haven't looked into it and don't propose to do so. You can settle it as you think right."

This must be the subordinate's dream if he feels capable, and Duff never felt otherwise. He was always unfaltering, and I never outgrew my surprise at his self-confidence. So certain am I always of defeat for myself and those I love, that generally when Duff came home from his back bench or his Ministry I would ask: "Any bloomers?" Worthy liked Duff and was very pleased with his first speech on Army Estimates, delivered, as were all his speeches, without notes, and said that he had made a "splendid dayboo."

We could ask no more of life. No more could my mother with her four children all happy, and her sixteen happy grandchildren. She repudiated age, disliking its perpetual obstructions to active plans and schemes. Like Bess of Hardwick, who was told that she would die when she stopped building, my mother found brick and stone rejuvenating. She had sold the majestic old house in Arlington Street for a king's ransom and therefore had money that burnt her pocket while she hesitated whether to settle it on me or to build me a home. For her happiness and mine she built.

Mrs Fisher of Bognor had died, aged ninety, and the house, that by rights belonged to the Duke of Portland, as he had lent my mother the money to buy it (she had honestly repaid him a yearly £150), now belonged to me. It was Duff's terrestrial paradise, and it became one of mine after some of the saved-and-scraped hoards had gone into furbishings and paint and baths and a gardener to garnish it. My mother's foundation-stone was laid, and a wing of two rooms, larger than the others and lighted by Gothic-topped windows in character with the house, was erected. We could, with squeezing and using the lodge, house thirteen people. Now began the Sundays and holiday weeks that have left a memory of sunlight and *agrément* (I do not like to use French words, although this book is pretty well peppered with them) to everyone who stayed with us. Chiefly I remember Maurice Baring there, reading his new novels aloud—*C* and *Cat's Cradle*. I was, as usual, agonised by my friends' or Duff's literary *chefs-d'œuvre* and quite incapable of fair criticism. For some reason I felt this discomfiture less about Maurice's poems, which he loved to read, particularly one to the memory of Lord Lucas, killed in the first war, and one to his nephew, Cecil Spencer, lost at sea. I never felt it at all with Belloc, who would recite his ballads as though they were songs, and his sonnets and nonsense rhymes, and later his *Heroic Poem in Praise of Wine*, which he dedicated to Duff.

At Bognor on a Sunday morning I would sometimes, to please Maurice, go with him to Mass. Then, Mass over, we would buy as many little lobsters as there were people to eat them. Before lunch there was bathing, and after the Channel-shock the bag of big Bognor prawns, bought on the beach with the lobsters from the local character Billy Welfare, was produced. These we would eat on the grass, clad in bath-towels with wet hair, and drink rum ("rum for the sailor") shaken up with real limes and sugar, and hear the sea, a blue background to the lupins and roses. After lunch there was sleep for the early birds, and bracing walks over the Downs for the lie-abeds, reading aloud, crosswords and *Spectator* competitions. Duff was a constant competitor and was often first or second prize-winner. The following entry, a sonnet-receipt for an excellent cocktail (later engraved on a crystal shaker), brought him a first prize:

RECIPE FOR THE MIXING OF "SUNSHINE," A WEST INDIAN COCKTAIL

Rum, divine daughter of the sugar cane,
Rum, staunch ally of those who sail the sea,
Jamaican rum of rarest quality!
One half of rum this goblet shall contain.
Bring Andalusian oranges from Spain,
And lemons from the groves of Sicily,
Mingle their juice (proportions two to three)
And sweeten all with Demerara grain.
Of Angosturan bitters just a hint
And, for the bold, of brandy just a spice,
A leaf or two of incense-bearing mint
And any quantity of chinking ice.
Then shake, then pour, then quaff and never stint
Till life shall seem a dream of Paradise.

It was at the end of this year of 1928 that King George V, very near to death, recovered and chose Craigweil House, Aldwick, as his place of convalescence, and Bognor was dubbed Regis, and soon afterwards the cornfields gave way to villadom.

After this disaster we would often move our Sundays to the

Shell House at Goodwood, a temple-folly guarded by two stone sphinxes. We would take our lobsters and meats, fruit and wine, roses and candles, to this delightful pavilion, and there by sun or moonshine revel and sing. I can hear Olga Lynn and Jimmy Smith singing descants, and Belloc I can hear too, and Duff acting Browning's "Light Woman" or intoning the sonnets of Shakespeare and Keats, and Maurice puling atonal Chinese scraps translated to fit the occasion. The young would crown the sphinxes with red roses and mount them on race-days, and when the candles guttered out we would go home to the garden, and at last to bed to the sound of the eternal waves.

Later, when the guests (all but Maurice) grew older, they got very out of hand and would voice their complaints loudly. The poor little house was breaking under them. There would be messages: "Tell Mr Johnston to have his bath in the less good one," "Mr Johnston says he won't," or perhaps a telegram: "Arriving 6.15 won't have room top of stairs," or worst of all an aside to another guest, but meant for my ears: "Bedtime! I suppose I must go to Ironers" (a reflection on the mattress). Lord G. complained that there was no room for his knees in the downstairs lu, he being so very tall.

The Bognor cottage is crumbling, and few today remember gathering rosebuds and making hay there.

Maurice never got older or laughed less or resisted the lighted candles at any grand London ball. Almost nightly in the summer season we ate our quail and drank our champagne together, while his trembling hand wrote verses on the back of menu-cards. Here are some of them:

> He drank too deeply of your eyes too kind:
> Small wonder that the god of love is blind.

The presage of all beauty that shall be,
The ghost of all dead beauty in the past,
Have met together in mortality:
This is incarnate beauty come at last.

Diana, wise and watchful at the feast,
I love you: you the loveliest, I the least.

The god of love, to his fair mother's isle,
Took you to be his playmate for a while.
His mother looked, and wept, and weeping she
Resigned to you her lost supremacy.

When Beauty with the gods left Jove's high place
She wandered homeless till she found your face.

Maurice always called me Mrs C, because once I had referred
to Duff as Mr C to get a laugh, so now I have shelves of his
books (everything he ever wrote) each inscribed in his shaky
calligraphy "Mrs C's collection." Once outside the Embassy
Club, some London wedding or Ascot day (for I remember
him in a grey top hat), he snatched a large basket-tray full of
gardenias and violets from the rich one-legged flowerman and
threw the lot into my open car. *The Times* was twice the paper
to me when Maurice was alive, for any morning the Personal
Column might have a message:

Mrs C.

I told her she was beautiful, it's true;
But I said nothing when I wrote to you.

I, no poet, could only quote:

Nothing shall come of nothing; speak again!

Next day's *Times* brought Maurice's answer:

Yet out of nothing God made time and space,
The stars, the sun, the summer and your face.

CITY OF EXILE AND ROMANCE

In September 1928 Duff went to Geneva as a delegate to the League of Nations. He was a believer in, and an active worker for, the poor League, and he gave twenty-eight lectures about it in 1927 and 1928. I went with him to Geneva and saw Switzerland as a microcosm of the civilised world as it should be—the one-in-three of countries, languages and costumes, federated and tolerant. Ever since I have had perhaps an exaggerated love for this peaceful town and its traditions of exile and romance, for its toy steamers, its Coppets and Ferneys, its Protestants' Wall, and for the hope that the League was there fostering. (With my little eye I saw it die, for I was there again at Munich-time.) The whole set-up I found inspiring and diverting; the delegates' difficulty in accepting alphabetical *placement à table*, the miraculous interpreters (faster than echo and more intelligible), and hearing Aristide Briand (in gloves) speak with a voice too harmonious for the words to count. Duff enjoyed it less. He gave a magnificent second-sighted lecture on the imminence of barbarians. He was in serious vein and had not time to share my freedom of the Lake or to join a Dalcroze eurythmic class, or to go to the circuses and concerts, nor could he quizz the stuffier delegates. But we had Belloc to delight us both. He was what he called "walking over the Jura" with his faithful "Bear" Warre. From their account they had done more singing than walking. We had Pertinax for seriousness and Arnold Bennett for humour and diversion. Bathing in the Lake of Annecy, I introduced him to Lady Horner. They shook hands treading water. They were both over sixty.

We had motored to Geneva and thought now of driving to Sicily for the last summer sun, so beneficial to Duff. Finding that it was too long a drive, we thought to board a ship at Genoa that would land us at Syracuse. Such a boat there was.

the *Ausonia*, bound for Alexandria, but unwilling to take passengers further than Sicily. I appealed with little hope to an Italian colleague, who asked for time to telegraph. The next day he told me that all was arranged. We had but to call at Genoa for the tickets to take us there and back. At Genoa they were handed to Duff together with the money paid out in Geneva and a free return-berth for the car. Aboard we were shown into the bridal suite. I see it now as carved out of ivory, with fluttering white silk and a crystal bath. This was my first whiff of Mussolini.

It must not be imagined that I did not pay for all these rainbow windfalls. They only sharpened my anxieties. If Duff was late in Taormina, I would imagine that he had gone on his own to Etna and been sucked into the crater. How many times in London have I not, after hours of Sister-Anning at the window, rung up the police-station to ask if there had been any possible accident to one A. D. Cooper with his name stitched in his suit-pocket? I thought: "If I am like this about my husband, it is as well that I have no child." Indeed, I had made the best of my barrenness and persuaded myself that children were sharper than serpents' teeth. Girls were sure to be plain and without virtue, boys dishonest, even queer, and certainly gambling drunkards.

To be free of nurseries gave me liberty for adventure, so that when our great friend Sidney Herbert, who was starting the cruel illness that was to rob him of his youth and life, asked me to join him on a health journey to Nassau, I went, torn as always by old devotion and by loathing the separation from Duff. Sallying forth this time had some kind of duty in it, that warranted crossing the Atlantic. Through our sea-journey we read aloud poetry and *Elizabeth and Essex* by Lytton Strachey. At Nassau we lived in the finest hotel on American-planned hygienic food with bad service, instead of the old ant-eaten "digs" with rocking-chairs and tin-openers. The palms and humming-birds had been swept away by hurricanes. Hog Island was already overbuilt. The little town was suffering a horrible earth-change of brick and concrete. Gone was the primitive atmosphere. Where it once consoled, it now irritated. Gone too were the spontaneous parties, the old friends, the turtle-feasts and the market. Even the sea, though still volatile as ether, and the blinding coral beaches, could not compare with the old New Providence of 1924. I could find no calm. Sidney was not improving in health. Besides, my mind was all but closed to outer things. It was totally wrapped in whether or not I was going to have a child. I was alive to that thought only. Not daring to give Duff a hope that might prove a dupe, I wrote to him of the day's doings, and his letters tell of the War Office, visits to munition factories and to Oldham, Army Estimates, all-night sittings at the House of Commons, the fever and fret of politics taken so blithely, and also of scandals and parties:

There was a fancy ball at Ava Ribblesdale's last night, and all the women looked 50% worse than usual—S. as Little Lord Fauntleroy quite awful, P. as a street Arab just dirty. Venetia and I had been to Michael [Herbert]'s where was Willie Clarkson with brilliantined beard and frock coat, his whole apparatus and a lot of French porters' clothes. Rosemary [Ednam] looked well in your "Artful Dodger." The rest of us were porters. We thought we were pretty funny all dashing into the room shouting "*Porteur, porteur!*" Gerald Berners was good as a hunting man with a marvellously funny mask by Oliver Messel. He had announced his intention of going as Nurse Cavell but was dissuaded. Winston as Nero was good. F.E. went as a Cardinal. The dressing-up was of course the best part but spoilt by your not being there, as everything is.

I was not long away, being every day surer of my secret and anxious to curtail the excursion. Sidney's brother Michael arrived, so I left my charge in capable hands and fled home. I knew that Duff, not having had to invent a consolatory philosophy as I had, would be happier at the prospect than I, who was only slowly appreciating what was coming to me. I was singing the Magnificat for Duff, not yet for myself, but as the months passed I became obsessed with joy and pride. "Late in time" made this child more to be adored.

Grotesque in appearance but feeling healthy and unapprehensive (for a change) I flung myself into the General Election of 1929 at Oldham. We never had a hope. The greedy Liberals had determined to run two candidates. Mr Wiggins, the sitting Member (Ned Grigg, the Liberal of our former election, having been translated to the Lords as Lord Altrincham), wisely backed out. As a newcomer he was right, but we felt that forsaking the seat would be a betrayal to our Oldham friends, with whose support Duff had fought and won, and who had been most loyal and undemanding. Once in the fearful fight one loses reasoning-power and is easily blinded to the truth by zealous workers and primrose-wearers. The town was plastered with a picture of Stanley Baldwin, looking as shifty as a coward caught, labelled "Safety First" (the most uninspiring, un-English slogan ever shouted). No longer the knock-about turn that I had been in 1924, and unable to clog-dance or be merry, I dragged myself around, a conspicuously expectant mother. The night before the count we were called back from Manchester after the polling-booths had closed, to have our silly hopes fanned by the scenes of enthusiasm in Oldham. I suppose that the Labour Party felt too secure to demonstrate and had gone to bed, leaving the streets free to wildly shouting Conservatives waving their colours confidently.

Next day the defeat was announced. I was so preoccupied
with myself that I could have taken it calmly had it not been
for the tears of the women and girls. They wore blue hats, and
we called them "the bluebells." Their disappointment after
so determined and tireless a tussle nearly broke my heart, to
say nothing of the handsome bouquet, prepared and inscribed
to the victor's wife, that the vanquished must accept. Thank
God I was never again part of a lost election. We were not
the only losers. The tide was against the old Government, and
the Labour Buggins had to be given his chance.

Our seaside haven was still unravished, and there we retired
from worldly labours, Duff to start his book on Talleyrand and
I to marvel and dream about my child, very happy though a
little apprehensive, marking auguries and omens. A sitting
hare would not get out of the way of our car. This, to one who
had read Mary Webb's *Precious Bane*, augured a hare-lip for
my baby. Most disquieting to me, though worse for the reader,
was a short story by Max Beerbohm read aloud to us by Desmond MacCarthy.* It is graven on my memory because I knew
before he did how the story ended, yet I dared not stop him. I
should have created some diversion. The tale described the
lodge of a seaside house (the actual one in which we were
living) where dwelt William and Mary, the loving husband
and wife—he the "man of genius" in her eyes, she the "brave
little woman" in Max (the gentleman from London)'s banter.
The story stood fair for tragedy. William and Mary were too
happy, and when that happiness was fulfilled and a child was
expected one knew the end. Mary had no misgivings, but
it was destined that her child should live only for an hour
and that she should die bearing it. William wrecks his world-
weary bark on some war rocks and the story-teller comes back

* "William and Mary," included in *And Even Now* (1920).

to the forsaken Bognor cottage, to the house that he had known once littered with books from William's shelves and bright with flowers from Mary's garden, and finds the grass obliterating it, the stucco fallen from the walls, the once-open door shut and knockerless, only the keyhole to peep through into "darkness impenetrable," and the bell that he rings and rings to hear again Mary's enchanting laughter echoing out of the past.

In September 1929 we moved to London, I into Lady Carnarvon's nursing home in Portland Place for my Cæsarean section. Silently I said goodbye to Gower Street for ever. It was a lovely evening, and I felt how sad it was for us both that such happiness should end. I sent a lot of telegrams by telephone to nearest friends announcing the operation for next day, and ending: "Pray for me." A telephone girl said: "May I do the same?" Next morning I went to the operating theatre and when I woke I was told that I was the mother of a boy, but I could not, I suppose, believe it, for I asked over and over again all day. I had prepared Duff for the hare-lip and when in a state of great emotion he asked to look at his son they told him that he might not see him until he had spoken to the doctor. This seemed to confirm the dread, but John Julius was a perfect child and has in my eyes remained so. I was very ill for a day, very near death, but soon was gloriously well and taken on a stretcher to my home. Crowds outside the clinic door, all wishing me well, made me cry terribly, because I was still weak. Some of the hundreds of letters written me by strangers were from mothers who had just lost their newborn child. I remember minding so much that I was no longer allowed my letters unopened.

I asked a great many people to be godfathers and godmothers, as they did in fairy-tales, and no bad fairy came.

There were Maurice, Otto Kahn and the Aga Khan, brother John and Sidney Herbert, J. M. Barrie, Margot Oxford (because she asked to be), Max Beaverbrook, Betty Cranborne, Ethel Russell in America and, of course, Kaetchen. I hated to have the baby out of my arms and used to take him shopping, wrapped in a swaddling cashmere shawl with his monogram in blue, lay him on the counter and buy what I wanted while the shop-girls worshipped the bundle. I had the best of all nannies, Nanny Ayto, to care for him and teach him goodness. She still at times looks after his own child Artemis.

Duff and I took Sidney Herbert to Nassau again in 1930, and this time it was still sadder. He was getting no better, and was soon to lose his leg. It was staying with him earlier this year at his pretty house at Lympne that I feared a tidal wave might drown Duff, and in fact it almost did. The Sunday afternoon was unusually hot and still, so still that lying on my bed I got up to look and wonder how and why the trees had become like a painting. Even animal-sounds had ceased. I felt it too eerie to bear, and as I looked a bank of black cloud rolled up from the distant sea, bringing with it a rustle that turned to a tempest of sound and movement. I tore down to the others, playing bridge and unconscious of anything but trumps, to ask where Duff was. He had gone to bathe with Bobbety Cranborne, they told me. "O God, he'll be in the tidal wave!" I shrieked. Roars of laughter and accusations of "really going too far this time," and a painful wait for me—no news not good news, as there never would be news of men taken by a tidal wave. At last I saw them arrive and heard to my triumph of the South Coast's famous tidal wave that had swept away bathing-huts and chairs for miles. Duff was in his half-depth when Bobbety on shore shouted to him to look and hurry. He looked back at a wall of water and ran in the nightmare obstruction of shallow water. "He came up the shingle white with exhaustion," said Bobbety.

Recovered, Duff was offered a new constituency at Winchester. He nursed it for a year, but with all its beauty and accessibility, one could not put one's heart into Winchester as one had done into Oldham. One's shoulder, yes, and a lot of shoulder it needed. Country constituencies are far more demanding. Every flower-show and little bazaar claims one's presence, and more is thought of the Member's attendance and social grace than of getting him to the top at Westminster. Oldham had been very proud of having Winston as their Member; I am sure that they still feel in part responsible for his zenith, and they were inordinately proud of Duff when he reached the Admiralty. I took a four-roomed panelled Queen Anne house at Winchester, a workman's dwelling in a churchyard of crooked gravestones bound in briars. The rent was a pound a week. No sooner was the bath installed and the panels painted than a hullabaloo started about the by-election in the St George's division of Westminster, caused by the death of Duff's former chief, Sir Laming Worthington-Evans. The back-benchers, impatient with Mr Baldwin's leadership of the Opposition, saw an opportunity (with the help of the noisiest Conservative newspapers, already in full cry) to bring him down.

Duff was lecturing in Sweden. I was enjoying the tour to the top of my bent, enjoying the snow and the ice-floes, the unfamiliar towns, the food of reindeers' tongues and Baltic shrimps, and the warm hospitality that lapped us round in small provincial houses as well as in the Royal Palace at Stockholm. (I remember seeing the King riding a bicycle and one day, taking us to the door after his family luncheon, asking us whether we would walk or wait while he fetched us a taxi.)

Suddenly, by telephone from London, a new fervently loved friend, Lord Ashfield, told us that no challenger had appeared in St George's. The lists were open. No one seemed prepared to fight this safest of all Conservative seats. What few considered taking up their leader Mr Baldwin's cudgels feared to fight that two-handed engine, the *Daily Express* and *Daily Mail*. No giants could frighten Duff, who came home hell for leather like St George himself to fight the dragons. My timorous heart quailed, not without cause. Besides, I loved Lord Beaverbrook and it was a fight to the death with him personally, since Sir Ernest Petter, the Press Lords' candidate, was but a man of straw. Lord Rothermere, the other dragon, fought with his newspaper, but Max Beaverbrook had his oratorical dynamism as an extra and formidable weapon. Mayfair, Belgravia, Victoria, Pimlico and many other wards in the heart of London were up in arms, and it was civil war, brother against brother. Lord Ashfield put a motor at our disposal. In it every morning lay a white camellia to pin in my cap (strange what things are never forgotten). As against this encouragement Lady Hartington, thinking me a normal candidate's wife and not platform-dumb, booked me for a series of meetings. I was to be responsible, if I remember rightly, for the domestic staffs. It not being thinkable to let her down, I managed somehow, by reading aloud endless messages from Duff with (I hoped) comic interjections, a sort of Charlie Chaplin turn. It was all far more like an election in a Disraeli novel than the Oldham and Winchester campaigns I was used to. Mayfair went mad. Never for a century had they had a fighting election, and they were feverishly excited. *"Aux armès, aristos!"* Duff and Max met before the fray like knights before a tourney. Max advised Duff not to blunt his lance. "Say what you like about me. I shall mind less than you will mind what I say about you." It was nobly said, though in the end Duff's armour had the fewer chinks, for Max never quite forgave him his victory. I was in touch with the enemy by telephone all through the battle. Again he behaved with nobility when Duff in a speech overstepped some limit, and Max deliberately overlooked the solecism. It could have had no effect upon the election's outcome, but it could have put Duff in the wrong and made a great coil for him.

I think that everyone but myself enjoyed the fray uproariously. Members of Parliament were thumping the tub and bawling their lungs out at street-corners. This was no baby- or butcher-kissing election. The gloves were off. My mother and Lady Cunard used fearlessly to attend the opponents' meetings, which were sometimes very rough. I remember hearing of one that was held at the Grosvenor Gallery, where chairs were flung and broken. My mother calmly described herself as having been "all right under a table." Emerald Cunard would go early, take a front seat in the hall and ostentatiously read a pro-Baldwin paper. The *Star* was one and the *Daily Telegraph* another. Whenever either Lord Beaverbrook's or Lord Rothermere's name was mentioned, she would look up and and mutter loudly: "Degenerates; they're both degenerates!"

After the hurly-burly some great or lesser house, the Londonderrys' or Juliet Duff's or Portia Stanley's, would spread an open supper-table with hot soup and restoratives for the fighting men and women. Prognostications were fifty-fifty. It was entirely guesswork. One night there would be bad news about Bond Street, another day about the domestic staffs or all Pimlico. It murdered my sleep, but Duff enjoyed it and with cause. The *Daily Mail* called him "Mickey

Mouse," meant pejoratively, though Mickey is as gallant a mouse as ever gnawed a lion's net.

I was at Queen's Hall when Mr Baldwin made his memorable speech. I saw the blasé reporters, scribbling semiconsciously, jump out of their skins to a man when he unfalteringly said that the Press Lords "were aiming at power without responsibility, the prerogative of the harlot throughout the ages."

On the telephone Max had given me no encouragement. As all fighters should be, he was confident of his victory. On the evening of polling day, the voting ended, we talked by telephone and he said that we had won. He told me roughly the situation in every ward, and it proved a very accurate summing-up. Then came the count, and Duff had won by over five thousand votes. I see little that night in the blur of fatigue except a weirdly lit mob-scene composed entirely of familiar faces distorted by yells of enthusiasm, waving enormous flags dragged from house-tops. I see a Delacroix picture on a cyclorama—no less. So we had a last tired triumphant supper with Mr Baldwin, who, to honour his champion, walked on Duff's right as his sponsor when, a week later, he took his seat in the House.

CHAPTER FIVE

Politics and Parties

WAS it in 1931, *annus terribilis*, that the pound fell? Whenever it was, Duff and I were in Dorset staying with the Cranbornes. Lord and Lady Salisbury were of the party, and so were Mr Baldwin and others. The news then, as now, was always bad. Times, we all thought, had never been worse or England closer to the abyss. On that Sunday morning at Cranborne an atmosphere of great unrest pervaded the house. Some secret crime seemed to be clamouring for exposure. Strange motor-borne messengers had come and gone. Mr Baldwin, once churched and luncheoned, was to return to London. The Salisbury faces wore looks of "We could a tale unfold . . . to harrow up your souls." The rest of us knew by whispers that we must assemble in the front court after lunch for some pronouncement to be made by Mr Baldwin.

"The pound has fallen. We are off the gold standard. I think it right to tell you immediately." The sentence, delivered with hesitation of voice and nervous stick-writing in the gravel, came as an anticlimax, but Mr Baldwin's gravity reduced his audience to two minutes' silence, broken by Lady Stanley's saying: "What exactly will it mean?"—a question that we were all burning to ask. The explanation was unsatisfactory to most of us, but it set them all talking of short rations and sacrifice and resolve to stiffen upper lips, tighten belts and pull in horns. In a few weeks the pound's insufficiency turned to golden hopes of prosperity. Were the dejected or the buoyant right? I have never asked, nor have I thought of it again.

We went to the Lake of Annecy that August while Mr and Mrs Baldwin were taking their yearly cure at Aix. Duff, who never lived down his schoolboy's bashfulness before masters, was strongly against asking them to luncheon beneath the chestnut-trees at Talloires on the lake. I was determined to leave no precious stone unturned that might lead to preferment for merit recognised and rewarded, so they were invited and they accepted, but Duff said that I really could not wear trousers. I said that I must, and he said that he would lift his ban if I promised to say nothing embarrassing at luncheon. I promised.

It was a prayed-for day. The swans floated past the green banks, and luncheon was the best that a fortune could buy. I had my trousers and a fisherman's shirt, and the usual vast straw hat to give me confidence. Mr Baldwin had just been back to London at a moment's notice for a crucial interview with Ramsay MacDonald, the Prime Minister. We had hardly sat down before I said, with a total lack of inhibition: "Come on now, tell us every word Ramsay said, for Duff tells me nothing." There was a smiling grunt as answer. Duff's face blazed into a sunset of shame and embarrassment, and Mrs Baldwin, astonished and horrified, said: "My husband tells me nothing either, but then I would *never* ask him." I felt more remorseful at having betrayed my promise to Duff than worried by Mrs Baldwin's snub, but I did not feel, as Duff did, that I had murdered his political future. For the rest of the sun-flecked meal of unique dishes and wine we talked of the uncontroversial news-less swans.

From Annecy we sped to Venice via Garda, where we passed Mr Leo Amery running at the double down from some

Tyrolean mountain-top, London-bound to be in at the Labour Government's fever and collapse. The dear good conscientious man got no office in the Coalition reconstruction, while Duff's calm patience led him on to Venice and promotion. He left me at Venice for the House of Commons' sudden reassembling. We hated being parted that August. Duff wrote from Brescia, speeding away in the train:

26 August

I was never so miserable at leaving you as tonight, not even that first time when I left you in New York. I had again that horrible homesick feeling which makes everything seem vanity and vexation, not because I have ever ceased to love you as much, but because we never had such an unexpected and anyhow beastly parting. We have been so very much together these last ten days, and so wonderfully happy. In all our twelve years of marriage I do not think there has been anything to equal it. You grow always not only dearer to me but more necessary, and you become all the time better, wiser and more to be adored.

I hate writing in the train and I can't do it as cleverly as you can, but I wanted to write to you before I went to bed. Every yard that I travel from you I become more and more determined to return on Saturday . . .

P.S. I had just stuck this in the envelope when the train stopped and I popped out my huge head and saw we were at Desenzano. I looked north. The lights were twinkling all along the shores of the lake and I sighed my soul towards our San Vigilio.

London   *28 August*

I went straight from the station to Buck's where I found David Margesson. He gave me the gossip and implied, though he wasn't sure, that I had not got a job. He said definitely that Oliver [Stanley] has. George came in and said how furious his cousin was at not getting the India Office.

I went to bed feeling disappointed but at the same time happy at the prospect of return to Venice. This morning I was busy making arrangements to return to you. I found that I could get to Venice tomorrow night at 9.30. I imagined your meeting me, and our going to "Olympia" on the Piazza, and my telling you all the news. Then the telephone rang. Mr Baldwin's secretary wanted my address. I felt sure that his letter would only be explaining why he could not give me a job, otherwise he would have telegraphed. The letter arrived just as I was leaving for the Party meeting and was giving money to our old friend, the drunken gaolbird, in the street.

My dear Duff, I am afraid your holiday is going west too. I want you to go on as Financial Secretary to the War Office under Crewe, who will give you a warm welcome. Let me have a telegram and come home as soon as you can. Give my regards to your lady. Thank her for her letter. Ever yours, S.B.

I received it with feelings as mixed as it is possible for feelings to be. I saw a crowd of politicians over cocktails at Quaglino's. Oliver pretends that he hasn't heard it yet, but I believe it's quite settled that he goes to the Home Office under Herbert Samuel. E. is dithering with disappointment, so are many others. Another must give up all his directorships and serve under one he loathes. It shows what people will do for office and it reconciles me to mine. It will be much more amusing than it was, as I shall be alone in the House of Commons and have the Estimates.

I've just rung up Haddon and spoken to John and your mother. John said that it was all a big mistake. We ought to have refused to coalesce. I said (which I believe is true) that within a few hours the pound would not have been worth twopence. "And a good thing too," said John.

I was looking forward this morning to coming back to you. I had got the motor-trunk ready and looked out the *Baedeker* of Northern Italy and everything.

So I was alone in Venice, missing Duff cruelly, praying for his return and (incompatibly) for him to get office. A wilder season Venice had not seen since pre-war days. Laura Corrigan had that year married the Adriatic and seemed to be holding most of the palaces in fee. I scarcely knew her, and I wanted rather priggishly to keep out of the maelstrom of her loyal and disloyal guests. But once Duff's fate was sealed I got lured to the festive Mocenigo Palace and never regretted it, for there Chips Channon became a diverting, lasting friend, and many younger people pleased me and frolicked me along with them. I wrote to Duff:

Grand Hotel, Venice   *30 August*

They are pressing me to join them. I suppose I'm for it, in fact I'm there. I dined with them last night and my plate was pyramided with birthday presents, including a really noble cigarette-case from Laura. It's all a modern fairy story, with everything that Beauty wants in her new palace—twenty backgammon-boards, rare *friandises*, and, since there are flesh-and-blood servants and many of them, placards on all the bedroom-tables warn you to tip them at their peril, and whatever we do we mustn't buy stamps or cigarettes, or pay for washing or cleaning or *coiffures*, and above all we must remember not to pay for drinks at the Grand Hotel or Lido Bar. The brutes have kept from Laura that Harry's Bar exists, so there they may spend their own money and feel untied.

Palazzo Mocenigo   *Later*

Today has been wonderfully typical. Luncheon on two wide fishing-boats about a hundred yards from the beach, with forty or fifty people taken out in speedboats and others on *pedalos* or water-bicycles or floats, and some actually swimming. Ourselves in the lifeboat with red-shirted mariners. Music on board, and spaghetti. Charlie de Beistegui the host. Baba d'Erlanger in very tight white linen trousers, a white linen glengarry and some great gems newly-dragged from the ocean. Mrs Corrigan left early to arrange for my arrival here. The arrangements consisted of taking another palace floor, along with eight more servants, another gondola and another super-charged launch-de-luxe. The arrival of the Christophers of Greece has something to do with it. Laura is in a frenzy of thrill—so sweet really. She has bought a huge new bed for Victor Cazalet, a dozen pillows or "cousens" as she calls them, and fifty "scrap-bǎskets." At all hours new scrap-bǎskets roll in.

I'm writing on the beach and it's impossible, but it's never impossible to tell you I love you, not even if I were on a grid like St Lawrence, or without a tongue like Lavinia, or in hell itself.

Palazzo Mocenigo   *31 August*

The scrap-bǎskets continue to arrive, a spate of them to-day.

Laura went to meet the Christophers yesterday and curtsied on both knees. She took a retinue of guests and footmen and gondoliers. "But, Sir," she said, "where are your servants?" "We have none," was the answer. It was sad, as the palaces had been turned upside-down to lodge them as befitted their serving rank. She couldn't help but explain: "Why I, Ma'am, have two body-maids and Mr Corrigan never crossed the Atlantic without two body-men."

Everyone pretends to have a birthday since mine. Colin tried it on yesterday and was given a lovely shagreen pull-out watch. Laura really has the world's happiness at heart. We all look filthily rapacious, but I don't feel so at all, and probably no one does.

Palazzo Mocenigo   *2 September*

A diver has gone into the Canal to find my brooch, the one that my friends gave me when John Julius was born. It dropped off me from the Volpi balcony while I was watching the *Galleggianti* and (because the sea's the street here) I feared that it was irrecoverable. I'm sitting on my balcony (Byron's). It's 8 a.m. and a stainless sky above. At 7 nothing was doing on the Canal, but now things are moving. The gondoliers are coming out to tend and burnish their gondolas and little sea-horses. An English tourist has just passed with a shooting-stick across his knees. Very incongruous!

I'll motor home with Kaetchen, who will fetch me from Salzburg. That way I'll get four or five days quiet before I come home. No one goes to bed here and the drinking is formidable. Last night Chips threw a party at Murano about twenty strong. You never saw such an orgy of dancing and *pas seuls* and plain shouting, plus the commotion of home-coming too, yelling "*Sole mio*" with a view to waking the dead as well as those sober-sides who had bedded down earlier. I feel a little bit of a drag through it all, but it's wonderful how I keep going.

Palazzo Mocenigo   *4 September*

Yesterday we were all marshalled into a group on the beach to be photographed. Seventy-year-old Jane San Faustino, dressed as a white Marie Stuart, was made to walk half a mile through deep, blistering, powdered sand to join it. The backgammon groups were broken up, the sleeping woken. No one made much demur, recognising it as Laura's hour.

The poor dear complained to Chips yesterday, as she buzzed round the three *cabanas* in a frenzy of tidying up and counting the dice, and searching for losses in the sand: "I don't feel I am getting the vacation I should be getting." She surely isn't! A note on her table of "Don't Forget"'s said: "75 *couverts* for Saturday. Servants fitted for white. Pot for Beck's room" (this last to take the place of one shivered for a joke on the orgy-night).

Palazzo Mocenigo   *6 September*

I missed writing yesterday because I was in my typical fancy-dress-frenzy from dawn to eve. I was also turned out of Byron's bedroom and put in the dining-room, to allow eighty people to dine in it—two tables of forty, everyone in white, a Cartier-bag prize for the best lady and links for the lucky man. I went as the Ghost of Byron's dream of the Levant, and was admired by artists (Lifar, Oliver Messel and Madame Sert). The party had no *entrain* and there are a lot of complaints on the beach this morning. The funniest is one going round the bars where the hang-overers are having hairs of dogs. Their headaches are attributed to too many tuberoses.

In October 1931 came a General Election in which the St George's division was as usual not contested. Duff and I went buzzing all over England and Scotland in aid of candidates in difficulties, shaky seats or the Central Office's whim. On election night we had a party at Gower Street, where from little radios in each room we listened to the results. It was the first of as many such parties as there were General Elections until the second war, and no parties have I enjoyed so much. The Prince of Wales, I remember, was at this one, and so was Winston Churchill, who cried when he heard that Randolph had been defeated. Newly elected London Members would roll in after their successful declarations to be toasted, and those who had lost were revived with stimulating wine and kisses.

Politics dominated our life, but they were never really predominant in mine, except vicariously for Duff's sake. John Julius was growing up with cotton-white hair, gloriously healthy and gay, still dressed in frill-hemmed spotted muslin frocks or checked rompers. I did not apprehend disaster for him as I did for Duff, but then I had Nanny Ayto in whom I had more trust than in myself. John Julius was learning to read very young as I had done, and I saw no fault in him. "Poor old baby," his monthly nurse had said, "he really seems to want to please." He did.

The Miracle was again in the air. I went as an emissary from C. B. Cochran to conclude an agreement with Reinhardt in Berlin. Iris met me there, and together we stayed with Raimund von Hofmannsthal, now released from Hollywood's apprenticeship and fluent in English, having held his own and made a livelihood in that most difficult world. His father had died, alas! and now he was on his own, to be an enduring pride to Iris and to me, for we considered him our creation, "brought up by hand" (to quote *Great Expectations*). A contract was signed and *The Miracle* planned for the coming year. It was the first time that I had been to Berlin, and I thought very little of anything there except the paintings and the Palace of Sans Souci.

So I went back to the stage in 1932, this time at the Lyceum Theatre, rat-ridden but romantic with the shades of Irving and

Ellen Terry and all my mother's youthful enthusiasms. These seemed undimmed when it came to *The Miracle* and she was in her old element again.

My mother's chief ardour at that time was building. With the huge nest-egg laid by Arlington Street's sale, she had bought 34 Chapel Street and later the next-door house. This remarkable residence had a double garden with a sky-high ivy-mantled wall instead of houses at the back. Doris Keane, famous for the play *Romance*, had owned the house and built a long room into the garden. My mother doubled its length, lit it with high orangery windows, joined the two houses and built a second orangery drawing-room on the opposite side which still left a large garden with a terrace, a lawn, flower-beds and a statue. It was all designed for me, and as I watched her building and her dreaming of my princely grandeur to come, I could not bring myself to restrain her ebullient extravagance, although I knew that her visions would never materialise. The many rooms were filling up fast with the Shannon family portraits, her drawings and the cream of the Arlington Street furniture, none too big for the spacious proportions of her building. The Hatley brocade curtains, at last bleached to her desired faded blue, were hung. The lace drawer, the feather drawer, the one for ribbons and the one for furs found their places, as did the immovable chest for stuffs and dress-lengths and patterns, a yard square, taken on trial from furnishers and never returned. Shelves were filled with Tauchnitz books bought on journeys in the '70s, '80s and '90s, bound extravagantly enough in half-vellum and marbled paper. Tables were crowded with statuettes in bronze and clay by living sculptors, and works of art very unlike the Unknown Political Prisoner. There was nothing ordinary in her house, not even the meals, which would have been unusual had they existed. She disapproved of spending money on food, and still more upon drink, so it was abandon hope the greedy and the alcoholics. She herself nibbled Marie biscuits and sipped Ovaltine, living comfortably and healthily upon nothing. Her appearance had altered little and her clothes not at all. In fact, they were the same ones. Phyllis Boyd, a girlhood's companion and now a beloved neighbour in Chapel Street, said, peering into a photograph dated 1894: "Tell me, Noona, what stuff is your shirt made of? Can you remember?" Noona (a name given her by her grandchildren and used by her younger friends) twiddled with finger and thumb the shirt she was wearing and said: "Voile." When these dear relics fell from her back she would wear my less flamboyant clothes, but I never knew her buy a dress.

After my father's death, my mother took the pretty manor house of Eastwell near Melton Mowbray, where she would harbour John Julius when I was on my travels. She was the best of all influences, and I was for ever pestering her with directions for his education. Lines must be drawn three-quarters of an inch apart for his writing and he must be given funny sentences that amused him to write. He must practise the piano regularly with scales and four-finger exercises, holding his thumb *down*, and learn by heart. He must be scolded if he is sick in the car and there must be no spoiling. He must always say that he is sorry immediately, be demonstrative, say his prayers with meaning and not have ugly toys—in fact, the same injunctions as she had herself instilled in me. She would have given her life for the little boy, so I felt that with her and Nanny Ayto he was well protected.

My mother rarely left the Lyceum Theatre while I was there. The biscuits and Ovaltine came with her, and coffee or chocolates from the bar kept her going. Tilly Losch was the Nun and the first professional to take the part. I had always admired and liked Tilly. Kaetchen was our go-between, but on the stage we were far from happy, though the bad-fellowship did not last long enough permanently to destroy my nerves or my admiration for Tilly. Massine was the Spielmann, as inventive as Krauss had been and more trustworthy. The play was less of a success than it had been in the United States. It cost far less and was produced with less taste, and Tilly shattered the story by insisting upon dying. Cochran being wax in her hands, she was allowed to die, and by so doing the Madonna's sacrifice in taking on the Nun's duties, that her broken vows and shameful vagaries might not be known in the convent, became unnecessary. It was Winston Churchill who was most irritated by this travesty of the legend and its symbolism, and it was King George V whose praise for my effort was most unfortunately phrased. After a performance which he and Queen Mary attended, I was sent for, as is the custom. In the Royal Box the King said that he had enjoyed it and asked how I managed to keep so still and all the expected questions. But my laurels wilted when instead of: "Wonderful that you can express so much with gesture only," he said: "Of course, you've got no words to learn or say, and that's half the battle." I felt that he was right, but wished he had not said it.

The Miracle always brought me good things in its train, and one night after the performance it brought me Evelyn Waugh. There was a treasure-hunt in full cry and the kill was to be at the Café de Paris at Bray. When we arrived the hunt was up, but the merriment was still there and I knew then that I wanted to bind Evelyn to my heart with hoops of steel, should he let me. Treasure-hunts were dangerous and scandalous, but there was no sport to touch them. Carefully laid with intricacy and invention, they could be made beautiful and need knowledge and concentration to follow. A clue might lead to a darkened city court, there to find a lady in distress, with a dead duellist at her feet, who would hand the next clue through her tears. This might lead to a far plague-spot where a smallpoxed ghost would whisper a conundrum that took you to a mare's nest in Kensington Gardens, and thence to a Chinese puzzle in Whitechapel. Quick thought, luck and unscrupulous driving might bring you first to the coveted prize. Duff disapproved and disbelieved in the wild ecstasy until one night when the meet was at Gower Street and the Prince of Wales was to be a hunter. Duff must have felt it loyal to join in, for he went with me in our little open car, caught the fever, and shouted "Faster, faster! It doesn't matter about the bobby! What's the matter with the car? Step on it!" He was quicker than anyone at guessing the clues, so we won. We also won a scavenge-hunt, a derivative of the treasure-hunt that was less dangerous and equally exhilarating, in which the prize went to the first to bring home a collection of objects all-but-impossible to find in London at night—perhaps a horse-shoe, a gentleman's boater or a life-buoy. The last item on the list had to be "something unique." I cannot remember what we found, but Michael Herbert (I can see his face, shocking-pink with pride of certain success) produced that night a coutil-busked corset belonging to Mrs Lewis of the Cavendish Hotel, signed, cross-signed and undersigned with the names, quips and quizzes of her noble and notable clients.

In the autumn *The Miracle* took to the road. I did not live in digs, but in the best hotels, and in those days there were none better—the Midland in Manchester, the L.M.S. in Newcastle, the Angel in Cardiff, the Caledonian in Edinburgh and the North British in Glasgow. In these towns I was happy enough, though alone but for faithful Wadey. A ceaseless procession of influenza-funerals in Cardiff, and Tiger Bay less coloured than it sounds, were depressing, and Southsea was not up to much. There the maid asked me if I had brought my cruet when she served me my dinner of a boiled egg. Duff would join me for Sundays when I was near London, and from the north Glen Byam Shaw and I would take six-shilling sleepers so as to spend one day at home with those we loved.

I was in Manchester with Evelyn Waugh when Duff's *Talleyrand* was published. He had been writing with diligence and calm for three years, much of it at Bognor, pacing serenely up and down the sea-washed garden, planning the construction of his sentences, polishing and burnishing them until they could be written in his scarcely corrected manuscript. It cost him no pain or anxiety. He spoke little about it and read it to me very rarely. He knew how it disturbed me and how my critical sense, never strong, took flight through protective love before his literary style. The book was to come out about the same time as Evelyn Waugh's *Black Mischief*. Dread was in all my bones that Duff's book would be pilloried while Evelyn's novel would soar into literary and lucrative fame. Fears were liars, and they both had glowing notices and fabulous sales. Evelyn had expected acclamation, but this was Duff's first book and he had feared for it, as I had done for his disappointment. Pride and relief filled my heart to brimming.

Evelyn had come to Manchester to help me with my rather lonely life, though there were two friends in the cast of *The Miracle* whom I have never lost—Glen Byam Shaw, then playing a decadent prince, now the strength and taste of Stratford, and Simon Fleet, with whom I would eat Mars bars in the interval, and with whom I still eat chocolates in the stalls of theatres or while gardening, every happy time we meet. Evelyn was splendid with my mother, who came for the Edinburgh and Glasgow runs. She was very fond of him, and more fond when he had had a stiff whisky-and-soda. She approved only of the sober, yet never differentiated them from the tipsy. Evelyn introduced me to *The Wind in the Willows*, reading it aloud in the rest hours. Together we would motor over the wild Derbyshire Peak and look at famous houses. In the evenings we supped at the Café Royal in Edinburgh, where a cricketer holds his bat straight in a stained-glass window and where the Scottish Nationalists gathered.

He who came to help my loneliness and stayed to become the noblest and dearest friend of my middle-age was Conrad Russell, and he must have a chapter to himself.

CHAPTER SIX

The Gothic Farmer

CONRAD belonged to that distinguished and most unusual family of Russells in which no member resembles another and one and all are unlike any other people. His father, Lord Arthur Russell, was a brother of the ninth Duke of Bedford, and his mother, formerly Laura de Peyronnet, was French. They once took their six children, with two nurses, over the Alps in a berlin to broaden their minds. At the Pass of St Bernard, Conrad remembered his father taking them into an icy barn where the frozen victims of exposure and snowdrift lay stiffly in rows. So much for his childhood. Later, like all Russells, he was educated at home by private tutors. No school, four years at Oxford and one at Cambridge had given him a sound classical grounding and a generally cultivated mind. Like his three brothers and two sisters, he enjoyed an allowance of several hundreds a year from his Duke, and with this and what he made in the City he had no money-worries. After the 1914 war he discovered that his unrobust health had improved with exposure to heat and cold and rain, so he determined to shake the City dust from his feet and tread a farmer's field. Now he was living in his cottage-farm at Mells and I suggested, when staying at the Manor House one Sunday, that he should return with me to Cardiff and see *The Miracle*. I was surprised and, truth to say, a little taken aback when he agreed to come. Knowing all his family well and him so slightly, my old fears of responsibility for his enjoyment returned—fears of my shortcomings. He came and I loved him. It was as cold as Christmas when we walked round that unusual Welsh town. He held my frozen fingers comfortably with his well-shaped farmer's hand, warm in the pocket of his Inverness coat, and his tender benevolence and humour made the civic palaces look more Utopian, and the stone animals scrambling over the machicolated castle-wall more grotesque.

Conrad was very tall and a little bent, though not with years. His feet turned out like a penguin's, his hair was white and crisp and even, his face gothic: "The Gothic Farmer," Kaetchen christened him. I could not know in Cardiff how much he was to mean to me, but even then he meant something to be esteemed and cherished, someone for whom to improve. I felt anxious to give all I could in exchange for his wit, his richly stored mind, his powers of pleasure, his truth and devotion. Conrad wrote letters with an incomparable flavour—annals of the parish and of the daily doings of his labourers, of life at the Manor House, where lived the Horners, and of his neighbours, of unusual angles on current events or on the cream of the book that he was reading, of plans for meetings and of presents.

Presents started right away and played a very important part; into their selection it amused us both to put unusual thought and inventive taste. Conrad had once been a jobber in the City, and while he had been unhappy in his work it had left him with an amused interest in speculation. These flutters, so often successful, were linked with presents. Jewellery was his choice, while my gifts to him were for his curious little five-room house. His sitting-room held a most unusual and characteristic crowd of objects, pictures, books and papers. There was a long shelf of saints and sages in china, glass or lead,

Confucius and Kant, I remember, were among them; Tycho
Brahe, the sixteenth-century astronomer, hovered somewhere;
and there were two large Staffordshire figures on the chimney-
piece of Cardinal Manning and Mr Gladstone. Under these
fixed stars were many lesser ones, cut out from reproductions
and stuck on to his dark-green dado-height cupboards. To this
gathering I added a Samarkand rug, a bust of blind Homer
with green wreath and pink drapery, and a coloured print of
the Woburn sheep-shearing. For his austere bedroom, suited to
a monk, there was a counterpane quilted by miners' wives in
Durham, holding strictly to an Elizabethan geometrical design.

No subject was too mean to be made twinkling and touching
by Conrad, not even systems for making money at race-
meetings or by flutters in the City. The clear frank hand and
what it wrote were, I think, Greek in measure and proportion
of living. Every week he came for twenty-four hours, to London in winter and to Bognor in summer, and that day we called
our *Tag* for treats. He would bring me the first primroses or a
palatable cheese of his own making, or butter and eggs, for he
was my poulterer and dairyman and was to make me a small-
holder in 1940 to fight against starvation, following blockade
and invasion. His farm wove through every subject, and I liked
it as a theme as well as any. Our letters start in 1933 and grow
in bulk and intimacy until Conrad's death in 1947. I have long
wondered how I could show Conrad as he lived, and being
artless and craftless, I have thought that snippets from his
letters might act as facets and when assembled show the gem.
I am not hopeful of succeeding:

Little Claveys, Mells

The *Tag* was a lovely one. It was nice too to be doing the same
old things—loafing in the Strand, mooching round Woolworth's,

buying oranges, going to the pictures, eating before the drawing-room fire, Cordon Bleu potatoes, dirty jokes at the Victoria Palace. There is nothing to touch the pursuit of pleasure.

I will come to Gower Street (or anywhere else you choose) at 5 on Thursday next. What fun! But what if it rains? I suppose it will have to be the waxworks or the Indian embroideries in the Victoria and Albert Museum.

Hyperion (trained by Mr George Lambton at Newmarket) has won the Derby. Many, many months ago I put five bob on him for a place and truly my foresight is richly rewarded.

I have sold some more indifferent shares—rubbish, but I got £270 and the Inspector of Taxes returned me £106 today. Dear Diana, will you consider this question of a present from me? Keep in mind that I am rich, childless and affectionate. Sparklers, jewels, rings, *baguettes* or a fur coat for the winter? They say if you buy a fur coat in August for two or three hundred guineas you can get one which looks as if it must have cost 1500 guineas if winter comes.

I very nearly bought you a tiara at Cartier's which you said cost £10,000. It was not the price that deterred me but I feared to embarrass you by giving it, and I thought I might look a bit sheep-ish if I arrived with it in my hand at Gower Street and there was another man calling on you already. No one likes to be made to look sheepish.

I read Benson's Miss Brontë * with passionate interest. How extraordinary about Monsieur Héger! Do you think she was his mistress? What did she go to confession for? And why did Madame Héger hate her so and piece together the torn-up love letters?

As I sit here I can see part of the yellow Samarkand rug that you gave me, but I haven't the power nor enough ink to describe its divine beauty. It was sweet to talk to you again last night. Now you're in the train going to Wales.

I think it was Mademoiselle Claire (not Louise) Héger who used to say it was a woman's first duty to be amiable, and I thought about it on Salisbury Plain yesterday, and I thought if there is a more

* *Charlotte Brontë* by E. F. Benson (1932)

amiable woman than you in the world, it is that I haven't met her. From the moment the train left Bristol for Cardiff last winter to the moment yesterday when we two parted, in silence and tears, I've never seen you cross or grumpy; I've never had a harsh word or unkind look from you; I've never even seen the shadow of a shade of impatience with me cross your face. And I know that I must be a trying man.

A propos of Henry VIII:

The Duke of Buckingham calls himself "poor Edward Bohun." His family name was Stafford. Some people have thought that Shakespeare made him say "Bohun" because he was descended from the Bohuns on his mother's side, but the most likely explanation is that Shakespeare made a stupid mistake.

When Wolsey was a young priest and rector of Limington (Somerset) Sir Amyas Paulet put him in the stocks. We don't know why. Do you think drabbing likely? Anyhow when Wolsey became Lord Chancellor he summoned Sir Amyas to London and shut him up for six years in the Middle Temple.

I did enjoy the play very much, but I thought Laughton poor, and Wolsey ought to have been much prouder and more magnificent. He was as proud as Lucifer.

I've sold 100 more American Celanese, and some of the previous sales were higher than the calculations we made together. There is now £3649 realised and I still have 350 shares. I am putting £2000 in the preferred shares of the same company to get a bit of income. But what is money? Only dross, and the temptation to a life of idleness and lechery is, goodness knows, great enough already.

I've been reading about gold-crested wrens being fed in the nest. There were seven fledglings and the feeding was mainly done by the cock. Each bird ate 150 times a day. The droppings were collected and the weight equalled half the weight of the bird. The two parents and seven young weighed together ONE OZ. Yet they fly from Norway to England in mid-winter.

I made butter in the morning and pulled mangels in the afternoon. Nothing like half pulled yet. I hope I don't get caught by Jack Frost.

The three women who went as old ladies to George I's Court were Lady Dorchester, Lady Orkney and the Duchess of Portsmouth. They had been mistresses to James II, William III and Charles II respectively. Lady Dorchester said: "God! Who would have thought we three whores should have met here!"

A cart-horse is lame, and a sow supposed to be in pig isn't in pig. "She's come on hogging again," we coarsely say. It will throw out my contract for December baconers. Do you think it's morally wrong to mate a sow with her own father? If not morally wrong, is it undesirable? I wish I knew. The only book which mentions the point says: "To mate her with her own father sometimes turns out a boomerang." What does that mean?

Conrad's old cart-horse Prince had some repellent disease (hoof-rot, I suppose) and became because of this loathsome infirmity an outstanding animal figure.

There is one thing that everyone is agreed about. I mean Prince. "Worse than ever" is the universal opinion. There are horses to be sold at Nunney on Thursday and I must get one and have poor Prince shot. His epitaph will be:

> Good night, sweet Prince,
> And flights of angels sing thee to thy rest. R.I.P.

Later: I bid 46 guineas for Smart and dropped out. So Prince breathes again, but his offence is rank and smells to Heaven.

Just got Norah off to the dairy show, accompanied by her great friend, another dairymaid called (believe it or not) Miss Bullock.

In the morning I went to Holcombe to my old dairymaid Doris and brought home three Khaki Campbell drakes which she had got for me, price 12/6d. each. I had expected to pay a guinea each. After dark they were thrust into a black hold with twenty-one ducks (their wives). It will be O! what a surprise for both sexes. To-morrow I'll let them out and hope the drakes decide to stay in their new home, where their domestic happiness is assured until I eat them.

Latest Prince news: this morning it was my fate to lead Prince (87 in the shade) up and down the mangel-drills and it wasn't a bed of roses.

Often came enclosures neatly cut from papers and pasted by Conrad on a spare sheet of paper:

Here is another newspaper extract: "Canon Hayes in the witness-box said: 'It is an abominable lie, and here before the Court I declare most solemnly that in my life not at any time has even the shadow of a dishonorable thought towards a woman come even remotely towards my mind.'"

Bravo, Canon! I wish I could say the same.

Norah won the second prize for butter. Mrs Pobjoy was first, and Mrs Pobjoy is the brightest star in the butter firmament.

Periodically there was an account of the Mells Women's Institute activities and, more quaint, the Bright Hour Association at Vobster, a nearby village. Lady Horner was the Lady of Mells Manor, and Mrs Gould was her cook. With the Mells guests, they carried away the prizes impartially in the Bright Hour competitions.

Today's competition: "Eating an eggcupful of jelly with a wooden skewer." Lady Horner in chair ably supported by Canon Hannay and Lady Wilson. Roll call answered to "Uses of Eggs." Lady Wilson told the famous story of "The Happy Prince." Prizes won by Lady Hulton and Mrs Gould.

We no longer shopped at Woolworth's. Conrad gravitated towards Cartier's and there bought me a powder-box for my handbag, in black enamel with baroque stones. There was a looking-glass and lip-salve inside. I lost it at once and had to confess. Another was quickly offered. I wrote:

Darling Conrad, I think that if you give me a box to paint my face with, I shall lose it as I have twenty other valuable ones. Would you like the present to be part of a suite of furniture—white-and-gold sphinxes and swans holding cushioned curves? I couldn't very well lose those. It's prodigiously expensive.

Conrad replied:

Norah got nothing except her portrait in the *News Chronicle*. She was the only dairymaid photographed out of hundreds. It is better than a prize. I really don't mind the butter being rancid as long as I have a pretty dairymaid.

Last night at dinner I told the Marchioness the fun we had had shopping together, but she seemed unable to capture our rapture, and she said rather gravely: "Do please be careful. You mustn't spend too much of your money on presents for Diana." And I answered: "I'm afraid your advice comes too late, as I find giving Diana jewellery just the most roaring, stamping, cracking, galloping fun I ever had in my life. It is a pleasure I don't mean to deny myself."

We'll talk over the suite. How lovely it sounds! Only I don't like your saying "part of a suite." Isn't that niggardly? Stolen suites are best.

The mangels are gathered in (statement enclosed) and I've been pulling swedes today. It's harder to pull swedes than mangels.

The income tax man has repaid the Canadian money. It is less than I reckoned (£49.6.8) but it's a gift. Let's blue it together and buy you a paint-box for your face from Cartier, which you can lose when you like. We could put your address in it, then only a robber would keep it. The other money would roll up for your drawing-room's sphinxes or swans. I'd rather like to do this.

You were right not to reread your letter. It was incapable of improvement. I had hoped you would write but I knew it was wrong to hope, as you wouldn't write if you were happy and amused. Now it looks as if I was grumbling that I only get the worst of you. If it was true I did, I could only be flattered. And indeed, dear Diana, if you so choose, depression, melancholia, crying-fits, cancer-trouble and suicidal leanings can all be put on me. I'm as tough as an old bull and I can bear troubles, as long as they are other people's, with equanimity. And I can listen with more attention than you give me credit for, perhaps with sympathy, but it is rash to claim that.

Duff and Conrad were naturally my repositories of hypochondria. I could not alarm my mother or victimise less tried friends with outpourings of gloom and despondency. To one of these Conrad replied:

I was unhappy to hear you had had melancholy again, but I like you to tell me about it. The first object of life is a quiet mind and you haven't got it, and I am terribly sorry for you. It doesn't help to say that it is idiotic. I suppose we both know that *in reason* you have less cause for despondency than anyone in the world. No one so beloved as you, no one with more grounds for being pleased with themselves than you, and I never have known anyone so free from self-complacency. I believe you are if anything too brave and uncomplaining about it. Depression of the spirits is an illness like any other (only worse for the patient) and I believe it has a physical cause. I mean that the disorder is situated in the spleen or bile or gall or something like that, and can be cured completely. My opinion is that you ought to see what doctors can do. The difficulty is to find good ones. So many are silly men, but not all. I don't believe you ought to go on too long simply trying to fight it down. One is wise to be sensible about health, and wise and sensible I think you are.

When Peter the Great came to pay a visit to Frederick William I, he brought with him four hundred *soi-disant* ladies and nearly all of them (nearly all!!) carried richly-clothed babies in their arms. So says Wilhelmina, daughter of Frederick William, who was present on the occasion. I find it hard to believe. She might be a woman prone to exaggeration, but it would be quite eccentric enough to bring twelve women and six richly-clothed babies on a visit.

IF IT'S NOT ONE THING IT'S ANOTHER

I wrote to Conrad:

I meant to write on Monday, and here is Friday and I've done nothing about it, due to feeling too miserable, nervous, melancholic and insane. I got the doctor in the end, very ashamed at doing so, and he said that I was quite well but had better see a mental specialist. I haven't faced that yet, thinking every night to wake up metamorphosed. One day soon, of course, it will happen and I shall look forward again. Every afternoon when there is no matinée I go to sleep with a hot pad on my chest, and I drink maté tea, full of glucose, and at night it's the sedative, so I *must* get new-spangled ore by next week.

Nothing to report, but a lot of love to send you and thanks too for a beautiful encouraging letter. I make too much "to-do" about everything, I know. If it's not one thing it's another. If I were told by God (directly) that the scheme of the Universe was sensible and Eternity perfectly charming for all, I should worry that perhaps I wasn't going to like that kind of thing.

Conrad replied:

But, O dear Diana, this waking early and worrying about what may happen to us all but has not happened yet! It's no good scolding you. I might as well scold a camel for having a hump on his back. But all the same, how wrong it is! It's your only fault and it is one only against yourself. I pray always for you to enjoy a serene mind.

It was silly to groan as I did. I had always sung a song of Willow, sigh on sigh, and waning youth was not enlivening me. Yet age was no bogey. The youngest of a family remains a baby until she dies. I still automatically sat on the *strapontin*, accepted inferiority as normal, loved chocolates, found many books "too grown up," and until now I had relied upon being older to understand better. Forty years had dragged my face, no doubt, but I had not counted them. They had not brought me grey hairs or weariness. Some are born old, some achieve it naturally. I had it almost thrust upon me, lately, with a jolt of surprise. Those middle years were so full of riches that I should have been thanking my God, my stars, my husband and my conditions with ardour, night and day, but born with me was a rift in my defences that could not be mended, so the jeremiads are lightened only by snippet-anecdotes and shining love. I wrote to Duff:

I've worked my silly self "up." Black cats cross my path. I am so afraid of harm befalling you. It's 11 o'clock and I've just come home, promising myself the treat of writing at your comfortable table. I light my way into your room and find it decked in white, not for Eastertide like the cherry-tree, which would be seasonable, but shrouded against the sweep. I rush to my own library and find it the same. The baby increased my apprehensions by informing Mother that: "Papa *will* come back, I *know* he will, in a few days." My blood ran cold. I'm bound to be in more distress than ever I can tell you, when you are away. I pray you'll be happy and make my fears and desolations worth while. Our freedom binds us. I know I am as glad to hear that front door banged by your hand after a long day's absence as after eight months, my longest separation from you, and in the same way (badly expressed!) every day you are away holds an unchanging degree of pain. Remember me and come back soon.

In the Slough of Despond so perpetually stumbled into by this poor Christian, Conrad's letters, with their healthy farm tang, were as helpful as the firm hand of Faithful.

Took the cows to bite down hard the old grass which rots and forms a mat. Believe me, Diana, the pastures of England are not grazed down hard in autumn as they should be.

I live here with Father Felix, a Benedictine monk and a sad serious man. He has not smiled since he came, and God knows I've been funny enough to make a cat laugh its ribs out. When I go to bed he sits up and says his Office. When I light the bedroom candles

he says: "Oh, I haven't said my Office." Then I say: "Not said your
Office, Father? That's bad. You must say it now." When I am
snug in bed I like to think as I go off to sleep "There's a monk downstairs saying his Office." You mustn't think that I don't like him.
I am very fond of him indeed, and I have promised to go and stay
with him in his monastery, where he assures me that "no one will
worry you." If so, it will be pleasanter than some of the houses I
stay in.

My No. 1 pig was marked "AAA" i.e. perfection, the very flower
and nonpareil of pigs, and paid for at 13/- a score. My first thought
when I heard of the AAA pig was of you. "How pleased Diana
will be" rushed like a flood into my mind.

Father Felix in his Collins says: "I hope I may have the pleasure
of seeing you in detail at some later time." See me in detail? It's a
vile phrase, isn't it?

Queen Mary came to lunch with B's mother and wore (Queen
Mary did) a very large fur collar dyed purple and a toque made
entirely of artificial pansies.

Talking of Queen Mary, when the Queen went to Holker she
brought nine people with her—two dressers, one footman, one
page, two chauffeurs, one Lady in Waiting, one maid to Lady in
Waiting, and one detective. The Lady in Waiting wrote before and
made these requests:

(1) A chair to be put outside the Queen's bedroom on which
the footman or page could sit by turns all night. N.B. the page
was a man about fifty years old.

(2) Fresh-made barley-water to be put in the Queen's bedroom
every two hours during the day.

(3) Ice in the bedroom at 11.30 p.m.

(4) Six clean towels every day. The Queen brought her own
sheets and pillowcases.

Then I took the cows on the Green and did the crossword and
finished it, and read some of your Tchekov. You don't know what
a fountain of pleasure these books are to me and especially suitable
for reading on the Green.

Social news: A vet came to see a sick cow called Isis. As animals can't talk, diagnosis must be difficult, but this is what he says: "Perhaps it's indigestion, or perhaps it's tuberculosis of the spine, or perhaps she's swallowed a piece of wire which is working towards her heart. Anyhow give her a red drench" (a powerful purge, though constipation never seems to me to be apparent in cows).

I've finished Winston's book and can turn again to *Oblomov*. How good the bit is when they discuss what the different kinds of itch forebode, and one man says that an itching of the back of the neck presages a rise in the price of butter.

Liz Paget's thigh being tweaked by the Italian makes me think of Lord Uxbridge's leg lost at Waterloo. I told Liz at Plâs-Newydd that I'd send her the poet Southey's epitaph on the leg, and never did. Here it is:

> This is the grave of Lord Uxbridge's leg.
> Pray for the rest of his body, I beg.

I can't say that I think the lines either good or amusing. Southey was Poet Laureate and I suppose that it was the best he could do. Masefield would probably do even worse. Leg-pinching is commoner among the upper classes than anyone would at first suppose.

Topper, the new horse, has turned out a confirmed and incurable kicker. It was a well-planned swindle. There's tricks i' the world, and men who sell horses are a byword. My own carter said to me: "You have been properly sucked in, sir." I thought it unkind, as Topper was his recommendation. She was in fact bought to please him.

Bognor is a lovely memory. If ever I say: "*Verweile doch, du bist so schön*" to the fleeting moment, it will be due to a fine day at Bognor in your sweet company, and quite certainly not to watching men at work on anti-coast-erosion operations.

I used to say that all Duff's loves had cows' names—Daisy and Betty and Dolly and Molly. Conrad wrote:

A WOW AT LONGLEAT

You may like the enclosed list of cows. Many will recall faded beauties of your husband's seraglio. Old Fillpail (Lot 3) is for me, but what of Lot 40—Handlebars? I hardly feel that I could love a woman called Handlebars, but Duff is a lion-hearted man. He is afraid of nothing.

The Marchesa Origo was brought over from the Manor for sherry. She is highbrow to the marrowbones and a siren to chaps. I showed her over the farm and dairy.

Then I got ready for Longleat. I felt less shy as it got nearer, and marched as bold as brass into the great salon carrying my cheese under my arm. They were all assembled waiting for me, viz. Lord Bath, two Weymouths, two Nunburnholmes, two Stanleys, Lady Alice and Sir Hugh Shaw-Stewart, Miss Stevenson (a Wiltshire character), Sir Aubrey Hugh Smith, children, and five or six others never identified. I walked in and said: "Lord Bath, many happy returns of the day and please accept this truckle cheese made on my own farm." A WOW! *Effet bœuf.* Sensational silence and then a bout of applause and chatter. I escaped into a corner with Lady Weymouth and hit back a quick sherry.

Luncheon went splendidly. Lady Wey (on my left) a real good crack. Roars of laughter. Lady Wey lovable and lovely. I stayed until 3.30 when I refused a kind invitation to stay for the picnic and took a tender farewell, Lord Bath holding on to my hand and patting my shoulder. Renewed thanks for the cheese and: "So kind of you to come." Grand finale: Lord Bath and Lady Weymouth on the *perron* waving handkerchiefs and blowing kisses until I was out of sight. I left in a blaze of glory. A red-letter day.

Conrad did not smile for effect or misplaced good manners. His silent laugh was better far than civil grinning, but strangers found the still face alarming, and this increased his shyness in new surroundings.

I mind the country house visiting and the parties less than I used to. You must keep me up to my mark. It's good for me and best for me to be where you are. But even when it all comes right and I'm next to you, and the hock and lobster pilav are good, I'm not

enjoying it much. I would rather be having cocoa with you in
Goodge Street and walking together through the rain to bad seats
at a second-rate cinema. I can't explain why and you must think me
wrong in the head.

R's hiccoughing during dinner last night was terrible. It was
nice when you came to fetch me to breakfast. No one else before
has seemed to notice whether I am at breakfast or not.

I had the same idea (too late, too late) of you driving me to
Cheltenham, foie gras luncheon together on a fallen oak in Wych-
wood Forest, robins, holly, squirrels, babes-in-the-wood touch.
I'm an incurable romantic.

I make Caerphilly every day. I make it rather badly and it is a
great sweat. But if I lived in London and only strolled about Club-
land I should be miserable, and drinking and drabbing would be a
great temptation. I don't believe you would be so fond of me, and
you wouldn't get presents of eggs. And I think being a novelist like
Maurice Baring or Evelyn Waugh hardly a fit occupation for a man.
Just scribbling. So I suppose it's got to be farming, sweat or no
sweat.

On and on Conrad wrote of everything beneath the sun—
of what Dr Johnson said derogatory about *Lycidas*, of Spi-
noza's house (asking for a picture of it when I went to The
Hague), of religion and country matters, the farm ever the background. I think that we never finished with Prince, and the
tale of the dread change, the awful dissolution, was never told.

Tomorrow Prince performs the trivial task and draws a hogging
sow to the boar. Let not ambition mock his useful toil and destiny
obscure.

After tea I was arranging to move the statue of Immanuel Kant
from above the fireplace to make room for your sheep-shearing
picture. It is to have the best place, where I can feast my eyes
continually on it.

Norah went off to the Bath and West Show with her butter and
cheese amidst a flutter of handkerchiefs and cries of "Good luck!"

and "Don't forget to telegraph!" She only goes as far as our country town and is back again tomorrow.

Historicus [Duff's pseudonym]'s letter was much to the point and good. You notice that he made an error of ten years in calculating how long ago the Franco-Prussian war was. Figures aren't the Financial Secretary's strong point. Homer nods sometimes.

Her Grace wrote me a very sweet letter—slightly nuts, or it wouldn't have been in your mother's style.

Slender continues ill and stands about staring and eats sparingly. I said to Ernest: "Does Slender eat her cake?" He said: "Well, she's not exactly cheese on it."

The last month of 1935 worked out like this. Dividends received: £141. In hand: £166, i.e. £307. Cheques drawn in December: £303. This leaves £4 to the good at the end of the year. When I say "cheques drawn" they include the Dominican's money, my godson's present and your £100 present. You must keep your eyes peeled in Paris for ideas, or if you saw any pretty little tiny kickshaws in Paris that you specially fancied you could spend part of it there. Or ought we to keep the whole thing to blue in one go? My actual income in 1935 was £1683. It is a high record. £300 goes on my share of Oxford Square and commitments before I start spending. The farm takes £300 pretty regularly. As far as money is concerned, I am most fortunate and I think that you are too. The third anniversary of going to Cardiff together will be January 13th, and I can't remember what my life was like before.

Today *un soleil d'Austerlitz*, and I'm making a Christmas calendar for Katharine. I've done your page in the calendar (Cupids all round your picture, verses underneath) and I've got a good picture to illustrate "the dark house and the detested wife." Some version reads "the detected wife"—a very poor reading.

The electric light is in tonight and Mrs James [general servant referred to as Mrs Jimjams or Mrs James of Sutton—see *The Diary of a Nobody*] says: "It is awfully bright but perhaps we shall get accustomed to it." She was nearly killed in the first five minutes as she fiddled with an electric heater and a knife. Some bluish forked-lightning came out and played round her person but did no harm to her. It looked like "the chair" for Mrs James of Sutton.

The cold continues. I have the same job every morning now of going round the cattle-troughs with cans of hot water to thaw the pipes. How did mammoth elks etc. drink in Siberian Arctic waters? Did Nature teach them to suck ice? Our southern bullocks simply stand round the trough and moo in dissatisfied tones and wait until I arrive with the boiling water.

I see that two thousand swans have died of cold at Copenhagen. Did they all sing first?

I wear vest and drawers made for East Coast wild-fowlers, mittens and two pairs of gloves and earflaps of deerstalker tied down always. The postman at Chantry went out on night duty with exposed ears and is frostbitten. His ears will turn black and then fall off.

The carter and I went out after luncheon and brought in the yearlings. I was afraid that the cold might possibly kill them. The carter kept saying to the yearlings as we drove them through the deep snow: "Poor little toads, poor little toads."

The cold is less bad and I enjoyed taking the milk to Mells Park before breakfast. Quite still, sparkling sun and lots of rime. This is my Christmas letter. Forgive me my trespasses. I am not always as nice to you as I ought to be. I see no fault in you, and you are nicer to me than anyone has ever been. After that I can hardly ask you if you are fond of me, nor need I say whether I am fond of you. I expect we both know the answer, and I greatly hope that the answers are true for all time.

Calendar-making progresses, but I must leave the task and go to Bowood. I mean to take the party in carefree devil-may-care spirit. I mustn't make this fuss about nothing.

The man who made me the (refused) offer for sows is dead. I said: "Was it sudden?" The answer was: "He was riding home from Trowbridge market and he said: 'I'm going to die' and with the same he did." I repeat the actual words.

I forgot to say that I have left you £1000 in my will. Affection is the only motive.

DUCKS' EGGS AND HOLLY-THIEVES

Next Conrad writes of old Teddie, a labourer, in the Temple Club Workhouse, and of how

He praised the food, the nurses, the concerts and wireless, the sweets and tobacco. A foretaste of Paradise. He only asked for "a duck's egg or two, from running water." I thought that I could not have heard right. "Don't bother, sir," he said, "I've written to Mrs Dando about it. They have beautiful running water at Mrs Dando's place." I asked if ducks in running water laid nicer eggs than the ones in ponds. He stared at me in bewildered astonishment. It turned out that he wouldn't dream of eating an egg from a pond-duck. He couldn't believe that I didn't know the difference, as though one asked Duff if French Burgundy was any better than Australian. Did you know of this important distinction?

The policemen caught two Frome men stealing my holly and on Sunday morning they are coming from Frome to throw themselves on my mercy. Of course I don't want a prosecution. But can one stop the police prosecuting if they insist on it?

Mr Miller spat repeatedly and said that he couldn't get Prince's smell out of his nostrils. An owl is hooting in the firtree as I write. I can see his body against the sunset. It sways each time he hoots.

The electric-light men came back to work, the lousiest set of apes I ever struck. We have used fifteen units at ninepence in sixteen days. Poor Mrs James is appalled at the cost.

Now the Manor House has gone off to Longleat to see the "Longleat Follies"—Lord Bath as the "Big Bad Wolf," Lady Wey in tights. It's slapstick and all the fun of the fair and a howl of fun from start to finish. I'm glad I'm not there.

Yesterday the two holly-thieves appeared to ask for mercy. They were straight out of Shakespeare (*Henry IV, Part II*), Bull Calf and Mouldy, the recruits. One had a semi-idiotic defect of speech. I forgave them and bade them sin no more. Mrs James of Sutton couldn't have spoken more seriously of their crime if it had been incest or simony.

My sister sits by the fire embroidering and doesn't know that I am writing you a love letter. She said of the Duke of W. that he had "an illicit love for another man's wife" and perhaps she meant me too. Anyhow, I felt guilty.

In the Revolution of '48 Lamartine took Aunt Sligo (aged about eight) driving round Paris with him in his victoria. In the victoria were a number of *lévriers* (his favourite dogs) and he made speeches to the Paris mob from the carriage. Aunt Sligo saw the Tree of Liberty planted in the Place de la Concorde and the mob dancing round it with hands joined. The burden of Lamartine's speeches was that the millennium was at hand, that peace, goodwill, liberty, prosperity and purity would rule. What would he think of France now? He was Secretary of State for Foreign Affairs in the Provisional Government.

If I die please prevent Maurice writing any poetry about me (if you can) and don't cry or wear black or send any flowers. If you wish you can light a candle for me at the Catholic church in the square near the Jardin des Gourmets. Man is born unto trouble as the sparks fly upward. It is all in the Book of Job. We must try to keep calm and enjoy the good bits of life, which after all do exist too. I think that you have done splendidly so far. Goodness, harmony and wisdom are the pith of your being. It would be a very queer thing indeed if we knew what the purpose of the Universe was, and even if God explained it, should we catch vaguely at what His drift was, seeing that we often can't understand the crossword puzzle even when we see the answer?

K. Charles Martyr. He nothing common did or mean etc.

The Journal of the Society for the Preservation of the Fauna of the Empire has come. I've been reading about the Lesser Bush Baby, a lemur from the Gold Coast only about two inches long. They will sleep in your pocket all day, but at night they grow lively. Though so tiny one of them can take a standing jump six feet high! Before jumping they spend a long, long time estimating the leap and mentally measuring and bending their tiny knees. If they fail in the jump (a fairly frequent occurrence) they don't fall lightly like cats. On the contrary, they crash down like aeroplanes and hurt themselves most severely. They eat termites, pawpaws and avocado pears. Later I shall be telling you something curious about wolves and badgers.

Ah! I was to tell you something about wolves. The last person devoured by wolves in France was in 1918 (October, so not very cold weather) and then not in the Alps or Pyrenees but ten kilometres from Chalus (Haute Vienne). Wolves always increase when there are wars. I suppose because gamekeepers and all vigorous young men leave their homes. When wolves get hydrophobia they go into villages and bite everyone they see. Thus in a small Russian village a wolf bit thirty-five men and twenty-three women. More than half of them died of it. The office of *Lieutenant de Louveterie* is said to exist in some of the Départements "down to the present day," like the Pest Officer in our own country. The *Lieutenants de Louveterie* were abolished in the French Revolution, but the depredations of the wolves at once became so terrible that Boney had to re-institute them.

I do hope that your cold is mending and that you are established at Belvoir with your husband and your son and are happy there. I didn't give your little boy a present for reasons which you would think good. I think he is a very nice boy. I am genuinely fond of him, though I am not one of those men who get on well with children. I like the mothers better.

I learnt at luncheon that we have negro relations in Grenada. As black as soot they are, and the descendants of my grandmother's uncle, Mr Ross. He kept a negress and their bed was unusually fruitful.

It's Christmas Eve and I am sending off this delightful and witty letter with all my love. All, all, all.

Our Saviour's birth is celebrated

I lay abed until 8.30 and I wondered if our lives had any purpose, or do they signify nothing? And I could come to no conclusion. If your life has been a happier one because of my life, that ought to be enough. I think it is enough.

THE GOTHIC FARMER

On the Feast of Stephen

Very hard frost. Bright sun. Lots of glittering rime. I caught the third rat at Wheat Mow.

There was the taximan Lane's row about a sudden refusal to supply paraffin. Mrs Jimjams says that Lane lately drove a friend of hers to Frome and "what he didn't say about you, sir," was "something awful!" It seems that the Borgias were saints compared with me, and that it's doubtful if a sixth-century Pope could teach me a new vice. O would some power the giftie gie us etc. etc.

Russet has calved, so all the four heifers have calved. We shall sell the calves tomorrow and then we shall know how the mothers milk. I took Ernest into the field and taught him their names. "Is that Diana with the white rump?" he asked me. And I said: "Yes, Ernest, it is. You can tell Diana by her white rump." Oh dear!

In winter-time Conrad had long hours for his books, and I would get the cream of his reading:

Tonight I finished the *Aeneid*. I began in February and calculated to take a year. As you see I finished five weeks before schedule. I don't quite know whether to read it through again or read the *Georgics*. I suppose it would really be more sensible to read the *Georgics*. This might take three or four months. Or I might read *De Rerum Natura*, which would take two years.

I've been reading in Gooch about Madame de Remusat and Napoleon. He was a horrible man and I've never thought him anything else. Everyone who knew him hated him. It's curious what frightful oafs his family were, including his mother. Josephine thought that Napoleon "had seduced his own sisters one after another." I never heard it, but I suppose she thought what she said and meant incest. What is odder than this though is that Bishop Burnet thought that Charles II committed incest with his sister Henrietta. The Bishop was in a good position at Court and wrote a *History of his own Time*.

I've finished Volume I of Mahan's *Nelson*, taking me to 1790.

HOW FAT WAS LADY HAMILTON?

His character has begun to deteriorate under Lady Hamilton's influence. I find it a painful story. He has been openly disobedient to the orders of his Commander-in-Chief, Lord Keith. It isn't easy to see why he was ever forgiven.

We've got Lady Hamilton on the scene now, hot and strong. Mrs St George (mother of the Archbishop of Canterbury) said of her: "Bold, daring, vain to folly. Her dress is frightful. Her waist is absolutely between her shoulders. Her figure is colossal. Feet hideous. The bones large. She is exceedingly *embonpoint*." Lord Minto said: "Her person is nothing short of monstrous for its enormity and is growing every day." Others comment on the dirtiness of her hair. One of the naval officers said: "I thought her a very handsome, vulgar woman." It is a curious case of infatuation, as the doting certainly went to extreme lengths and ruined his character.

"Pick up hay in Brown's Bottom" is the order of the day. The word "day" makes me think of *der Tag* which is the day after tomorrow, I hope, so don't forget, my sweet Diana, to tell me if I am to arrive for luncheon or at some later hour.

And now I must thank the Major [Maurice Baring] who has sent me good Father d'Arcy's great work on the real and the supposed Nature of Belief, in which many errors and fallacies are exposed. Bless you, sweet Diana.

I should very much like to have seen Lady Hamilton, not for her beauty but for her fatness. How fat was she? About 1801 people who saw her in 1797 were saying: "She is if possible more immense than ever," and "an unusual degree of corpulency" is mentioned. Nelson and Lady Hamilton had codes for writing to one another. Nelson was "Thomson" and Lady Nelson was "Thomson's aunt" and so on. People must have been either bigger mugs or more charitable in 1800, as a great number believed that the relations of Nelson and Lady Hamilton were innocent, among them her husband. Didn't they notice anything when she had a baby? And I'm not sure that she didn't have two. I can't make it out.

I went over to Bulbridge where I found the affable Pembrokes. Then came Lady Horner and then Katharine from London. She had waited 1½ hours for you, an appointment that you didn't keep. So I spent the evening and part of the night wondering if you had been in a motor accident.

Lady Horner asked me at breakfast where I was going for Sunday and I said: "Bognor." She did not smile at all into her beard. She merely said: "D'you know Grandi?" I said: "No." She said: "Never meet him when you go to London?" I said: "No." She said: "He is a great lady-killer." I said: "Oh!" She said: "Oh, yes, women are simply mad about him. He is a great charmer and so fascinating. Women simply can't resist Grandi." I said: "Oh." Katharine to tease me said: "Don't you meet Grandi at Bognor?" I said: "No." Katharine said: "I suppose Diana doesn't ask him the same Sundays as you." I said: "I suppose not."

Nelson has left England for the last time. Lord Minto went to Merton to see him on the last night and Lady Hamilton assured him that her love and Nelson's were pure. They had had two children and one of them was asleep in her cot upstairs at the time. Nelson signed his letters to her "Your loving father." Do you think that we would put up with this nonsense now? Shouldn't we simply say: "Come off it"?

Nelson called Napoleon "Mr Buonaparte," and Wellington called him "Napoléon," using the French pronunciation. Nelson pronounced Edward "Ed'ard." Was it the usual way at that time? Nelson's daughter was called Horatia. At first they called her "Thompson" or "Tompson" or "Tomson" as a family name. Nelson's last letter of all was to her, signed "Father" and telling the tiny child to obey "our dearest Lady Hamilton." So odd to admit the fatherhood and deny the mother.

Horatia grew up and became the wife of Rev. Mr Ward. Her grandson is living in Bath (Mr Nelson Ward). A most unattractive man. I know him. The other brother I knew too at Pulborough and he was an Admiral! As like Nelson as two peas. I always believed that Clarkson made him up for the part. Lord Nelson (we went to Trafalgar House together) simply descends from

Mrs Bolton, Nelson's sister. Oh! and I knew George Matcham too, the great-grandson of Catherine Matcham. She was Nelson's favourite sister. Old Mr Nelson (Rev.) had *eight* sons, and there was not one legitimate descendant of any when Nelson died, so an earldom was created and passed to the dreadful, underbred Boltons. And I could write pages on how the Dukedom of Brontë (in Sicily) got into Lord Bridport's hands, but I am sparing you.

I've done the death of Nelson. Impossible to read it with a dry eye. I didn't know that he called it "telegraph" when he sent a signal. "Mr Pasco, will you telegraph?" he says. Collingwood was very much irritated by it all—"I wish Nelson would stop telegraphing." I think "Kiss me, Hardy" a most surprising episode. Hardy wasn't surprised and kissed him on the cheek, but a little later when Nelson's eyes were shut he kissed him again on the forehead and Nelson said: "Who was that?" Hardy was the only man who spoke his mind to Lady Hamilton. She hated it. *She* never said "Kiss me, Hardy," I'm sure. I don't think that Lady Hamilton loved Nelson. He was a tiny man, always ill and feeble and not naturally brave. Like you he suffered from fear and mastered it. Vanity was the sin that did most beset him. And boasting.

My grandmother acted charades with Lady Hamilton. Lady Hamilton did enact Medea and my grandmother one of the children that Medea murdered. This was at Dresden (with Nelson) in either 1800 or 1801. She was very frightened by Lady Hamilton.

The Times hadn't much to say about Kipling. He was the greatest English writer alive, but they were very guarded about it. I remember his beginning, and Mamma talking about him to Aunt Madeleine and saying: "It can't be his real name." Aunt Madeleine said: "It's impossible. It can't plainly be his real name." Mamma said: "But why choose a name like that?" Aunt Madeleine said: "It might be a sort of joke on drunken stripling."

The King's health worse, I take it. The next thing, I expect, will be: "Go bid the soldiers shoot."

Chinese Gordon was murdered fifty-one years ago today. Wolseley (son of "All Sir Garnet") and I were sent to the War

Office to ask if it was true. I see myself just as I am now, but suppose that I looked like John Julius.

Cuckoo-pint and dog's mercury are showing in the woods, the first signs of spring. I shan't be able to find you a primrose for some time.

I read today in Gronow's memoirs: "Some of the most magnificent fortunes of England have, in the first instance, been undermined by an extravagant expenditure on jewellery, which has been given to ladies married and unmarried who have fascinated their wealthy admirers and made them their slaves."

It is true, and the cheque for five jimmy o'goblins enclosed is giving you the snail-shells for your ears. They are my favourite jewels. I like them better than either of the paint-boxes, and when I think of you I like to picture you with the earshells and a bang, better even than the aquamarine drops.

The head of Conrad's house was the Duke of Bedford, grandfather of the present Duke. His wife, "the Flying Duchess," often "flipping about the Gold Coast in her Puss Moth," one day did not return, and the old Duke, then lonely, began to invite very occasionally members of his family to Woburn Abbey in Bedfordshire. When Conrad received his summons I made him promise to leave no detail unnoted. The following description of the Duke's paramount rule compares strangely with today's mobocracy:

Dinner was a choice of fish and a whole partridge each. No drink except inferior claret and not much of it. Nothing else. The second that I had swallowed my peach Herbrand [the Duke] sprang up and we all trooped out. He read the *Evening Standard* for 1½ hours. Miss Green (companion librarian) had been reading the Flying Duchess's account of coming to my farm in her diary. She had liked it more than any she had ever seen. "She was envious of having a house like that." Odd! it's an ordinary sort of very small house and suits me all right. When we arrived Herbrand was wearing a white silk tie, tweed coat, dark waistcoat, gabardine trousers (much stained and frayed around the bottoms) and very thick black buttoned boots. For dinner he wore a long-tailed coat, black tie, black waistcoat. I've got a lovely bedroom, all rosebud curtains and rosebud chintz. It's the room that Papa always had at Christmas. The bathroom is huge and stinks fearfully on account of rubber flooring. Herbrand said: "I've put you on the first floor so that you can see the birds and squirrels better." As it's dark I can see neither.

This is how the day passed. At 9 minutes to 9 we are all assembled in the Canaletto room. At 9 the butler knocks loudly at the door, comes in and bawls: "Breakfast on the table, Your Grace." Herbrand says: "Well, shall we go to breakfast?" We all file in then. There are five men to wait on us, one for each. Everyone has their own tea or coffee pot. You help yourself to eggs and bacon. The butler takes your plate from you and carries it to your place. You walk behind him. It makes a little procession. As soon as the last person is helped he leaves the room. Herbrand eats a prodigious number of spring onions.

Glasses of milk, apples and biscuits at 11.30 to keep one going until lunch, which is at 2. Later a comic-opera Rolls dating to 1913 picked us up. Man on box as well as driver, and the back wheels fitted with chains as if for snowy weather. Miss Green held a small butler's tray on her lap and on the tray stood a Pekinese the size of a basset hound. The tray was supported by a single leg and hitched to the front of the car by green baize straps. By this means the dog's behind is brought to within a half-inch of one's nose. There's no escape.

We called on Constance and Romola, Lord Ampthill's daughters. They were sitting indoors in immense beefeater hats and thick cloth coats with brown braid. We all talked and screamed and said the same thing over and over again for forty minutes. Lunch at the Abbey, and afterwards Herbrand offered to send me to Whipsnade: "There's nothing to do here, you know." I refused and walked to the Chinese Dairy alone.

Dinner a repetition of last night. Rough claret, and Herbrand puts a lot of ice in his. Miss Green's stinking dog sits on a tray on a high chair next to me. On the table is a wooden bowl hollowed out to hold a glass bowl full of ice. The dog licks the ice from time to time during dinner. Clear soup, choice of two fish, grouse, ice, peaches. A.1.

I enclose a card stolen from my bedroom: "You are particularly requested to refrain from giving a gratuity to any servant."

It's been an experience coming here. Poor Herbrand! What an extraordinary business it is, and how odd that the world should contain places like Woburn and people like Herbrand. It sometimes strikes me as quite unnatural. My family is a zoo, only instead of lions and bears in the cages there are unicorns, chimaeras, cockatrices and hippogriffs.

After Herbrand's death Conrad wrote:

Woburn makes anyone believe in the curse on Church property. There's been no happy normal life there since Great-Uncle Bedford died in 1861. Since then we've had old William, Uncle Bedford, Tavistock, Herbrand and Hastings. It makes six in succession all unhappy, tragic figures. If I had Woburn I'd make it a show place with restaurants, swimming pools, dance-halls, car parks, guides, for four summer months and let the public have a good time, and I'd live there for three months myself in autumn and winter and have huge rollicking house-parties run alternately by you and Lady Wey, and the remaining time I'd live unchanged at Little Claveys with a small London flat.

CHAPTER SEVEN

Pride of Boot

A FEW elderly admirers helped to keep me young. My letters bristle and burn with gibes and pretended indifference to their gallantry, yet on them I depended for spoiling and merriment. There was one whom we knew as "The Hound." On nights when I dined with him Conrad would put me up a candle. "Candle please from 9 p.m. Friday" my telegram might read, and his answer would be "The candle burns brightly for you. I dare say you have need of it." I placed great reliance on that candle.

Another admirer loaded me with presents and exciting surprises. An obscure clue over the telephone might lead me to an unused drawer, there to be dazzled by a birthday jewel, or to find a pair of doeskin gloves. Scent from France would be left casually on my dressing-table. Furs in the cupboard at Christmas would dumbfound me, or telegrams on summer evenings at Bognor would send me in a flutter to the station, there to pile up my car with hampers of wine and meats and fruits from Fortnum's and boxes and boxes of flowers, too many for the cottage to hold. I wrote to Conrad:

Gower Street

B. offered me, between 5 and 7, an ermine cape. I fumbled the acceptance with my usual Betty Boop eyelid-drop (disgusting!). All this nonsense sinks into insignificance compared with the way I coped in the taxi with W.G.'s long-anticipated declaration. I could not have dealt more idiotically with a simple situation. I am at home now ashamed and slightly scared.

Seriously, I wish you would laugh me out of this "*âge dangereux*" wallowing state, which drags me into a futile, useless and *undignified* way of living. Reviewing it this morning, I was *appalled*. And in this chaos of juggling I am only truly happy with you.

Conrad replied:

I wonder if you would be happier if you had occupation and spent less time "wallowing." It's a problem. I don't think you'll ever have men friends who don't make love to you, and if you did I don't think you'd like them. The object of life is happiness. I don't mean that life is a happy condition. I think it is radically wretched, and that misery, suffering and disappointment are the common fate of man. But we ought to aim at being happy, and what makes one happier than being with congenial people one loves and being loved in return? And in moments of gloom and self-abasement it ought to be some alleviation of misery to think: "Conrad is a man of good judgment and knows me well, and he adores me and thinks me perfect."

It is all a question of proportion, I suppose. How much time should be assigned to philandering and how much to graver pursuits? I think you are rather inclined to be morbid on this question of wallowing, and as a man who keeps pigs. I don't think that "wallowing" is a very good name for it. Seeking the society of people who like one is only common sense.

I wrote to him from Belvoir:

You will be at your sister Flora's and I am on the lordly terrace yet. My cold is only a little better. The eyes are bulgy and tired and I feel like the proverbial rag.

Friday night was A. over the fire at home. Sir Richard Cruise frightened him about his eyes and has stopped him, for the time being, playing golf and reading (his only solaces). He pretends courage and cheerfulness but I (in my belief that everyone reacts exactly as I do) imagined him a soul in torment and treated him with extravagant and very unusual solicitude. If one could see other's thoughts one's behaviour would be O! how simplified. He must have thought me mad, but I visualised him all evening stone-blind with a white stick and a dog.

Saturday was chores in the morning and, after lunch at Emerald's, Dame Ethel Smyth's *Mass in D* at the Albert Hall, followed by Ethel's tea party composed of nobs (i.e. Beecham, Virginia Woolf, Laura Lovat and famous musicians) in the open tea-room of Lyons's shop in Brompton Road!

I should refuse another present so soon. I should help my fool and his money to keep together, but there it is—I am as weak as water and can't but be excited to death about the present. It must be called my birthday present (August 29th) and as it's the equinox, and after the equinox Winter rears its shivering head, do you think it should be furs? One can get a rare lot of good ones for the money this time of year.

Presents were taken and given too. I loved to give them, cunningly designed and worthy of Conrad only. Kaetchen too had to have his own confections, and Duff only the very best. Rex Whistler, that inspired craftsman, developed my crude ideas into works of art—bookplates and drawings that held many and hidden meanings. Presents at the Belvoir Christmasses had become super-abundant. "The young Duchess" (my sister-in-law), in her radiant beauty clustered round with five starry children, would dole us out our share of her generosity beneath the topless Christmas tree. Servants and tenants had their fat shares. Traditions were dying hard at Belvoir. My wise father had ordered his sales and affairs in such a way as to leave his heir money to prolong largesse. Aunts and uncles in fearful decrepitude and deafness assembled at Christmas. The children camouflaged them. Now there were five Mannerses, my sister Letty's five sons and my only child, four years old and my eye's apple. I wrote to Conrad:

The train to Belvoir went in five parts, and Nanny and I and the baby sat alone in a first-class carriage while the corridor was jammed-packed with tired standing thirds. What does one do? I pressed them in but they refused for fear of having to pay. I could not pay for them all, could I? Nanny, with a jaundiced eye, was looking as though she should have been carrying a basin on her thighs. At Belvoir no old horses yet except my darling mother. Uncle Charlie too ailing to come.

Christmas Eve all preparations and stockings and "Don't come in's." Presents have grown to excess this year. Duff's present from Kakoo, a fur-lined Chinese dressing-gown (designed by me) an enormous success. The young Duchess delighted with it, so I felt relieved. All the snow had gone on Christmas Day in the morning, but the sun shone through the chapel windows and John Julius went to his first service and sang lustily.

It was in the abundant year of 1933 that Duff and I motored in the summer holidays to stay with Chips Channon in an Austrian schloss that he had taken. We stopped *en route* in an exquisite German town called Montjoie. There for the first time I saw Nazis—a dreadful revelation. I had not thought that the new temper would be so blatantly apparent. I had not imagined washing-lines of red-and-black swastika flags, nor the tramp-tramp of unarmed Brownshirts. Our next stop was to be at festival-less Bayreuth, but there we found unexpected trams and congestion.

Inns in forests, I felt, must be near by. Duff, never one for changing plans gleefully, showed patience, and with what German I had picked up from Reinhardt I managed to learn, through questioning a sympathetic crowd, of the hotel that seemed to fulfil my hopes, forest-built by a trout-stream, bath-roomed yet simple. So Berneck became our destination, but who would have thought that it held all we asked for and Hitler too? A myrmidon of the Führer named Rosenberg who had met Duff in London, hearing that he was in the hotel, invited him (but not me) to the Chancellor's suite upstairs. I encouraged him to go and sat for a long while twiddling my thumbs and picturing Duff reforming anti-Christ. When he at last reappeared he brought only tickets for the Nuremberg jamboree and the (to me) disappointing news that he had not seen Hitler. I could do better than that, I thought. I discovered from the porter that his horrible Führer would be leaving at 8 a.m. next day for Nuremberg. If I came down before then, he said, my eyes would see the glory.

I woke late, and only by throwing on a dressing-gown and tying my hair in a handkerchief to hide the curlers did I get down by eight. There I hid my sordid appearance behind the curtain of a window that looked on to the front approach. A motor-car was drawn up and remained so for a full hour. Meanwhile the lounge was filling with the coffee-drinking faithful who had come like me to see the departure. I dared not come out of my hiding-place, bedraggled slut that I looked, yet in the end come out I had to, and I ran the gauntlet of surprised pilgrims with my eyes closed like an ostrich's. "Quick," said the porter in German. "The Führer is leaving now by the back door. Go upstairs and you will see him from the window." I was up the flight in a trice and in another trice I had opened the first door to my hand and run to the window. There I saw nothing but the cloud of dust kicked by Hitler's heels, and turning, I met the horrified gaze of an old Hun in bed. He was more flabbergasted by me than I was by him. I scuttled away mumbling apologies.

At Nuremberg the beautiful town had an extra million Nazis in possession. The organisation impressed us. No cars were allowed within a certain periphery, but parking was painless. Luncheon in some vast restaurant was smoothly planned and

deftly served. True, we had Hitler's permits to flourish. I ate
my trout in excitement and also in nervous apprehension. I
knew Duff's feelings too well to hope that we should get
through the day without trouble. Luncheon swallowed, we
walked a long hot way to the meeting-hall, where we were
ushered into outer chancel seats. It was not long before thun-
derous acclamation announced the Chancellor's advent, but it
was a very long time before we heard his guttural, discordant,
scrannel-speech. He passed, alone and slowly, two feet away
from me. I watched him closely as he approached, as he passed,
as he retreated, compelling my eyes and memory to register
and retain. I found him unusually repellent and should have
done so, I am quite sure, had he been a harmless little man. He
was in khaki uniform with a leather belt buckled tightly over a
quite protuberant paunch, and his figure generally was unknit
and flabby. His dank complexion had a fungoid quality, and
the famous hypnotic eyes that met mine seemed glazed and
without life—dead colourless eyes. The silly *mèche* of hair I
was prepared for. The smallness of his occiput was unexpected.
His physique on the whole was ignoble.

Slowly he took up his position on the platform alone, while
we listened to forty delightful minutes of Wagner played by
an orchestra. Then came the speech, read into a microphone.
It was not the main speech of the meeting (that was made later
in the Square) and in fact I do not know what it was, as we
neither of us understood a word of his cacophony. My wish
to see Hitler now fulfilled, Duff was only too delighted to leave
the hall quarter-way through the oration. We crept out, not
unnoticed. Trouble came. It was bound to, and I am only
glad that it was no worse and that we did not land in a cell.
The roads were empty when we emerged guiltily from the hall.
I was footsore and hot, and the way that we had come was

closed. A much longer one was indicated to us. Duff asked a Brownshirt to allow us the shorter way. The request was refused gruffly. An older official, not a Brownshirt, came up to help. The young Nazi told him to go to hell. I could see Duff's temper flaming into his dear face, and only by tearful entreaty did I get him away from the loathsome Nazi-boy. But I am glad that my eyes and my memory obeyed me, and that I can see Hitler and his background as clearly as a photograph.

I did not see Mussolini, but Duff did the following spring. We went to Rome, I think semi-officially, and Duff had an interview with the Duce. We made great fun of the preparations, dressing him as one might a child for a party, with clean socks and injunctions of good behaviour and final queries of "Are your nails nice? Where's your clean hanky?" I deposited him at the Palazzo Venezia's colossal entrance. He was dreading the long walk, so often told of, on slippery surfaces to the Duce's desk, but this he did not have to negotiate, because Mussolini met him at the door and laughed at his jokes. In his autobiography Duff has given him some charity.

It was after our visit to Nuremberg, when Duff told the Junior Imperial League that Germany was preparing for war on a scale and with an enthusiasm unmatched in history, that he was labelled (by, I am sorry to say, the *Daily Express*) "a warmonger." We were due to lunch with the German Ambassador, Leopold Hoesch, on the day of that press outburst. Duff asked him if he still wanted us to come. He treated the matter as a joke and said that he was expecting us. It was in his instructive arms that I had waltzed all 1912 and 1913, and I was fond of him through war and peace. Two years later he was liquidated—through foul play, I have personally no doubt.

Duff would never agree with this, but there is good evidence. Besides, Leopold Hoesch was no Nazi.

Financial Secretary to the Treasury was the last step to Cabinet rank, it was said, and in June 1934 Duff was given that coveted post. I was becoming more ambitious for him politically, but I did not yearn for 10 Downing Street. The thought, if I did think of it, appalled me. The old fear of "bloomers" being made, with constant gruelling work, no time for writing and no leisure of our own, easily dispelled aspirations for Prime Ministership. Duff was writing an official life of Haig. I cannot see how he had had the time (week-ends and holidays, I assume) but now at the Treasury there were to be more free days. My ambitions led me to giving a series of dinner-parties at the House of Commons. There one could take a private room and, with trouble and careful ordering, arrange a very good meal. Enjoyable I found these candle-lit dinners with a nucleus of twelve friends. During the evening Duff could return from a division with Winston Churchill or Walter Elliot, Shakes Morrison or Brendan Bracken, Ministers or back-benchers, to drink a glass of champagne and jaw and smoke and argue. Only in England could this happen, and it is what most I miss living abroad. I even dared to ask Mr Baldwin to dinner at Gower Street. To Conrad I wrote:

Well, the *Tag* went wonderfully well, and the old friends behaved splendidly. Sister Marjorie arrived first. Duff and she walked up the *enfilade* of rooms, turning switches on and off and straightening rugs, while I was reducing the inch-thick paint on my face. Ettie [Desborough] came next, bringing confidence to us, and then Stanley Baldwin and Lucy. She was in a new dress—white satin slashed with blue. A *Rigoletto* page.

We served no cocktails (too fast, we thought) but old sherry was on tap and Mrs Baldwin said: "That's a thing Stanley can't resist," and Mr Baldwin said: "Then just half a glass."

THE BALDWINS TO DINNER

Desmond [MacCarthy] came next in white-tied gala get-up, but with studs missing and laundry-kisses all round the crooked tie. We couldn't wait for your Minister [Walter Elliot] and he arrived, like the unnervous man of the world he is, a proper quarter of an hour late. Hilda the cook surpassed herself. Politics were not touched upon in front of the ladies. There was a little pig-talk to Walter Elliot (Minister of Agriculture) because I was thinking of you. Here's the table:

Me

Mr Baldwin	Walter
Marjorie	Ettie
Desmond	Duff

Mrs Baldwin

You can't make a dinner without eggs, and yours were the basis. Maurice sent a forest of gardenias—too exotic really, but I strewed them on the table all the same and it helped to allay that appalling corpse-smell in the dining-room. A. weighed in with too-good fruit, a gigantic foie gras which I didn't let appear (too rich from both angles) and a dessert service which I was able to send back before it arrived.

Mrs Baldwin "took twice" of the savoury roes (soft). They (the Baldwins) left at 11.15 and we had a post-mortem for half an hour and read some purple patches from Stanley's book. Then Ettie went and Marjorie imitated her. Then Marjorie and Walter Elliot went and Desmond remained until all hours.

I kept beautifully quiet through everything and no one got drunk. God bless you.

Conrad replied:

Your letter describing the dinner-party arrived this morning. It is a good letter, a very good letter. It is the best letter I have received in my life. I am a good judge of that kind of thing. You have brought the dinner before my eyes. I had to bring your letter to the mangel-pulling with me. It is Carter's Lord Wardens now, as I've finished Kirsch's Ideals. I would pull about twenty Lord Wardens, then stop and wipe my great red dirty hands on the seat of my trousers, take your letter out and read a few paragraphs. The men thought it odd, and I heard Bert say to Ern: "Maaster tarnashun funny smorning Ah think." And Ern answered: "Zim zo." They talk like that.

Down on the ranch in the Far West I had become horsy— an enthusiastic rider with an uncertain seat and no "hands." Here in England, gone were the chaps and the dude-stuff, the Western saddle and the Spanish stirrups so hard to lose. Only the jeans and the good Armada boots remained, and whenever I had a chance I would ride. Tommy Macdougal had lent me an Arab-blooded white hack called Cerise. I kept her at Goodwood and, while Duff wrote about Haig, I would ride alone in Goodwood Park, ambling through wild roses and honeysuckle, with the song of larks and the smell of hay about me, and so taste ecstasy. Sometimes a party of us would gallop along the close-cropped watershed of the Sussex Downs from Goodwood to Steyning, over Amberley and past Chanctonbury Ring, where on Midsummer Eve many fear to go. It was a wonderful ride uncrossed by traffic. I rode it once with Evelyn Waugh, but it was marred by a hang-over. Staying away and being mounted on any old horse was not so happy. I wrote to Conrad from a stately home:

This house is in a sad state of disrepair. *None* of the lu-lus work. Everyone complained after being seen running down the passage with jugs of water and anxious faces. The bedrooms are pitch-dark, although there are plenty of lamps. The bulbs are at fault (superannuated!).

The stables too are a disgrace. Crocks covered in stinking stained horse-blankets, old dung all over everything, harness without a shine and reins sticky. E. said that we could ride and that I had better have Sooty. So I had Sooty, who was a sort of Queen

Victoria's *Highland Diary* pony. Venetia had the Master's bay hunter. We mounted in the stable-yard. A half-witted boy got me up. Then out of a sty leapt Venetia's charging Tom-Webster animal, with mean rolling eyes, 200 hands high, mouth and groins a washtub of suds. It was raining. All the gates were padlocked. We had not been offered a key. Venetia's brute bucked and plunged and pulled and made the noises that stallions make, and when we got in the head groom was waiting with an ashy face, saying: "I never thought you'd get home unhurt. It's the greatest brute ever bred. His Lordship's been trying to sell him and can't. He's not fit for any lady to ride, nor any man for that matter."

Max Beaverbrook became a riding enthusiast too. He bought Cerise from Tommy Macdougal and gave her to me. It was a great relief to ride my own directable darling, who tried to do what she was asked, instead of Max's rough self-willed strangers. Valentine Castlerosse had stepped up the "hands" of the Cherkley stud, as he had to have heroic horses to carry his great weight. Max was very brave and I very timorous as we rode (never *con brio*) in his Surrey woods or galloped away from Calvin Lodge, his house at Newmarket. "I shall never ride again," I say now without sorrow. "I shall never play tennis again," I said at twenty-five with glee. "I shall never ski again," I said when the last war was declared. None of these renunciations do I regret, so unproficient was I at all athletics.

Sport took us yearly to Euan Wallace, the best and dearest of men, who with his wife Barbie and his five sons made me love and understand Scotland. There somehow I kept my end up. I wrote to Conrad:

On the high road to Scotland   *September 1934*

Health bulletin first; excellent. Miasmas over-ridden, soaring spirits, glowing body, boundless schemes and plans in profusion.

Even looking forward to autumn fashions and furs and Molyneux. Plans include a tunny-fishing expedition (not for you). It would have to be Venetia (who might get bored but never cold, never tired, never sick) or Raimund (but his wife might snivel) or Mr Wu [Evelyn Waugh], but what would Kommer say? "Wooing Mr Wu?"

Another plan—a visit to the Soviets. I can go with Barbie Wallace and Maureen Stanley, but this entails flying to Leningrad. I could join them by train and see what Tchekóv and Maurice saw —moujiks and tea and introspective passengers reading Milton. I would be alone for that part, unless you came with me. We must put it off until snow-time. Very keen I am.

My melancholia left me on my birthday. It's all been good since. Seeing you again was an excitement and a calming.

Kildonan

Here by 7. A huge house built since the war, very nice and very comfortable with water (tap and filtered) as dark as cocoa. All the boys—Duff, Euan, Seymour Berry, Sir John Milbanke, Loel Guinness, two Loughborough boys, two Wallace-Sackville boys, three Wallace-Lutyens boys—played golf. I read Mr Wu's book aloud to Barbie, Joan Guinness and Sheila Milbanke with overwhelming success.

In the evenings I play backgammon and in two I have won a tenner. Today I went shooting with the boys, leaving at nine in my silly blue cotton trousers and still sillier Mexican boots. Duff was a little cross early, as he so hates the unusual, poor beast, so he told me that there was a hurricane blowing and a lot of rain about. But I thwarted him and went, partly because the tone always is when I get out of a Mayfair drawing-room or Venice or Salzburg or bed: "Whatever are you going to do to amuse yourself in these wilds?" and I can't bear it. Also I have Pride of Boot, Loyalty and Amour Propre for the old kangaroo-skins and they proved their worth on the moor all right. It was an almost heatherless bog. The other girls (only two of them came out to lunch) hated it, and Duff was pleased in the end, but will be every bit as bad next time.

KILDONAN AND CHARTWELL

14 September 1934

It's rainbow weather, a lot of rain and shine. I've just had a hot bath. Immersed one looks like chicken in aspic.

Another less sporting visit followed closely, this time to the Winston Churchills at Chartwell.

Well, my darling, we got here very late for luncheon, both speechless—Duff with rage, me with skid-anxiety and general distress at rudeness. I had had a wearing morning taking the baby and Nanny to my idea (not Nanny's) of an acrobatic dancing school, where he would learn cartwheels. It was the squalidest thing ever I saw. I dared not meet Nanny's eye. Old sponges and rags and ends of grease-paint lay among clouds of dust and pools of sweat. They pulled out a rug to make a ground for the baby's cartwheels and it was like opening the desert. John Julius said: "A bit crummy, isn't it?"

Then I ran for the car and Chartwell. Forty winks in the afternoon and then (unexpectedly) bathing at 7 in pouring rain, intensely cold with a grey half-light of approaching night, yet curiously enough very enjoyable in its oddness. Freda Ward, Winston, Duff, Clemmie, Randolph and a child, in fact the whole party, were splashing about with gleeful screams in this sad crepuscule. The secret is that the bath is heated, and it is Winston's delightful toy. Just now, again, twenty-four hours later, he called for Inches, the butler, and said: "Tell Allen to heave a lot more coal on. I want the thing full blast." Inches returned to say that Allen was out for the day. "Then tell Arthur I want it full blast," but it was Arthur's day out as well, so the darling old schoolboy went surreptitiously and stoked himself for half an hour, coming in on the verge of apoplexy. Again we all had to bathe in the afternoon.

Then "feeding the poor little birds" is a huge joy to him. They consist of five foolish geese, five furious black swans, two ruddy sheldrakes, two white swans—Mr Juno and Mrs Jupiter, so called because they got the sexes wrong to begin with, two Canadian geese ("Lord and Lady Beaverbrook") and some miscellaneous ducks. The basket of bread on Winston's arm is used first to lure and coax and then as ammunition. The great aim is to get them all fighting. "We must make a policy," he says; "you stone them and we will get the five flying fools on their right flank."

Soon after this came my journey to Rome alone as an emissary of government to deter the Italians from attacking Abyssinia. This unusual assignment grew from a mustard-seed dropped at one of those House of Commons dinner-parties, just before the policeman shouted "Who goes home?" Amongst others sat Duff, Winston Churchill and Lord Tyrrell, former Ambassador and Head of the Foreign Office, all of them heated and anxious about Italy's coming violation of Ethiopia. Methods were discussed of discouraging Mussolini's unnecessary resolve. They could think, at dawn, of no better way than to depute me, due for Rome two days later, to inform those in dictatorial power how strongly England was against the aggressor. This journey can be called the real Failure of Mission—just as well send a tramp. What hope had I of harnessing Italy from beneath the hospitable roof of 3 Foro Romano? My tickets for the canonisation of our English saints would get me nowhere but to St Peter's. The only opportunity that offered itself was a luncheon-party in my host Lord Berners's house, when several close friends of Ciano, the Foreign Minister and son-in-law of the Duce, were present. The burden of my message I must have spluttered out too vehemently, for the Princess San Faustino made a major exit before the meal was eaten, outragedly banging the door as she left, and the aggrieved Lord Berners found difficulty in forgiving me. I don't blame him—he had the Fascist vengeance to face.

Then came a General Election in which a Labour lady opposed us in St George's. Although we spent most of the three weeks' campaign touring the country and revisiting Oldham, we still won by a good majority.

Duff had hardly dug himself into his room at the Treasury before he received his summons to the Cabinet. It was the War Office. This was excellent, for he knew the ropes, the Army and hierarchy. While he was Financial Secretary I had trembled for his mathematics (Duff was no wizard with figures), but with the Generals and the Army Council all would be "Sir Garnet" and I would fling myself into reviews and tattoos, and re-read the decisive battles of the world, learn the ranks and distinguishing marks, and try not to fall foul of anyone. I had not known many Generals. The first I had seen was General Buller, helping Queen Victoria out of her carriage in the courtyard of Buckingham Palace on some black day of defeat in the South African war. "Bobs," gartered and re-splendent though little bigger than myself at fourteen, I saw on some gala occasion. Kitchener's insensitive strength had crushed an antique ring to twisted smithereens when he had wrung my adolescent hand, and I could never forgive him. French I had known as an omnipotent uncle in youth and war, and Freyberg as a dedicated boy, the inspiration of my fighting contemporaries. Generals de Gaulle and de Lattre de Tassigny I was to meet, study and admire ten years later (that is for another volume), but the brass-hats of 1935 were unknown soldiers to me. When, subsequently translated to another element, I found myself among Admirals, I remembered the Generals as being more unusual and unexpected (even eccentric), more surly and heated and generally less serene. The Admirals seemed to be all moulded, no doubt by the restriction of their island-ships and solitude, into a sameness. Now must I learn the soldiers' distinguishing marks—crowns, crossed swords, sphinxes, grenades, pips and stripes —and above all the perplexing alphabet language ("What's C.I.G.S.? What's Q.M.G.? And A.G.? And D.M.S.?") in

those smaller pre-war days more easily acquired and differentiated. I must remember though not to show off by talking
in initials to the uninitiated. I must buy new clothes for
Camberley and manœuvres and Trooping the Colour, and
remember not to fall into the perennial temptation of delving into the dressing-up box for trappings and symbols suitable to the occasion, to eschew khaki, scarlet and high fur
hats, to avoid trying to look like Boadicea or pretty Polly
Oliver, and to be demure, as suited a serious newly arrived
Cabinet wife. Indeed, I did feel serious and aglow with pride
and resolve to conform and please. It would not be difficult
nor fearful to walk the brilliant path by Duff's side. In every
way we were blessed. I must never again tire or sicken or
moan.

The publication of the first volume of Duff's book on Haig
received vicious press reviews but paeans of praise from those
who mattered—from Trevelyan and Kipling, John Buchan and
Maurice Baring. Conrad wrote:

You made me feel that I didn't say enough about *Haig*. Who am
I to praise it? I admire Duff *enormously* as a man of letters. The
book is in the grand manner, but all his own. You never feel that
he's imitating Gibbon or Macaulay or Froude (all Whigs, so add
Hume) and never, never, never, never, never, is there a phrase even
remotely influenced by Lytton Strachey. It's very dignified and the
very way that good biography is written. If the book isn't praised
it will be caviar trouble—not enough educated people to see how
good it is. The man Haig is somehow dull—dull compared to
Marlborough, Nelson or Wellington—but the book seemed without flaw to me.

Margot Oxford wrote:

Dearest Duffy, I would *not turn a hair* were I you over the spite-
ful criticisms of your *Haig*. My autobiography was cursed and

abused by everyone at the time, but on reading it again the other day (for the first time!) I think it *very good*.

I wish I could think that on re-reading this book of mine I shall feel the same.

CHAPTER EIGHT

The Fort and the Cruise

IN January 1936 King George V died. Duff was perhaps the last Minister to receive the seals of office from his dedicated hands. He faded gently out of life, and when the bulletin was issued that "The King's life is moving peacefully to its close," his subjects were unexpectedly moved.

At Westminster he lay in state for several days. From morning until night a procession of tearful mourners passed through from west to east, silent on the thick felt that had been laid on that pavement of history. The queue stretched for miles, and had to be stopped forming three or four hours before the time when one hour must be given to regarnishing the Hall, renewing the tall candles and freshening the flowers. I went almost nightly. Through a secret door one could slide into the centre of the moving masses, and there I would lead, in patriotic and monarchic pride, any foreign friends visiting London. The night that I took Henry Bernstein the sentinels at the four corners of the bier, heads deeply bowed, were the dead King's four sons. Later we saw the small coffin pass with the crown laid upon it, and noticed that the cross had fallen from its summit. We saw the four Princes, cold and disconsolate, following their father in the London drizzle. We saw his body laid in the vault at Windsor, and life begin again at Westminster.

Neither my family nor Duff's had been at all intimate with the Royal Family, not at least since Duff's uncle, who was a

neighbour of Queen Victoria at Balmoral, was made Duke of
Fife that he might marry the eldest daughter of King Edward
VII. My mother's father was the old Queen's equerry, so she
was often at Balmoral, where she had been petted and even
painted by the Queen in water-colour. I own the picture. It is
of a tall girl, her auburn hair knotted low on a slender neck, in
a black, trained dress, probably of silk.* It is the only portrait
I know that the royal hand drew, though it painted in hundreds
the Balmoral moors.

But neither of these connections had brought friendships.
The Prince of Wales, now King Edward VIII, was the first of
the family that we both knew intimately and had admired and
loved for several years. He had turned a royal folly near
Virginia Water into a liveable house, where he could rest from
his labours at the week's end. It was called Fort Belvedere and
was a child's idea of a fort. Built in the eighteenth century and
enlarged by Wyatville for George IV, it had battlements and
cannon and cannon-balls and little furnishings of war. It stood
high on a hill, and the sentries, one thought, must be of tin.
Here Duff and I had sometimes stayed. It was completely
informal. I wrote to Conrad in July 1935:

This stationery is disappointingly humble—not so the conditions.
I am in a pink bedroom, pink-sheeted, pink Venetian-blinded,
pink-soaped, white-telephoned and pink-and-white maided.

The food at dinner staggers and gluts. *Par contre* there is little
or nothing for lunch, and that foraged for by oneself American-style
(therefore favoured, bless him).

We arrived after midnight (perhaps as chaperones). Jabber and
beer and bed was the order. I did not leave the "cabin's seclusion"
until 1 o'clock, having been told that no one else did. H.R.H. was
dressed in plus-twenties with vivid azure socks. Wallis admirably
correct and chic. Me bang wrong! Golf in the afternoon, only the

* Reproduced in the first section of illustrations.

Prince and Duff playing, Wallis and me tooling round. It poured and we took shelter in a hut and laughed merrily enough with other common shelterers. The social life at The Fort centres round the swimming-pool, which has an elaborate equipment (better than Bognor's) of long chairs, swabs, mattresses and dumb-waiters bearing smoking and drinking accessories in abundance. It is some little way from the house, so showers cause a dreadful lot of carrying in and bringing out again for the next fitful sun-ray.

Everything is a few hours later than other places (perhaps it's American Time. "The huntsmen are up in America, and they are already past their first sleep in Persia"). A splendid tea arrived at 6.30 with Anthony Eden and Esmond Harmsworth. Dinner was at 10. Emerald arrived at 8.30 for cocktails, which she doesn't drink although the Prince prepares the potions with his own poor hands and does all the glass-filling. She was dressed in a red-white-and-blue walking-dress, with tiny blue glass slippers and toes showing through.

The Prince changed into a Donald tartan dress-kilt with an immense white leather purse in front, and played the pipes round the table after dinner, having first fetched his bonnet. We "reeled" to bed at 2 a.m. The host drinks least.

The house is an enchanting folly and only needs fifty red soldiers stood between the battlements to make it into a Walt Disney coloured symphony toy. The comfort could not be greater, nor the desire on his part for his guests to be happy, free and unembarrassed. Surely a new atmosphere for Courts?

Spirits excellent. Can it be due to proximity to royalty? Surely not. I think it's being entertained and resting from the strain of entertaining. The Prince reminds me of myself at Bognor—over-restless, fetching unnecessary little things, jumping up for the potatoes or soda-water. I'm looking frighteningly ugly. It's Sunday and mid-day and the music must soon be faced. I quake a little. Lunch at 2. No more or I shall have nothing to tell you on *Der Tag*.

Now the Prince was King and everything due to change, but very little was different. Frock-coats were outmoded almost by law, but I cannot remember much else. We continued to go to The Fort and to exciting house-parties clustered round the King.

The Fort   *17 February 1936*

It's all been a great "do"—a successful "do." My health superb. Can't judge the face. The King unchanged in manners and love. Wallis tore her nail and said "Oh!" and forgot about it, but he needs must disappear and arrive back in two minutes, panting, with two little emery-boards for her to file the offending nail.

His Majesty's evening kilt was better than ever. I think it was a mourning one, although he denied it—anyway pale dove-grey with black lines, and his exquisitely-fitting jacket rather Tyrolled-up in shape and improved buttons, and instead of that commonish white lace jabot that is generally worn he had most finely pleated Geneva bands like John Wesley. On Sunday by request he donned his wee bonnet and marched round the table, his stalwart piper behind him, playing "Over the sea to Skye" and also a composition of his own.

He suggested on Sunday that we should all go over to Windsor Castle and see the library there. "No one ever sees it," he said; "I know Wallis hasn't. It's a bit off the beaten track. There's an awfully good fellow there called Mr Morshead. He's most awfully nice. He told me the other day to go over any time I like. He's got some wonderful things there too."

This glorious stationery is new. Nothing much else is changed. The servants are a bit hobbledehoy because H.M. wants to be free of comptrollers and secretaries and equerries, so no one trains them. Last night one brought in the evening paper which carried something about the Ascot Enclosure coming to an end, and said "Lord Gran*ard* (mispronounced) has just telephoned to ask Your Majesty if you know anythink at all about it?" "Well, I must say," said the King, "I call that the top!! I really can't have messages of that kind. Can you see King George having that asked him?" No time to write. I will at length on the train.

This was the train to Marrakesh, again to companion Sidney Herbert, whose health ever declined and who was now without a leg though with ever-increasing courage. His friends rallied round him tirelessly. To go to darkest Africa was the greatest of thrills, and we met Juliet Duff in Madrid, where the Civil War had that day begun but was not noticeable. I wrote to Duff:

Tangier   *22 February*

We've come to this very good hotel—your style, with a pretty Moorish bath in an alcove in every room and a lu-lu *à côté*. Good food, charming bar, space and patios.

There's a man called Wylie to whom I had a letter given me by the A.D.C. at Gibraltar. The other party had already picked up with him and invited him and his friend *High Wind in Jamaica* Hughes to a cocktail. A quiet attractive man with a beard. Alfred Mason had arrived by this time, having had an appalling journey in a single-engined aeroplane. The bar party was gay. I should have liked to have talked to Hughes, but I heard Juliet's infernal memory urging her to such glibness with him on the subject of *High Wind* that I felt I couldn't compete. She'd got all the children's names and characters pat, and she also had the link of having known well the man Harris, who was a great figure here and whose life Hughes is now writing.

Tangier   *23 February*

It was your birthday yesterday and I forgot to say so as usual, but I thought of you all day and sent you a telly calling you beloved, although I had no word from you in letter form, so it was like good wishes.

I'm thinking all the time if you would like it here. Some of it you certainly would. Dining at Menebe's you couldn't have failed to be amused by. He sent a smart car with an ordinary plain-clothes gangster as chauffeur. We had all tanked up at the hotel bar, knowing that there would be old Mahomedan customs. We were ushered into an immense white Moorish hall, with round the walls and darting out in T and E shapes hard kind of Wagons-Lit divans, with the hard Wagons-Lit bolster and cushion, all upholstered in a violent Midland Hotel cretonne. The party consisted of us four, Miss Jessie Green who interpreted, and Mr Gye, the British Consul, sweating dreadfully. His Consular servant was on the job and doing most of it with the help of two fat bare-footed women who clearly despised activity. My practised eye caught the glint of four gold-necks in the corner. Then the host sailed down to meet us off a raised alcove, where we were set to eat. A man of rare charm, very tall, with a twinkling dark European face. His arms wide open, something of a black Chaliapin about his grace. He led us to our seats; low corner *banquettes*, him in the middle and the others quite comfortable on Wagons-Lit divans. Menebe did the piling up of cushions round our bums and elbows and took one comfortable little fall in doing it. We were each handed a large bath-towel for our lap, and on a six-inch-high table were laid in rapid succession the most delicious foods ever I tasted, the first a boiling dish of pastry, so light that you could not get it to your mouth intact, from which peeped hidden quails. Between every three people was a shallow plate of clear honey and another plate with a block of butter on it. Each person had a large hunk of bread to dip into the dishes of butter and honey, and with which to keep their fingers dry. The dishes were so large that although we ate liberally of them, one made no impression. They were all rather the same, and there seemed little reason why the meal should ever stop, or why it should come to the abrupt conclusion it did. The twelve-baskets-full of fragments go in slow declension to The Wife, the wives, the concubines, the minions, the slaves, the dogs, and the blind beggars at the gate. There was a good deal of washing at a stand-up centre brass ablution-arrangement, with a slave pouring hot water from a smart kettle, and soap too. Conversation never lagged and of course there is no greater fun than talking to each other about the house and the host in his presence. Miss Green was very good at the interpreting—an unchangeable drone of voice that in the same tone passed you an oriental compliment or said: "Of course the old man finds it frightfully difficult to get his daughters off."

There were five grandfather clocks in a row in the hall and

endless photographs of the Royal family, Lord Ripon, Lord Lons-
dale, Juliet and her mother. After dinner we moved to an identical
room, only smaller, leading from the main hall. Same Wagons-Lit
divans and bolsters propped round us, this time covered in rough
plush from Birmingham carrying a design of "scotties." The old
Moor found it very difficult to get off his divan and always offered
us each a hand to crane him up, but he was so heavy that we could
only just do it. Gye, who tried once single-handed, failed, but
Menebe laughed through the botchery. Whenever Mason put his
hand into the common dish he pulled out mistakes such as bones.
"What do I do with this?" he yelled. "Lay it on the table," came
Miss Green's drone. Another time he got involved with a skewer
and to our shame made such a fuss that a slave brought a plate
and *fork*. We flew at him for letting us down, and Menebe had it
explained to him that Mason was the "butt" of the party, from which
time he took a violent fancy to him and at parting suddenly started
tickling him and saying: "Good man, good man!" In three of the
hammam rooms that lay off the hall the centre *pièce de musée* was
an English wardrobe like those to be seen in a Grantham hotel
bedroom, stained deal with two mirrors and drawers in the middle.
In the fourth was a painting of himself by Lavery. It was a great
night for me.

This year of 1936 seems to overflow with events and work
and travel. The tangle of threads muddles memory, at any
time a preposterously inaccurate recorder. Easter took us on
an official visit to the war cemeteries in France. I could not
keep the tears from my eyes. Never did I find the grave of
a soldier I had known, but to see those innumerable stones
with the words "Known unto God" engraved upon them, in
acres tended and planted by English hands with English flowers
(rosemary, lavender, violets, lilies, roses and stocks), to hear
the bees and see the butterflies, to find the gates of the
enclosures open and the children playing and hiding and
shouting among the tombstones and round the great stone

cross, made me half-wish to be laid in such quiet English company.

The air was already befogged with fears of war. I remember doing a Red Cross gas course and having for the first time an examination through which I scraped. Many people thought this a grotesque precaution, which anyway would be outdated when war came. Conrad wrote in September 1936:

The Adjutant of the 4th Battalion Somerset Light Infantry, to whom I have offered myself for enlistment, has sent me a form on which I have to say what size hat, boots and shirt I will require in the next war. It makes it feel dreadfully near, and I have to promise to turn out on there being danger of war, not only actual war. That seems to me White Queen trouble.

Are you happy at Bognor? My spirits droop rather in this painful cold wet weather. I sigh for your company and the comforting warmth of the London picture-houses.

Doors were opening and shutting too. Alan Parsons had died too young and left me with an aching scar. Maurice Baring was trembling even more than he used to. He did not speak of anxiety. His getting worse may have been too gradual for him to realise its force and speed, but the time would surely come when the disease it proved to be must conquer him. It may have been one day about then that he said, lightly enough, as I tried to help him into his overcoat: "I'm becoming paralysed. I'm sure I am." I felt it to be true, so could not force myself to say "Nonsense!" His eldest brother, Lord Revelstoke, had died and left his brothers handsome legacies. Maurice, who had never before had juggling-money, felt himself a Croesus and bought a villa in Rottingdean and a little house in Chelsea. Both were arranged in the taste of his young days, with the same William Morris wallpaper of spraying olive-branches, with water-colours of Italy and Switzerland and a grand piano (always open) on which he would quaver out lyric-perfect songs from the Gilbert and Sullivan operas. On the walls hung faded photographs of Sarah Bernhardt, famous beauties, Russians, Danes, literary Frenchmen and women—links with his diplomatic years and the countries and places he had visited. (One that I well remember was of the house of Count Benckendorff at Sosnofka. I remember it because Maurice told me that when he was asked to stay by his hostess she said that there were two trains, one arriving at 4 a.m. and one at 4 p.m., and asked him if he would do his utmost to arrive by the 4 a.m. one, as the servants enjoyed this so much.)

On the long refectory tables at Rottingdean were piled stacks of books holding snapshots, theatrical programmes, menus scrawled with verses and sketches, letters, Royal Navy jokes and touching mementoes (Maurice spent several weeks a year aboard His Majesty's ships and was known the Fleet over as "Uncle") and what we called "Unusual Scraps" of fifty years. Between these stacks stood blue-and-white oriental bowls of potpourri. In his rather suburban overlooked garden grew in abundance pinks and pansies—pansies whose faded heads he decapitated tirelessly with shivering scissors, that they might re-flower throughout the summer.

New friends from our widening life were made and kept or forgotten—Euan Wallace, David Margesson, Oliver Stanley, Brendan Bracken and Antony Head, now married to our cherished Dorothea Ashley-Cooper, were all fast friends. Randolph Churchill was growing up and threatening to be a lifelong one. Belloc was still much with us. Hutchie had taken silk, and his daughter Barbara had grown up and become beautiful. Kaetchen moved across the Atlantic like a

Clipper. He had the direction of my worldly life completely in his clever mobile hands. He was also my martinettish accountant. I loved him dearly, obeyed and honoured him, yet often quarrelled with him. Children I had been frightened of were now self-possessed adults and had become equals. My sisters and my brother, all taken up with their families, I saw less of.

Another new friend was Dino Grandi, the bearded Italian Ambassador. His Embassy was the happiest in London. Thanks to his magnetic charm, his wit and his true love for England, he weathered until the last day of peace the Abyssinian war and the hundred grievances his country was courting from ours. He had been sent to England as a punishment. He told me that when first he arrived he felt like a soldier imprisoned in a garden. Later he learnt to love the garden, to respect its privacy and even to resent autocratic ways. Once, on his return from Rome, he was still fuming with indignation because his Duce had told him to remove his beard, which was silvering, and worse had suggested that he should beget more children. After all the alarms and tribulations Dino Grandi is still a treasured piece of what remains.

These crowded days of Generals and functions and being a War Office wife left me less time for my real friends. There was too my dear little boy, growing ever gooder, to take up my thoughts. He was not precocious, though he learned very early to read and write and, curiously enough, to telephone. Once I found him (he must have been four) telephoning to the number of a conjuror whose box of tricks he had been given, to inform him that the magic wand was a bad one, and could he exchange it for one that worked? The conjuror, who answered himself, said that he would come round and see what was wrong. Sure enough the good man came, with the fine present of a shadow theatre, and fled before a new wand was put to the test.

I took John Julius as often as he liked to the theatre. The open-air one in Regent's Park was giving *A Midsummer Night's Dream*, and I bought the most expensive front-row deck-chairs, in which I looked forward to two ecstatic hours. It was a moment of acute disappointment when, after Scene I, a hot whisper in my ear from the child of five asked: "Mummy, may I go when I want to? (I nodded) which is *now*." At that moment entered a fairy, and my peace was restored.

He was musical and as a page at the wedding of Angie Dudley Ward to Bob Laycock, aged five or six, he reproved another toddler for exclaiming when the organ pealed out: "O! what a noise!" "It's *not* noise, it's music," said John Julius. He had not had much spoiling, in fact there was a certain spartanism in his upbringing. "Accustom the body" was used as a pain-killing hope of future detachment from petty irritations. Accustom it to missing meals, to nettles, to bites and stings, to sleepless nights and a bed of cobblestones. He was afraid (as I had been) of anarchy, but forgetting my babyhood, I would insist on the obedient child breaking laws that I considered obstructive. I remember making him pull up stakes put across Roman grass-tracks in Sussex to impede our wild cross-Downland motoring. But I remembered confession to crime and subsequent apology being horrible to me, with their accompanying tears, so John Julius was taught to be sorry or to pretend sorrow for misdeeds without hesitation. This method softens the scolder, but it leaves room for no true repentance or resolve to sin no more.

He was being educated first at a little open-air school in Regent's Park, by Mrs Milner at Wigmore Hall for music and, from the age of seven, at Egerton House, Mr Hodgson's day-school in Dorset Square. Duff and I had planned that the horrors of a preparatory school should be avoided and that he should remain a London day-boy until it was time for Eton, with perhaps a year in a Swiss school between the two. The war knocked this plan into a cocked hat. Egerton House was all that one could wish, with its sensible work, its ridiculous theatricals, its prize-fights, which I felt bound to attend, dreading the yearly sight of a child of seven trying to brush his tears away with the back of a boxing-glove, and the Sports Day, which took place at Hampton Court. This was a feast of fun, specially for me, who knew my capacity for keeping out of Mothers' Egg-and-Spoon Races and other humiliations. Duff, not so armed in obstinacy, suffered sweaty qualms at the fear of obstacle, sack and three-legged races, and the hundred-yards Fathers' Sprint. John Julius and I in our wisdom protected him when other fat fathers were pressed by their mischievous sons to butcher themselves for their holiday. These athletic enterprises never came for John Julius to any form of blossoming. This mattered little to me, who am no sports-spectator and prefer romantic bookworms. Mrs Milner's half-yearly pupils' concert would keep me awake for two nights with fear. The little boy on his piano-stool, with feet far from the floor hanging so touchingly limp, dressed in a Duff tartan, his hair Nanny-neat for the occasion, playing *The Merry Peasant* and an encore, I can see as plainly now as then.

A great believer in being sometimes alone with him and in another world, I began to take him abroad with me. I had thickets of obstruction to overcome, put up both by Nanny, who did not trust me, and by my mother, who did not trust God or the railways or foreign milk. We settled in 1936 to go to Aix-les-Bains, where I could do a bit of a useless cure for lumbago. I found a Mademoiselle who would join me and talk French. After the amusement of the child's first journey, pretending to be monkeys on the ropes of the Wagons-Lits, we arrived at a swell hotel and went on an immediate quest for something more to my taste. We found it on the beach of the lake. I wrote to Duff:

It's all lovely—one of the happiest things I've done for years. Weather perfect, *fond de l'air* cold, fresh and bracing, sun showy and bronzing. The hotel itself all that I desire, though I admit that it's no one else's fancy. There's no bath and the hot *eau courante* has gone irremediably wrong. The annexe in which we live is the shape of things to come. The *nourriture* is so good that with only one meal a day I'm getting fatter—*lait, fromages, volaille*, great *massifs* of the best butter, *brioches*, mushrooms, sweetbreads, brains and ices —all fresh and real. It costs eighty francs a day for the three of us. The garage is on the ground floor of the annexe, so I step out of my bed at 7.30, clap on the thick blue ulster over my nightgown, tie on my sandals and step into the car. I drive two kilometres to l'Etablissement des Bains, where I am given *traitement gratuit*. It's like the Palace of the League of Nations and I'm passed naked to the hot hands of two fat Fates, and they hand me on to other fatter Fates through waters and pommellings and heat and cold. At last I'm sat under a shower, hatted with a rubber billycock, and am quite unaffected when I should be exhausted, so they lift me up tenderly and lay me on a bed with care and pinion my arms in boiling blankets, and I cheat and get away without cooling down. On with the ulster and the handkerchief tied round my purple face like a gay Russian's, and off in the car again, first to fetch a bottle of purest milk for John Julius, then to get the *Times* and *Express* and buy a pear or a treat or a birthday cake. Back by 9.30 for breakfast.

I'm delighted with the little waif's appearance. He's pinker and fatter and very very good. The language is the trouble but it will improve.

As I write it's 11 a.m. and a glorious day. The baby is doing his class with twenty other exquisite shrimps on the very green grass, and afterwards we are going to swim and I'm going to swagger my diving. He's bad at palling up (like you) and says that he likes watching, but the class is a help. The Frogs are all wonderfully acrobatic and put our northern Metropolitans to shame, turning cartwheels and somersaulting both ways. I can see poor Mademoiselle now. She's an acrobat and can do the splits. John Julius is making her imitate an ostrich and she has her head buried in what sand there is, while he rides on her back bawling bad-French directions at her. His French is much easier but unfortunately he has copied my accent and idiom instead of hers. I'd give almost everything to have you here, not quite all because you'd hate it so.

Tomorrow seven years ago John Julius was born. Tonight seven years ago you were taking me to the nursing home and playing those ridiculous records that Betty gave us, with hearts shaking more with fear of death than with exultance of birth, and each heart from the other hidden. Well, he's a great success, the little boy, up to date. I've ordered him a cake (white, with his name on it and seven candles) as a surprise, and we've invited the *patronne* and her son and pretty daughter and the two instructors to tea, and you see how much better it is to be at Les Platanes than at the Splendide.

I get up all night keeping an eye on the weather. So does a darling old Frenchman in the window opposite (a great eater with a moustache, paunch and beret). We greet each other from our windows.

Every day there's a delightful *Ausflug*, rowing round or across the lake, a visit to Hautecombe, the monastery across the lake where they pray for me to be able to pray, or to any amount of gorges, and a terrifying excursion in an iron cage suspended on a wire thread, which stopped with my heart half-way, and the fair at Chambéry with a carousel and children dressed in enchanting paper costumes, and Les Charmettes to teach our child early about Rousseau. Excitements come to our door too. Today a fascinating group of nomads arrived, with a barrel-organ pulled by an old pony and turned by a young man and three young *forains* (two pretty girls and a boy of fourteen) all on high, high stilts, twirling faster than the eye follows, castanets and tambourines going full blast. Very Italian of Byron's date.

Duff's mind was ever occupied by war. He felt it not inevitable, though every action and inaction brought us nearer to the abyss, and too few cared to look into its depths. The speech that he had made this summer of 1936 in Paris was no blunder. It was framed with care so as to convince the Germans that if they fought they would be beaten. Many censured him for it and were wrong. The King's face was heavy with displeasure when we returned from Paris to The Fort. Duff expected a rebuke and thought that the King was preparing one, but suddenly the frown fled, giving way to his delightful smile as he said: "Well, Duff, you certainly have done it this time." My letter to Conrad of this date reads:

Blenheim

Winston, while being delighted, thinks that Duff's Paris speech will lead to good or bad. Duff is completely unconcerned about it; what a strange man it is! If he gets the boot, Anthony Eden must get it too, and Mr Baldwin won't survive, so I don't see what can really happen. The speech was only "between the lines." In actual words there is little to catch hold of. Winston's hatred for Baldwin is so violent that his wish fathers the idea that the Old Man will "fall" over this speech at a coming club dinner. I'm very fortunate in having Duff's serenity to live with. Imagine the state I'd be in, or Edwin or Winston himself would have been, in Duff's shoes!

When the air-raids start only the heads of departments are to be left in Whitehall. All the others are to be hurried off to different provincial towns or encampments, so if Duff is no longer Secretary of State all the better.

Now I must get up and face my King and the light of my common day. Back tonight probably.

I am naturally timorous and I felt the iron entering ever more relentlessly into my soul. I thought that the cataclysm would be what the next war will be, and not what people remembered the last one was like. I never thought to survive it, nor desired to. But there were three years of peace left us, and in June the King invited us on board a yacht he had chartered in the Mediterranean. Greatly excited and flattered, we joined the *Nahlin* on the Dalmatian coast, pausing at Venice, where our international troubles seemed to be over. We took ship to Split, and I wrote to Conrad:

The other passengers were madly excited about the King's journey, all eyes scanning horizons. The Captain saw three ships long before any of us did. They were sailing obliquely ahead of us and were soon out of sight again. The destroyers *Grafton* and *Glowworm* look a bit too militant, you know, but stirring to English hearts. A friend met us from the royal yacht, dressed very shabby —sloppy trousers, blue grubby little short-sleeved jersey, yachting cap minus badge. He told us that the only disappointments were no sandy coves for bathing (and indeed the sand is like the pumice you scrub your feet with) and the impossibility of landing because of the yelling, jostling crowd that does not leave the King space to breathe. If he walks to the sights (the churches and old streets) they follow shouting "Cheerio!" and surround him so that he can see nothing. We went aboard and there were greeted by the young King radiant in health, wearing spick-and-span little shorts, straw sandals and two crucifixes on a chain round his neck. Our fellow-guests are Helen Fitzgerald, Pootz and Humphrey Butler, Jack Aird and Wallis.

We did not see Split. The others could not face another forced landing, so we set steam for a near island through the magic light that makes a background of ethereal mountains, the same colour and consistency as the benign little clouds floating round them. I've got a sore throat. God help me!

No sooner was the yacht sighted than the whole village turned out—a million children and gay folk smiling and cheering. Half of them didn't know which the King was and must have been surprised when they were told. He had no hat (the child's hair gleaming), *esvadrilles*, the same little shorts and a tiny blue-and-white singlet bought in one of their own villages. The other girls were rather seriously fixed, but Duff and I followed our Sovereign's lead. I sported the old green zipped trousers, striped shirt and a straw hat bought at Le Puy last week. Duff wore navy shorts, too loose and sagging below his reduced tummy, the white sandals that we bought at Verona together, and the old blue-and-white top. The rather battered yachting cap on top (battered by my packing, not by wear) gave him a W. W. Jacobs bosun look. The crowds were handled fairly cleverly by the detectives with the help of a local policeman and the equerries, who held hands across until we were far away on a stony path up a hill. It was not very pretty, but at least we were free of the mob, and the detective was told to pick wild rosemary for the ship. Following the road over the hill took us back into the little town—a lovely church and campanile, Italian-but-not-quite, and all the bells ringing. The staff were sure that they were ringing for the King, but I was not so certain, and sure enough by great luck it was a feast day, and there passed a procession of clerics in their best, the Virgin and Child beneath a silver canopy, and a long procession of townsfolk which relieved the density of the "send-off" mob. Still there were hundreds left throwing flowers. One woman had a huge magnolia grandiflora, but by gesture she made clear that it was not for me and that I must get it to the King. I made a gallant effort and forced it into his hand when he was talking to someone else.

At last we were on board again, and it was considered to have been a great success. I thought that I would go and gargle a bit and put some ice on my throat, not that it was much worse, but it was no better. I found that I had all but finished the gargle, so I sent for the doctor who is on one of the Nanny-boats (as the destroyers are called) to prescribe me a new one. He came, took my temperature, found it ninety-nine, said that I had tonsillitis, gauged it with a stick and said that I must stay in bed.

It's maddening! I feel perfectly well. Appetite, and no pain, only a lump in the throat and fearfully ashamed of arriving on the yacht as a liability. The doctor said that these things take two or three days to clear up. I can't think that I must stay in bed three days. O dear, O dear! I haven't got frightened yet, but that perhaps (being so unusual) is a bad sign. I shall gargle all night and pray God to let me be better in the morning.

SICK BENEATH THE AWNING

I am too unhappy. My temperature went up to 101 before I went to sleep and the stone in my throat got larger and sorer. In the end I took three aspirins, sweated like a pig and woke in great pain but without fever. By lunch-time it was 101 again, but I induced the doctor to let me be "with the sick beneath the awning." On deck things weren't too bad. I don't feel actually ill, but I'm in pain and ashamed. No one is sorry for me except Duff.

Tonight I had to cry with disappointment. We are in a new place. I think it is off the island of Lissa, but one can't tell. One never sees the Captain and there are so many thousands of these little islands. One always feels oneself to be in a kind of Garda, only without vegetation or habitation. All the others went off to see an old town and it has been a wild success. In fact they brought two Slav thugs on board and some yoghourt for me and some liquor of roses. Crowds had been well controlled, and it was what I had missed and was going to miss that made me cry. I can't be well enough to-morrow to visit Ragusa, so they'll do it without me, and tonight there is to be folk-dancing. Twenty monks came by in a long boat (ten pairs of oars). I've got a poultice on my neck and I can't eat or speak.

17 June

Another awful night of poultices, gargling, sweating and praying, but the morning brought no relief. In fact things looked worse, including the other tonsil which, Dr Keating informed me, had gone too. I dragged myself on deck with a thermometer and some gargle and a glass to spit into, and lay, too bad to speak, too overcome with self-pity to concentrate on a book. I could just swallow yoghourt with greed.

At lunch-time we reached Ragusa. The three- or four-hour journey there had been beautiful (barren, but there's a celestial light everywhere). From my isolated position I could hear them talking after luncheon about plans for going ashore and dining ashore, and I suddenly determined that I was doing no good brooding and coddling and that I'd rise above it all, so I joined the group and said that I was well, lied about my temperature (still over 100) and threw off my wraps. The cure was immediate. Two hours later I was 99 and the pain had lessened. It seemed like a miracle and I felt tipsy with relief and exuberance. I suppose the truth was that the corner was turned before I took the decision. The turning suggested it. Anyway today, twelve hours later, I am bathing and shouting and stamping and swearing.

To go back to yesterday, no sooner had we anchored than the King got into a row-boat and went off to discover a sandy beach, rowing through all the craft and canoes and top-heavy tourist-launches and the rubbernecks glaring at the decks of the *Nahlin* and not knowing that they were seeing what they were looking for. After some bathing and some sleeping and some gossiping and a cup of tea, we boarded the Royal launch respectably dressed (by that I mean trousers for the men only, no hats but sweaters, no naked torsos showing). When the Nanny-launches arrive, all the men stand to attention. I knew this but I didn't know that they saluted with their boat-hooks with much flourish, as bandmasters do with their long rods.

There's no traffic in Ragusa and there are baroque and gothic churches and palaces and monasteries. The people were mostly in national dress and on this occasion they were all out in orderly rows, both sides of the streets that the Consul had mapped out for our tour of the sights. They were cheering their lungs out with looks of ecstasy on their faces.

The King walks a little ahead talking to the Consul or Mayor, and we follow adoring it. He waves his hand half-saluting. He is utterly himself and unselfconscious. That I think is the reason why he does some things (that he likes) superlatively well. He does not *act*. In the middle of the procession he stopped for a good two minutes to tie up his shoe. There was a knot and it took time. We were all left staring at his behind. You or I would have risen above the lace, wouldn't we, until the procession was over? But it did not occur to him to wait, and so the people said: "Isn't he human! Isn't he natural! He stopped to do up his shoe like any of us!"

After sight-seeing, drinks in a hotel garden. The King makes the cocktails himself for Helen and Pootz. Duff and the staff have beer. I have white wine of the country. Wallis has whisky and water.

ASHORE AT RAGUSA

The staff say that they hate the King to see the Consuls the first day, because they are always so *émus* and in such a trance of ecstasy and nerves that all the plans the King makes with them are forgotten as soon as they are out of the presence. When we got back I found that the doctor had been and left orders that I was to sleep on deck. Nothing pleases me more. I always have to fight for it.

Dinner at the hotel, so we all repaired there at 9.30, along with the two Nanny-boat captains, Firth and Jessel. It went beautifully—a good time had by all. Again the orderly crowds, this time dressed up in all their national gewgaws, lining the long walk from dock to hotel. During dinner they did a peasant dance and ringed round our table (all alfresco, of course).

18 June

Duff and I got up early and went a proper English round of the town, entranced with every new prospect and discovery. Back at 12 and out with the others to bathe. After lunch siesta, and at 5 shopping in the town by the girls alone. I was rather tempted to buy an eighteenth-century embroidered Dalmatian coat, but didn't do it. The town remains permanently lined up, waiting for the King to walk through it. Venice dyed my hair canary without warning me. It's worrying—I look like a Pitcher jack-tart. No news, no letters, no papers ever reach the yacht.

The dinner was on the roof of a little fish-shop (local food, wines and songs), too crowded because it got rumoured that the King would be there. Afterwards we went to their fine municipal café. One of the Nanny-boats, quartered at Malta, carries a ridiculous but pretty little scarlet gondola (square, with two standing oarsmen) which they pretend is practical. It's really a mascot like the Welch Fusiliers' goat so we went to and fro in it. You cannot imagine how fantastic and lovely the whole thing is. I expected a lot, but the half was not anticipated. The rough side is not there and humours are easy.

19 June

Another night on deck with a 7 a.m. waking. After sour milk and foaming coffee ashore Duff and I hired a rather Heath Robinson motorcar driven by a "middy" of the Jugoslav Navy. We told him to drive to an old patrician villa twenty miles away. It took an hour to get to, and was a drive of the greatest beauty and the greatest danger—narrow hairpinned road, thick layers of loose shingle as a skidding-surface, and unparapetted. It was worth the pain. The little old owner of eighty-four received us in brown boots, good tussore trousers and a pyjama-top. The property has been in their possession since 1200 and he is the last of the line and thankful for it. He thinks the new world so abominable. He spoke only unintelligible French but managed to make me cry with a story of the Emperor Maximilian of Mexico and his wife Carlotta. They were having a meal under a great tree in his garden, and they took the knives from the table and carved their names and hearts on the tree. She threw her arms around him and said: "*O Maximilian, O Maximilian, nous allons toujours être heureux comme aujourd'hui.*" It was a Castle Ichabod all right, but the old man was so happy and alertly young for his age, and gay about things ending, and even death itself.

We sailed away at 1.30, too soon for me. There was a deal left to see, but the restaurants and bars were exhausted, so off we went. My clothes are standing up to the situation fairly well. The others never wear the same dress twice. I can't do that, of course, but mine are appropriate and sensible.

At five-ish we turned into the Bocche di Cattaro, the fiord of the Adriatic, very beautiful sinister country, the wall of the mountain so high that the light is depressing. We went ashore with the usual arrangements of Mayors. It's a very small town of only 2500 souls, very poor-looking, no shops, hotels or bars, Venetian influence strongly marked and a great deal of treasure owned by the Churches, both Catholic and Greek—silver tables, many silver arms and legs enclosing fragments of shins and funnybones of various saints. The party wanted to be off again at 7, but there were pathetic Japanese lanterns with single candles hung up and little pyramids of Greek Fire along the quayside, so thank God we settled to wait for such illumination as there was. And was it not lucky! You have never seen so sensational a display. Every mountain-peak was set afire, every house and every mountain-path lit with living (not

electric) lights. Guns from the forts booming and echoing through
the ravines. The same was done all along the fifteen miles of gorge.
So magnificent was it that we determined to say "Thank you" by
sending up some excellent S.O.S. rockets ourselves, and our Nannies gave a searchlight display, and in return for their serenading Mr
Fletcher, the King's piper, gave them "Over the sea to Skye," walking round and round the deck, the King shouting explanations of
bagpipes to the crowd.

Corfu   *20 June*

Two Kings tomorrow night. It's all a great treat. I think that
I'm enjoying it as much as (No! *more, much more* than) anyone on
board, partly because I'm so conscious of the occasion. The others
seem to take it in their stride.

I "took on" a lot about Greece. It looked wonderfully Homeric
—brown rocky earth, ships like Ulysses's (at least rigged the
same), mountains capped in silver cloud, one of which may be
Olympus. Some of the shipmates have never heard of the Olym-
pians, nor do those who may have done associate them with anti-
quity. Godfrey Thomas has got the inevitable *Baedeker 1906*.
The day was rather given over to fuss about the King of Greece.
The King doesn't say "George" or "the King" or "my cousin"
but always "the King of Greece" which sounds to me *La Belle
Hélène* musical-comedyish.

Once anchored in Corfu, it was dressing up Aird to go and call
on the King of Greece. We had sent a message to ask him to dine
on board and had the reply that he was bringing six English guests.
We can't cope with so many. We haven't covers or table-seating
for sixteen, so Jackie Aird had to try to get us invited to his board
instead. The same difficulty there—no time to get the crockery and
plates, but they would call for a cocktail at 6.30. The evening dresses
that had been brought out of their paper were put back and the *robes
d'après-midi* ironed. We fixed our King up in white flannels and
blazer and yachting cap. Wallis left us to arrange it all. They came
and stayed two hours, and we behaved badly and were cliquish,
catching each other's eyes and yawning and looking miserable. The
King played up best. The King of Greece seems quite altered by

Restoration. He had lost five stone and some of his affability. His life, they say, is a very sad one. He has not one man he can trust or take advice from, and not one personal friend. He's made himself more or less of a dictator, he says, though disapproving of dictators, and he is feeling the strain badly.

Everything here is ruin—not classical, modern. No rich villas left, the Kaiser's and the King of Greece's both practically roofless. I had a lovely bathe and scrambled very painfully over razory rock to feel the soil of Greece.

21–22 June

All my spirit has gone. I feel suddenly like Hamlet at his most lugubrious. I was incapable of writing all day, but tonight I feel at least not ill, so I'll try.

Friday 21st was too strenuous for me. I got up at 7, and at 8 Duff and I were ashore trying to get our money changed into 74 drachmas, and also to get a motor-car. We found a very shoddy open green Ford on the quay. Speechless we got into it and pointed in the guide book to the name of a monastery on the other side of the island. The driver chattered back at us like a monkey and it all looked hopeless until a lounger walked up and in fair English explained that the car had been hired by the King of Greece, but that it would take us to the bank for the money and find us another car for the drive. This plan worked. The new car had no windscreen and no springs or stuffing, but it had an English-speaking man at the wheel. No charm in the streets of Corfu but great beauty on the other side of the island. Our goal was a place called Palæocastrizza. Every mile of the way got more lovely—cliffs into green sea with always deep caves for sirens, immense olives, fragrant smells, and of course utterly unspoilt by people or pumps or posters. We had a nasty little breakfast on a bay. Breakfast over, we went to a monastery on a hill-top where the bearded monks gave us bunches of verbena and herbs with delicious brand-new smells. We walked down—a longish walk through cypresses and olives where Greek girls with headcloths and aprons and bare feet tended their goats.

Home again via the exterior of the King's two palaces, one in the town, the other miles outside, both deserted and broken by successive revolutions, both built in excellent taste by the English Governor in Napoleonic times. The villa is called Mon Repos and a very desirable Regent's Parkish (only better) house it is. The King of Greece means to restore these palaces but his throne is still too groggy to start spending money, and the country does not look as if it owned a drachma. Back to the boat pretty exhausted because the heat is prodigious. Poor Helen is wilting beneath it, but I don't worry. Duff is baked to a cinder and does not know that it is hot; no more does the King.

At 4 Wallis, the King, Duff and I went off in the launch to see the famous villa built by the Empress Elizabeth and bought by the Kaiser. We landed on the pompous broken quay and found to our horror that the gates of the demesne were heavily chained. The King began climbing, but there was barbed wire. A lot of peasants and fishermen were watching us when Mr Evans, the detective, and an Adonis dressed in the same clothes as the King, started fiddling with the chains, broke them, took pliers to the wire and opened it all up! I thought it a funny gate-crash for a King, but no one commented on it.

Then came a forty-minute climb of beauty—one endless flight of steps bordered by symmetrical cypresses culminating in a charming 1890 statue of the Empress Elizabeth in marble skirt and collar of modish cut. The top when reached (dead with fatigue) showed a tremendous view and a colossal figure of Achilles erected by the Kaiser, and a house the size of Chatsworth of such hideosity that it takes seeing to believe. Pompeian in style. The electric light is installed with great fancy—baskets full of electric-light flowers, groups of plaster cherubs blowing electric-light bubbles. An amusing piece of furniture is the Kaiser's own writing-table. It consists of a high clerk's desk, painted white and gold, and another little platform from which rises a pole crowned with a stirrupless saddle that revolves.

I wondered as I slithered down the half-hour's descent how the tight-laced and booted Edwardians had ever got to the sea. I decided that they never did, because why should they want to, non-bathers that they were? But I was wrong. It appears that they had a cavalcade of donkeys and bathed daily. Well, it's another Castle Ichabod and I don't want to see it again.

Back fatigued to dress for the King of Greece's dinner. Everybody making a great groan about it, but I thinking that "it will make a change." I wore the grey organdie, but I was too tired to look as spry as necessary for that material. A couple of cocktails before starting at 8.45 did no good. We piled into the slow launch called *Queen Victoria* and chugged across a very wide bay, an even slower Greek launch piloting us. Of course we were a good hour late for 9.30 dinner and found the King of Greece twiddling his thumbs on the quay. He packed us into two open cars, himself at one of the wheels, and we hairpinned up a steep cypress-lined road and came to a magnificent villa rented for the summer. We sat out to dinner on a lordly terrace and the dinner was A.1. I sat next to the Greek King. I never got going at all, but I observed everything and watched our King turn to Mrs Jones next him (an exceedingly good-looking Englishwoman, whose soldier husband has just divorced her, or been divorced by her) and turn the charm on full force. Meanwhile Wallis, on the King of Greece's other side, was doing splendidly, the wisecracks following in quick succession, the King clearly very admiring and amused. It went on until 1.30. I was nearly crying by this time. I suppose that I had done too much in too great heat: anyway the journey home made me almost unconscious.

I woke on the 22nd no better, in fact rather worse than the night before. Panic set in. Was I going to be really ill? I did not know all day what to do with myself. The deck was too bright, the cabin too stuffy, legs ached, hands ached. I could not read because I could not keep awake, nor yet sleep for nervous jerks. We had left Corfu at dawn and were sailing to Cephalonia. It's all very bare, but my eye was jaundiced. We tried to "make" a bay, nearly grounded the ship and as near as a toucher got rammed by a steamer.

At 5 I forced myself to bathe and felt a little better. The King was in high spirits. He took a walk to the top of a hill in the early afternoon, then later appeared suddenly with an old shrimping-net on his shoulder, looking like a child of eight. He ordered out a dinghy and set about catching jelly-fish, while we all leant over the ship's side shrieking "There's a big one, Sir." At meals he gets served last, with the result that there is never anything left for him. The fool stewards don't realise it and go on passing the sauces and extras to his meatless plate, so that every day he has to say at least once: "Yes, but I do want something to eat."

I feel a lot better this evening. Panic over, and I know now that it was too much energy in too great heat and that I shall be all right tomorrow.

Cephalonia   *23 June*

Woke up with new-spangled ore. The nights on deck are almost the loveliest part of the twenty-four hours. One is cool, breeze-blown, the stars are clear and one wakes up to new surprises every morning. Duff and I went ashore at 9, struggling to get a car to take us a drive round the island. The village was very primitive, so we were lucky to get the crazy vehicle we did get. We always forget what tortures of terror and vertigo we are taking on ourselves when we set forth on these expeditions. A man with a few words of English offered us a police escort. We refused in true British style, but under pressure we took a uniformed young gentleman along. It was a magnificent drive and took four hours. At one moment we had to get out and walk, for terror of the sheer precipice.

Duff is really worse than me. These goat-paths, no wider than a car's axle, with crumbling precipitous edges and a surface of shifting shingle, give him acute vertigo. I get only abject terror. He can shut his eyes at least, while I have to drive the car with hands and feet and eyes, but I can carry away a picture of the heights and cliffs and wine-dark sea. Poor Duff has only his lids to remember. We were well rewarded for our enterprise by hearing first a jangle of the most beautiful bells miles and miles away. They came from a strange Greek church with open belfry attached, of great architectural value. It seemed that anyone could run up and have a bang at the bells, and the result was a pleasant discord. The village was *mouvementé* to a degree. Even a few so-called cars were parked outside the church, and a lot of saddle-donkeys. We looked round the church which was empty and from there we heard the noise of a mourning crowd. We passed out through the opposite door, and there to our delight was Reinhardt's *Miracle* (Orthodox style) and all the props, banners, crucifixes, reliquaries, candles, staves, choir-boys, clergy, a tremendous bearded Archimandrite with a bulbous oriental gold crown on his head, an ornamental silver coffin with a visible Saint carried in a standing position, cripples and old chronics laid on the ground, moaning, praying, but alas! no miracle that we could see. Were we not lucky, though, to hit off the Saint's feast, and the actual hour of his procession? We arrived back with something accomplished before the height of the mid-day sun, to find the others just coming out into it from their airless cabins.

After lunch a siesta, well earned by us but the others have only just got up, so aren't as keen about it. They wander about trying to find a cool place on deck, while the mad-dog English King rows for an hour or two or takes a strapping walk.

Delphi

There was a sudden movement last evening amongst the few that we had better go and consult the Oracle on our own or we might easily miss it. So the three (Duff, me and Godfrey Thomas) went ashore at 9 and hired a car and a guide, and buzzed up the para-petless road, preceded by eight soldiers jammed into a Ford car and followed by the same. What made the whole thing funny, as usual, was our clothes and the fact that nothing would persuade the natives that one of us was not the King. The guide said that it was no good. The more explanation given them, the surer they were that it was an incognito stunt. Even though we signed the book, our names were shown to another batch of our party who went to Delphi as the King's signature.

At 5 we went over to *Glowworm* to watch the crew play water-polo, an extraordinary performance and one that moved me very much. These splendid young men behaving like so many porpoises for half an hour in a swelling sea, not allowed to touch even a goal-post for rest, shouting at each other in Yorkshire and Cockney and Hebridean, all backgrounded with Greek mountains. The Captain entertained us in his boiling cabin packed with pictures of his "kiddies" (three of them) and good prints and objects of art collected by him with taste.

At dinner (O the pity of it!) we watched the little town light itself up, and also the two villages, mountain-built in the middle distance, so the King said: "Let's give them a show." Up went half a dozen rockets, up went the White Ensign to the mast-top while the searchlight from *Grafton* played upon it. Godfrey ran in on the dinner-party saying "I'm afraid there's been rather a bad accident. *Glowworm* hopes you will excuse her if she fails to give her display." Captain Jessel, while bathing off the ship at twilight, had been run over by his own motor-launch and was most terribly injured. *Glowworm* had rushed him off to Patras, which was the nearest hospital. I think that we all felt sick and faint (I did) and Godfrey was so maddening in his sort of mysterious way about the injuries. "Most terribly cut about." "Will he live?" I said. "That's what we don't know." The mysterious tone gave one the idea that the wounds were unmentionable and Abyssinian, but before we went to bed we heard that both his legs had compound fractures, which (if that is all) is not too bad. The poor dear Captain with his *joie de vivre* and his "kiddies" haunted me all night. The King was greatly upset and fussed round sending messages and giving orders. When he settled down again, he said; "I've told them not to worry about us if we're delayed. It doesn't matter a bit."

Arrival in Athens. Looks better than expectations. Other girls scouring the shore with glasses for night-clubs.

Athens   *26 June*

The whole of Athens is a nice shape and colour. There is nothing atrocious to violate one's associations (from the sea, I mean). The Acropolis through the glasses looks wonderful. Excitement was great. As Duff and I were trying to slip away independently, Sir Sydney Waterlow and a young attaché called Nicholls and a herd of Greek geese came aboard, so we had to stay and be agreeable. Sir Sydney has everything I ask for in a representative of H.M.G. Immensely tall, voice like Hutchie's and Louis Mallet's in one, and a look of blank astonishment like Harry Tate's, yet completely uninhibited. On boarding the ship he said: "I've got plenty of splendid ideas"—this à propos of plans. He propounded them and the King accepted to go:

(*a*) to the Acropolis at 6.

(*b*) to the Legation for cocktails after.

(*c*) to leave with the Minister at 3 tomorrow, motor for two hours, walk over the mountain for three hours and be back in the summer residence at 8.30, where the rest of the party should arrive at 9.

Neither party quaked at the thought.

Because of a general muddle of plans, Duff and I got the Acropolis to ourselves, also the full attention of the Head of the Fine Arts, who took us round and showed us the most beautiful of the seven wonders of the world. It isn't only the proportions and the marble's warm tone and the wonder of it—it's the sky and the air and the arrangement of mountains and sea together with the human inspiration of the temple that give you a catch in the throat, and that strange restless sensation one had so often as a child (and very rarely now) that something must be done about it. Mere looking does not seem enough. This emotion disinclined me for a routine evening which lasted too long.

Everybody in consequence felt weak this morning, except those who never opened up until lunchtime. Duff and I, a bit irritable, plodded off at 9 to another temple and a museum where the Mycenæ dug-ups are kept. Most finely-chased cups that maybe Agamemnon drank from, and gilded masks for the faces of the dead, and much gold, jewellery and many swords. Actually the things that Homer wrote about. We bought handwoven stuff from an English weaving-lady that I knew about before, had an ice at the café and came back to the yacht less irritable to a lunch of first-class cold grouse. Good news of Jessel. It appears that it was quite dark when he bathed. No one's fault but his own. His legs are dreadfully lacerated and broken too, but only below the knee. Dr Keating operated at once, without anaesthetic as he was too weak to take one. He was conscious and "chaffing." This morning a message told us that he was a bit better, but they won't think that his life is spared until after five days. All are determined for his legs to go septic, but I don't see why they need. Sea is saline.

The King, dressed for his hike with the Minister, said: "I say, he's got the most awfully long legs. Do you think he'll walk me off mine?" At 2.30 the Minister arrived, a sight for sore eyes— six foot four, with white mustachios trained upwards Kaiser-ways and very short shorts with alpine boots and a stick with a spike. You felt that he had probably got an axe on his back. Our poor boy looked inadequate and went and changed into something harder, and off they went with the athletic detective behind. Time for a siesta and at 5.30 we were off again to the Parthenon. Better still tonight—all hills violet as we have been told they are for the last two or three thousand years. I would like very much to see it with you. I think it cannot disappoint.

Dinner at the Waterlows' a great success. I sat next Sir Sydney and was delighted with him and his wonderful Lucullan food and rare wines. Home and bed betimes. The King's walk had been a huge success. Conversation never stopping. Tonight is the last night.

27 June

Our last day and I planned an expedition. It was a complete success but it gave me anxious moments. The yacht was to sail at 7 a.m. and take us to the island of Ægina. So the pampered ones, if possible, were to be up at 10 and find themselves already there. I never thought they'd make it but they did, with the exception of Helen who didn't try. Tommy Lascelles arrived on board at 7 a.m. from *Grafton* and I had a little talk to him, self-conscious because I hadn't been down to my cabin, having just rolled out of bed.

The island when we got there looked quite insubstantial— *Tempest*-like and crowned with a solemn temple, improved by ruin. We landed and then a bad moment came to torment me. Twenty donkeys were waiting to take us up. The crowd fell on us, all of them natives who did not know about him being a King but thought that by grabbing physically they would be certain of a client for their donkey. So they shouted: "*Aristo, Aristo!*" and grabbed and pulled us about. They were old clean crones and young shepherd boys, and it was funny to see Duff being led off by two crabbed Fates. He looked under arrest and went quietly. But others didn't like being manhandled and panicked a bit. There was no means of getting onto a donkey for being pulled towards another. As we walked the gay pack jostled around us. I had had exactly the same experience six months ago in Morocco and enjoyed it no end, but this company is different. However it ended as bad moments do, and the donkeys got picked and the rest didn't follow and we rode (Wallis, Mrs Rogers, Duff and I), the others walking, to the temple, up a steep difficult path through pine-trees and views of sea and mountain. Everyone was delighted, not only with the temple and the brave old world but with the exertion and novelty. We took common snapshots and meandered down again. A romantic bay with translucent water and cavefuls of sirens called to us, and there we bathed. I got over-keen and fell on the rock, covering myself with blood, but I behaved splendidly. So, when it ended, as good things must, it was proclaimed the best thing we had done, and as scheduled we were back on board for lunch and steaming home to Phaleron Bay.

When I returned to London later in the year I was rudely awakened to the reality of what was soon to happen—the King's abdication. This has been written about so many times that my silence will be golden. It brought me a world of tears and sighs, and it brought King George VI and his spell-binding Queen to the throne.

CHAPTER NINE

The Price of Admiralty

THE new Sovereigns made a habit of inviting their Ministers for a night to Windsor. I had never been there before, and recovered youth's anticipation of pleasure. Duff, who had for many years idolised Queen Elizabeth, was equally excited. So off we went one early spring day, and I wrote to Conrad:

Windsor Castle   *16 April 1937*

We motored down in an Army car in grey rain. I slept most of the way, which I felt was unworthy of the occasion, but I was suffering from a headache, caused, I think, by the excellent Johannisberger 1900 which was given me by the Goldsmiths last night.

We were warned by the Comptroller's minion to present ourselves at the Castle at 6 or thereabouts, and that knee-breeches would be worn. We arrived about 6.30 at what looked to me the servants' entrance and Wade came in by the same door. I heard an impatient telephone-voice bawling "Trousers, trousers, I've said trousers four times" as we passed down a many-doored musty passage which led us to our suite. This consists of a sitting-room with piano and good fire, evening papers, two well-stocked writing-tables and thirteen oil-paintings of Royalty, the only charming one being an unfinished sketch of Queen Victoria drooping submissively on a merely "blocked in" figure of her dear Prince, the work of Sir Edwin Landseer. Besides the oils there are about a hundred plaques, miniatures, intaglios, wax profiles etc. of the family in two Empire vitrines, and two bronze statuettes of King Edward VII in yachting get-up and another Prince in Hussar uniform.

Communicating with this bower is Duff's very frigid room with tapless long bath, enclosed and lidded in mahogany. Through this again is my throttlingly-stuffy bedroom with nine "oils" of the family and a bed for three hung with embroidered silk. Next a large bathroom and lu with eight oil-paintings of the family by Muller 1856, a bronze statuette of Princess Louise on horseback 1869, and Princess Beatrice, Prince Leopold and "Waldie" (also in bronze) on the moors.

After a few minutes Lady Nunburnholme and Sir Hill Child knocked and came in for the smallest possible talk, and a minute or two later Alec Hardinge appeared. He warned me for my good that dinner was at 8.30, leave dining-room with gentlemen at 9.30, but gentlemen don't stop, they walk straight through us to the lu and talk and drinks. Girls gossip until 10.15 when the men reappear flushed but relieved, and at 10.30 it's "Good night."

A man has just come in and commanded Duff to go and see the King. O, I forgot! The first thing that Sir Hill Child said to Duff was: "Have you brought any trousers? No? Then you'll have to wear my secretary's." They had informed all the inmates, but had forgotten to warn those coming from London, that the King had changed his mind. Muddles obtain identically under all reigns and all classes. Luckily Holbrook had put in some trousers, so Duff will look dandy. There is a clock in each room, *all* synchronising.

Duff is now with the King and I must paint my face and go on wishing that I could have a cocktail. I arrived in the *Good Earth* hat and the pretty moleskin jacket, and tonight it's to be the "Queen's own blue." It's high-cut and modest in design, but I'm not sure that it isn't worse than "strip-tease" because for some reason it shows the minutest details of anatomy through its draping. Till bedtime . . .

11.15. It's Fersen, it's Tristan, it's Königsmark, it's Culpepper! The King and Queen said goodnight to the cringing company and the party broke up. I waited for my husband to escort me to bed, and waited in vain, and behaved as I behave only on race-courses, tearing round to one and all saying: "Where's Duff?" "Have you seen Duff?" and asking in vain. At last I'm down to a butler who replies with an inscrutable face: "He is with the Queen." I had the humiliation of being taken to my rooms through the meandering mazes of the Castle by a red-liveried man. I'm pleased of course, and it's a big story, but I cannot bear to be missing anything. Now I'm sitting among the family "oils" nursing a grievance. It's all been fine and the Queen in gloss of satin, a lily and rose in one.

12.15. Duff's not back yet. It will be high treason and the block. Through dinner they had what I thought was an inferior make of loud gramophone playing airs from *Our Miss Gibbs* and *The Bing Boys*, but from seeing a red-uniformed band playing after dinner I suppose it was them muffled.

I'm to be down at breakfast with the staff at 9 tomorrow, and then to take the Castle tour with Dick Molyneux. My admiration and love for the Queen did not stop me talking. The iron tongue of midnight, and still Duff is in the Queen's bower. It's d'Artagnan (no! Buckingham), it's Bothwell, it's Potemkin, it's Lancelot, it's boring.

He came back at 12.30. One hour so-called drinking tea with the Queen. She put her feet up on a sofa and talked of Kingship and "the intolerable honour" but not of the crisis. Shan't write any more. Too tired. Duff so happy, me rather piqued.

Shortly after this visit to Windsor Duff had a dream—a very vivid one. He told it to me on waking. He showed more distress than any dream warrants. Mr Chamberlain had sent for him and he knew in his dream that it was for dismissal. He half-expected as much, for a London newspaper editor had made him a handsome offer for articles to be written after he had left the Government and urged him to accept, knowing (he said) more than he could admit of the future Cabinet's make-up. In his dream Duff walked boldly to the Treasury, but his fears were for his face. He felt frightened at the thought of it puckering, the upper lip sagging and the crest falling. He opened the Chancellor's door, marched breast forward and was woken by the contortion of his face and his tears falling. It was a curious dream for Duff to dream, he who did not know fear of fiends, but he remembered it, and so did I when very soon afterwards an ominous message came inviting him to step into Mr Chamberlain's parlour. But there was no web, nor yet a boot, and he came out of the parlour with a smiling face, to a post that he was to like better than any other, that of First Lord of the Admiralty. He could not at the time exult wholeheartedly. He was too regretful at leaving the Army, for which he had striven with all his frustrated might for eighteen months.

Always surprised by the past yet never at the time, I do not remember any joy and delight at being given the most romantic house in Whitehall, looking on to the Horse Guards' snowy arch, the garden of 10 Downing Street and the pelicans in the Park, and also the *Enchantress*, a thousand-ton sloop to sail the seas. I felt sorry for the Army, as a loving wife should, and I was a little loath to leave dear Gower Street that we had been so gay in. Its mutations, its associations, its books and its atmosphere wrapped me gratefully round. It had grown with our fortunes. I wondered if it would wait for us and shelter and indulge us again as it had done for nearly twenty years. I never loved any house as well and I trembled for its future, with good reason. But there was such a tide running, water to tread and waves to dance upon, a Coronation ahead, Generals exchanged for Admirals, my mother's pride and enthusiasm, and Duff's own First Lordliness. There was no time, no time. We did not move into Admiralty House for many months. A lot was to be done, and Sir Philip Sassoon as Minister of Works was to be the most generous and interested of decorators. He gave us a fine bust of Nelson, and I bought for the hall a mermaid from Copenhagen. Conrad and I had been to Elsinore to see Laurence Olivier and Vivien Leigh play *Hamlet*. Rain had defeated the actors' hopes. The platform was too wet for ghosts, so the play was acted in the lounge of the Beach Hotel.

Never was there such a performance. Disaster leads to finest hours, and Lilian Baylis, in mortar-board and gown, told the audience in epilogue that they would never see a better rendering. It was there that the beautiful pair plighted their troth, and it was on leaving for England that we bought the naked mermaid carved in wood by Thorwaldsen's father. Her arms are raised to the skies, but her face looks repiningly into the depths. For all too short a lease she filled her Admiralty niche, surrounded by Trafalgar trophies.

The principal room in our new palace was furnished by its dolphins that sport, and support, each chair, table, screen and stool. They had been given by a generous Mrs Fish in memory of her husband. Their walls were *eau de nil* and their gleams needed little light. For the gaunter dining-room Philip Sassoon recovered for us all the pictures by William Hodges and John Webber of Captain Cook's voyages, the biggest of which I snatched for my bedroom, which was much larger than the dining-room. It represented war-galleys at Tahiti and hung over an elaborate marble chimney-piece, reminiscent of Arlington Street, that faced the bed of beds, which I wonder how I ever dared to erect. The room was at least twenty feet high, and from close to the ceiling hung a wreath of gilded dolphins and crowns. Blue curtains, lined with white satin and falling to the ground, spread open to reveal a headpiece of more dolphins, tridents and shells. At the bottom corners of the bed two life-sized dolphins, arch-backed and curved, menaced intruders—fishy sentinels. It was a sensational room in my eyes. I asked Rex Whistler how the bed should be, and he drew me a design that never was or will be, with me asleep and the First Lord coming too late to bed.

Duff transported his library to the Admiralty, which wounded Gower Street's pride. He was always very happy "battering his books" in his free hours, though now he had less liberty than ever before. On the second floor John Julius had his schoolroom looking on to the Horse Guards Parade and, of course, I made it a riot of fish, nets, tackle, barnacles, anchors and crowns, with actually a tank of sea-horses bought from the Zoo and particularly difficult to keep alive. Fresh fleas seemed to be their staple diet, which meant perpetual to-and-fros to Regent's Park, and we found them viciously pugnacious, erect like knights on a chessboard, strangling their brothers with their iron-spring tails. So many died that we gave up struggling for their lives.

Wade and Holbrook and our modest cook came to Admiralty House. Holbrook was anyway an Admirable Crichton, and absolute power had made him already intolerant and intolerable. He wearied us with his importance and long words. He could produce like a genie anything he was asked for. With a rub of his lamp would appear a pair of greyhounds on leashes for a Diana tableau, ripe mangoes or flood-lighting for the Gower Street fêtes. He could wait, valet five gentlemen, garden and drive the cars. He even made us several hundreds of pounds a year by forming the Holbrook-Cooper Company for transporting shingle from Bognor beach to waiting lorries on the road. The Company's office was a tin hut on the beach, its stock-in-trade an old white horse and some trucks. The deeds and agreements had green tapes and red seals. His profits were double ours. We always rather hated him, and were not sorry that the Admiralty daunted him. He rightly left us when it came to an end. He took his pension and came to dust.

The Coronation! Nothing but the Coronation. Clothes, uniforms, robes, ermine, miniver, rabbit, velvet, velveteen. Where were the coronets? In the bank, at Carrington's, or in the attic? There were fears for bad places behind stone pillars, absurd fretting over starvation and retiring-rooms, alternative routes to the Abbey via Ealing or Purley. A Coronation still, in 1937, belonged to the Peers. The Ministers did not feel so certain of ringside seats. Still we would be there, and Molyneux embroidered me a gold dress and Eleanor Abbey's genius fashioned me a crown of golden flowers. I looked faded but not, thank God, overblown. I wrote to Kaetchen:

Dear parti-coloured Kat, The family go fifteen-strong to the Coronation. There'll be no room for the Dominions. Brother John carries some sort of sceptre, so does Charlie Anglesey, Kakoo carries the Queen's canopy with three other *little* Duchesses, Ursula [Manners] and Liz [Paget] are train-bearers. Henry Uxbridge is page to Queen Mary, Charles, Johnnie and Roger are pages too, one to his father, the others to Lord Ancaster and someone else. Mother and Marjorie will be there, and Duff and me the "also rans."

Our places we found to be behind the Viscounts, not all I hoped but good enough. The many hours of expectation were relieved by exquisitely funny comings and goings. Peers without pages in a crowded tribune cannot cope with their velvet robes. One hand holds the coronet, the other gathers up the heavy folds in the most impudic fashion. Retiring-rooms dotted all over the Abbey are magnets. Our Viscounts were dodging in and out like water-carriers. Hunger obsessed them. One, returning from retirement, brought from some first-aid booth an enormous box of mixed chocolate-creams. He naturally stumbled (his velvet brought him down) and the silver-papered chocolates went careering down the steeply built-up tribune. There was an ugly rush to catch them by any Viscount within reach of their rolling.

The mediaeval ceremony of consecration passes all too

quickly. The crowned heads leave, the Archbishop's voice is still, and the present jars back through the loudspeaker. Let no one move before direction, was the order. I hate orders, and I persuaded Duff to sneak up to the exit so that, once it was opened, we would head the Viscounts. This anti-civic move was, of course, followed by many commoners, so that when at last the direction for the Viscounts' stampede was given, a hundred of us were pressing against a door that could be opened only to Peers. It was a moment after my own heart. The bewildered usher, desperately obedient, barred the narrow way. The Lords were protesting from behind, but ours was a spot of no return. We were allowed out at last by vowing to come back to our places as soon as the Viscounts were cleared. I suppose that no one kept that promise. Certainly Duff and I, the original culprits, never looked back but walked briskly to Brendan Bracken's lordly collation laid for friends in his Lord North Street house. Duff, who (as very often at such times) almost cried with shame and embarrassment, was regenerated with relief, good food and pride in my lawlessness. Conrad wrote:

To commemorate King George's Coronation Mrs Sykes has planted a Cornish oak at Cuckold Corner.

Back to Admiralty life and a second holiday in Aix with John Julius, and to September plans for the *Enchantress*'s official sailings. She was a sloop with a crew of a hundred and fifty captained by Peter Frend, with her stern converted into living-quarters for the First Lord, his wife and four friends. She had two big saloons, and later another superstructure was built for Duff to work in. The officers knew this as the Duff Cot. No one was so happy, so visibly aglow with pride, as Duff when we all assembled at my sister Marjorie's house in

Anglesey, complete with yachting-caps, Royal Yacht Squadron badges and buttons, and my eight-year-old son in blue with H.M.S. *Enchantress* written on his hat, to see the little white-ensigned ship sail into the Menai Straits. Duff adored the sea. Euan Wallace ("the Captain") and Tommy Thompson, Secretary to the Board of Admiralty, made up our party. The Naval Secretary, Admiral Whitworth and Secretary Peck were to join us a few days later. A needle had just been extracted from my foot, so I limped on board. The Paget family and Conrad cheered us out of the Straits into freshening seas, bound for sister Letty's island, South Uist. I wrote to Conrad:

From Anglesey bound for South Uist   *6 September 1937*

It was quite awful as soon as I left you. I unpacked valiantly and John Julius pretended that he always laid himself down after lunch. Everything was battened. The dining-room had all its chairs laid low—an after-orgy scene. Then I got sardinewise onto the bed with John Julius and read *Emil and the Detectives* aloud until we both fell into a sea-coma. At 6 it got much calmer and we could see a very mystical Ireland with broken sunlight upon it. The Quality dressed for dinner, and I undressed the poor little sweat-drenched boy, who had remained curled up animalwise, and put him to bed in my narrow cell. Dinner was dull but all right. Bed at 10.30. I moved my sleeping child onto his pallet and getting into my own read *Oblomov* with great enjoyment until sleep came. Smooth night, because of passing the straits and islands and in fact all the beauty spots arranged originally to be seen by day.

At 7.30 this morning Duff came in. "Isn't it wonderful?" I said. "Yes, but you're going to have two very bad hours—the Minch" and, my God, it was *three* hours of hell! My poor child was sick four times. Captain Wallace was taken very ill too. I'm thankful to say that Duff and I both felt rotten but were not sick. I had really no chance to be, from picking John Julius up and laying him down and holding his head and his poor heaving stomach. At 11 we arrived and now it's 12. It's a vile day—gale, rain and no visibility.

THE PRICE OF ADMIRALTY

You can't see the beauties (if beauties there are), only misty rocks and gulls and diagonal cold rain. Captain Frend said that we had the worst possible wind, and the forecast is bad.

Off Uist

The present idea is that we should not go back with Duff to-morrow to Oban, but stay here (Uist) until he picks us up Thursday a.m. I personally would rather stick to Mr Micawber, but I don't want to subject the child to too much. Duff and Euan have gone off in the launch to the port to find out what's what, as one can see nothing. As I write it is lifting a bit. They've been away an hour and I'm just warming up my anxiety. Good food, except that the puddings are over-fancy. First-class Hock. Mustn't grumble. If only the old ship didn't shake herself like a wet retriever in the middle or trough of her pitches!

7 September

What a life! I find even time difficult to follow. When Duff and the "Captain" left John Julius, Tommy Thompson and me on the ship to go ashore and connect up with the Bensons, they reached a dead harbour with no living man or craft in it. They stared at each other in a wild surmise and realised that it meant taking the only road (a crazy one) and walking the five miles to the Lodge. So off they started, muttering. After half a mile they came to a cottage where a bicycle (not conditioned) was found. They started to blow up the tyres, Duff no doubt vastly relieved, as he has never learnt to ride one. Just as old Euan was mounting it, a provision Ford came along and they hitchhiked the five miles. There they found the Benson family, who had been waiting at the port for one and a half hours and had just given it up.

Back on board it had become 1 o'clock and Tommy Thompson was talking of sending the second launch after the first one to see if she had piled herself up on the rocks, when it appeared with all the Bensons, Charterises and Wakes on board. The day was brightening and an uncertain beauty appeared of green barren hills, no tree, no shrub, only vivid velvet. We sat down to lunch about twenty strong. Smart made-up food with crests and panaches appeared miraculously. After eating, a serious *conseil de marins* took place as to plan-alternations. The weather being viciously inclement, it was decided that the child, Euan and I should remain at Uist while *Enchantress* took Duff back to Oban, and that she should return to Skipport to pick us up and rejoin Duff at Mallaig.

Off we set, first in the launch, then in two Ford vans and reached, after a wild drive through rock and water and velvet, this horrible little house. They all think it Paradise. It is within a mile of the Atlantic seaboard and the wind knocks you down and howls and whistles through the windows. The men went out shooting at once, all capped in deerstalkers and rubber attachments and cartridges Cossack-fashion, with even nets attached to spectacles over their hideous faces. Letty (who is dressed as John Brown, knees and great width of skirt), Mary Rose Charteris (born for a lizard's life in San Domingo and essentially not for St Kilda), John Julius and Jeremy Benson (carrying a gun and not yet eleven, which made me panicky) and I went off to a far loch to catch a fish from a boat with the help of Donald Macdonald. We caught four and landed only one. It was beautiful driving there through stretches of green corn; sun on the sea's blue; very green grass and a million spating lochs and streams. Tea and biscuits only, in a fishing lodge with (thank God!) a bit of a fire, for the sun had gone and rain was blizzarding down and a dreadful hurricane was blowing. John Julius got so cold in the boat that I had to put him in the bottom of the wet dinghy and open my coat and lie on him like Elijah and the child. No booze but whisky in the house. Duff and Tommy Thompson left at 9.30 for the ship and will sail at dawn. I went to bed but couldn't sleep after 2 a.m. for the wind's roar causing graver and more terrifying apprehensions.

Now it's noon and the wind is still howling and I am cowering over a very unsatisfactory peat fire. The men have been out already to shoot wild geese and failed, and have now gone to shoot duck. Letty has gone out alone for two hours to get a fish for the table. Only the "Lizard" is left painting her nails vermilion, John Julius typing a letter to Nanny, and me cowering and scribbling. I'm not suited to the Hebrides, it's clear. I don't understand how they endure it, far less love it. No papers, no radio, no gramophone, few books, no charm of house or rooms or garden, no culture. I don't like it at all, at all! Baths are not. No electric light; in this I rejoice.

This letter shall be posted from the misty island. I wish my heart was more Highland.

9 September

The last day at Grogarry was the best, because after another hideous night, again of bombarding rain at my window, apprehension and panic growing with the small hours, a magnificent rainbow was the first thing I saw, connecting a pitch-black sky with a celestially blue one. The gale was stronger than ever, but the glass was rising and the sun shining fitfully and brilliantly. This good news was bad news for the men, who sat disconsolately in the drawing-room all morning, as the weather had spoilt sport. Letty was disgruntled, poor darling, and when she came into my room and I said something about the gale, she snapped my head off with a "Don't go on about the wind. I can't help it blowing." She picked cruelly on the boys for the way they held their knives, and on Mary Rose for painting and smudging her hideous nails, and for mis-addressing her telegrams and letting nail-varnish get on the cushions. Poor Mary Rose! but nothing could distress her that morning. I was Perseus to her Andromeda and was bearing her away from a rock and a dragon, and sailing her over the sea past Skye to civilisation, four days before she was due to leave. Her eyes were dancing.

At 12, in the middle of Happy Families of Geography, Letty said that we took no exercise and no wonder we were liverish and devitalised. I said that I was neither and couldn't take a great deal of exercise on account of three big stitches across the ball of my foot. So we bundled into the comfortable Ford van and drove down to the Atlantic beach. Quite a sensation! I couldn't hear for the wind, nor see for streaming eyes, but the glaring white sand and dazzling sea and rocks and breakers on distant reefs trembled in my watery vision and seemed very beautiful.

Back to lunch. There's no waste, so those who should normally be fishing or shooting have to sit at table and eat their haversack rations out of their grease-paper, while the stay-at-homes gorge a nice bit of goose and pancakes. Poor Euan tried to swap a marma-lade scone for anything going, but no one was taking it except John Julius who had nothing to exchange and found that he couldn't eat it. After lunch the men went out to fish and the rest of us went into cottages after home-woven tweeds. I enjoyed that.

At 7 p.m. ten of us left for *Enchantress*. On arrival on board I was told that Duff's journey back to Oban had not been too bad. We had a tremendous dinner of trout and grouse and ice in boiling soufflé, and all the children got steaming drunk. The Liebfraumilch was beautifully cold and the service deft and silent. I did the honours well, I thought, and they all (except Mary Rose and Euan) packed off in the launch about 11. A lovely night of calm in harbour.

We sailed into Stornoway after a fine day. Stewart Menzies was waiting in a car at the landing-stage and whizzed us up to fantastic Lewis Castle, the most opposite to South Uist's lodge that can be imagined. Winnie Portarlington had furnished it with *objets d'art* for two months' occupation. The rooms were hung with old Chinese panels of silk, and museum clocks chimed from mantel-pieces. Modern American and *anciens meubles* merged harmoniously, radios hummed music and the last news soothingly. Great vases of auratum lilies intoxicated the non-drinkers. Huge salmon were shown and then given to us. The evening was short and happy, and the talk encouraging about the weather, which of course was constantly in my thoughts as we were due to sail for Cape Wrath that night.

They sent out a volley of fireworks as we left, and we answered with a few dampish ones and a fine searchlight. The wind, though strong, was said to be friendly to us, so I went to bed with a light heart. John Julius was sleeping deeply in his frail cot. At 1 o'clock I was woken by the dreaded creaking and groaning and swaying of a violent pitch. In a few minutes the child started moaning: "Cape Wrath! Is this Cape Wrath?" and said that he must be sick. It was a false alarm and I put him back to bed, where he lay uncomplain-ingly still, perhaps asleep. I noticed that it was getting distinctly rougher every minute, and I lay trying very hard not to start panicking, not to think of ghastly possibilities, but to keep reasoning and praying for another six hours, when we were due at Scapa Flow. By 3.30 the tide was rolling hysterically and I was bathed in sweat. It was only with difficulty that I kept myself from seeking help. Suddenly there was a super-roll followed by a series of crashes, and I leapt up and dashed into Duff's cabin opposite. What should I find but a scene of chaos! The bed had "got away" from its mooring, the whole of the bedding, mattress, blankets, pillows on the floor in a tangle and poor Duff picking himself up, bruised and bewildered. We got some scared-looking stewards to help put it together again. I swallowed three aspirins and a good big glass of brandy and went back to my cabin, where John Julius was doing a nice orderly "cat" by himself. It didn't take five minutes. Once over he was as merry as a grig and did me good. I thought, if my bed plays the same trick as Duff's it will kill John Julius, so I put him in mine and prepared to take his when another appalling crash-roll-and-pitch forced me out again. There I found old Euan green in the face, having also been pursued and bruised by his own bed and bedding, and in Duff's cabin the same chaos come again and Duff furious with the ship, the stewards and me. So I went back to my seclusion and hung on to the foot of the bed. The "Captain" (Euan) popped his head in and I begged him to go up to the bridge and find some comfort for me, or anyway news. He was nothing loath and disappeared above (coat over pyjamas). He was away about forty minutes.

Funnily enough time goes fairly fast in acute misery and crisis. It's anxiety that makes it drag so. The roughness wasn't moderating a bit, but I suppose that the aspirin was doing a little good. Euan came back at last with fair news. It wouldn't be any better for two hours (it was now 4.30 a.m.) but again it was all swell and not an actual storm, no water being shipped (this proved to be a lie as there were seven inches of sea in the wardroom and the radio was broken to pieces). I took this as comfort, feeling that it would not therefore get any worse and that two hours aren't interminable, so I got into bed with John Julius. There was no bed-rail on the outside, only on the inside, so I had to cling to that over the child, otherwise I couldn't have stayed put for a minute. They spoke true. At 6.30 it began to subside and I must have slept, for I woke at 8 to a calm harbour and a smooth sea, the engines still, and all well. Then how the spirits soared up, and what a breakfast we all ate of kippers and eggs, honey, jam, scones, toast and more scones. Everybody was saying that it was the worst ever, and that the wind instead of being friendly had been from the direst direction, and it all seemed long ago and not so bad, even at breakfast-time. Things lost were being recovered in the most unlikely places. I can't help thinking that the staff doesn't know its work, nor do those who converted this sloop into luxury. Nothing is secured half firmly enough. The drawers fly open when the roll is severe, the cupboard doors flap. Sixes-and-sevens is the order. Nothing shipshape.

We've reached Invergordon. It's Christmas-cold but mirror-calm, and the worst is over.

11 September

I've had no time to write since we got to Invergordon until now, three days later. I imagine I left the diary at the morning after the great storm, safe in harbour. We had a whacking breakfast and an exchange of experiences, and a look at Euan's bruise, coal-black already and the size of a kettle-holder. We made again for the open sea, waves still big but the wind friendly. The furniture was still laid down, but nothing will ever seem rough again.

In the evening we arrived at Dunrobin, dressed to kill. It was raining and I was wearing my red velvet, red hearts and your diamond trembler, when it was discovered that the tide was too low for landing except by changing into a dinghy with two oarsmen. I loved it, but it made the others cross. I felt like Mary Queen of Scots escaping from Loch Leven. It was early away because we were to sail at dawn for Invergordon and have early breakfast and stand on deck at the salute as we sailed past *Rodney* and *Resolution* and *Courageous* ("Curry Juice," the aircraft carrier) and many destroyers, cruisers and submarines. The sun was shining. *Rule Britannia* was played by each band, the guns banged and the soldiers were drawn up in toy rows as at a review. Later in the morning the

Commander-in-Chief, Sir Roger Backhouse, arrived in a swanky emerald-green barge, dressed with gloves and a clanking sword. He's a tall man shaped for my taste exactly—a freak, lama-like, yellow and shaven-looking and uninhibited, slightly lisping, with a suppressed zeal and an innocence. He has something perhaps of Trenchard in his independence and uniqueness. Duff was taken off to his flagship *Rodney* while I wrote you my account of the big storm. The Commander-in-Chief said: "We never thought you'd come by sea with those forecasts." Since then I have heard that there has been a row about it. Either the warnings were wrong or we should have waited. All this is very flattering to our courage, though really no alternative was offered us.

After lunch John Julius and I explored the town. It was incredibly dreary—nothing for any of those poor sailors to do, no cafés, no billiard-rooms, no music. One miserable cinema open only at night. A sad cripple playing a concertina was all the entertainment we could see. We had tea in a tea-shop, with midshipmen eating fish and chips and eggs and bacon in total silence.

The evening was crest-of-the-wave for me. I dressed as best I could in red-and-white silk with billowing sleeves and went off in the barge to *Rodney*, where the whole ship was dressed like me in red and white stripes, and the orchestra playing, and about forty officers to be introduced to and to sit down to dinner with, unhampered by any other woman. I loved it, but got a little rattled afterwards when I was given for five minutes to each of them in turn and they all looked identical, and I shall never know them or their names, faces or positions again. Euan is a godsend. He gets better every day and more cheery, and he's exactly what we need as a medium and a mirth-provoker.

12 September

Yesterday was Sunday and it started off with lovely church in the *Ramillies*. All our crudest, most favourite hymns shouted out stoutly and two perfect Lessons, and the 1500 of the ship's complement with two of the longest of the guns pointing at us. I did adore it and John Julius prayed with his face in his hands like an Elder of the Church.

WITH THE FLEET AT INVERGORDON

In the morning I was sulky because John Julius and I had been invited properly by Captain and Commander-in-Chief to go with Duff to sea on the aircraft carrier, and then suddenly we were not to go. Photographers were to be on board and it seemed that it would create a flippant tone if I were photographed watching the latest Naval Air Arm exercises. We went instead on a tour of inspection in the destroyer *Blanche* with our stunning Captain and were given tea in the Captain's cabin. Both captains very young and jolly and an atmosphere of "Cat's away" about it ("Cat" being the First Cat of the Admiralty).

Back at 5.30 for a cocktail party on *Enchantress*—boiling cocktails, sodden cakes, but no matter: it was short and sharp and orderly. Next a scramble to bath John Julius and to dress for another party on *Rodney*. My heart was rather failing me at a third meal next the Commander-in-Chief, but his was too, apparently, because he gave me two other sailor boys. One called Storey I delighted in because he had been blown up in the *Queen Mary* at Jutland and is one of nineteen survivors. After dinner we repaired to the Warrant Officers' mess, which was my cup of tea, playing darts and winning, and Duff playing table-tennis with the champion player, putting up a splendid show (19-21) and cheered to the echo. We've got very chummy with our shipmates, so returning at 11.30 we settled down to beer and a discussion of the evening.

This morning John Julius and I have been over the *Swordfish* (submarine) a great thrill and dreadful too, quite dreadful. I'm just back from it and trying to keep calm about Duff going down in one this afternoon, down to the depths of the sea. Will his bones make coral?

It's hard to write on account of there being but one sitting-room and always being called away to watch *Rodney* weigh anchor, or cheer *Blanche* on her way to Spain.

Now I have got home and Admiralty House is no nearer readiness. Next week we leave for the Pirate Zone (the Mediterranean) in that very tiny yacht.

In October we were off again, without John Julius and Euan, and in their places came George and Imogen Gage and my niece Liz Paget. We boarded *Enchantress* at Venice, where I began a long diary to Conrad:

Raimund von Hofmannsthal and Rex Whistler fly out to see the last of us. There are fears of submarines, incidents, ambushes and watery graves. The cruise is to be very official. Already I groan at the Fascist leaders, prefects and *podestas*, British Consuls, calls and dinners.

At the Mocenigo Palace, the scene of Laura Corrigan's extravaganzas, we meet the paragon Duke of Aosta. He is an extraordinary man, seems nine foot high, speaks eight languages, including whatever one speaks in the desert and in the Congo. His English is too good, with phrases like "not my cup of tea" and "now I suppose you want me to hook it." Two years at an English school, a fighting soldier at sixteen, back to his books, a bit in the Camel Corps to glamorise him, and two years as a fitter in Lever's soap-works in the Congo, so the common touch is not lost. A famous flyer, he is now the head of the Italian Air Force and sails his own ship (Master Mariner too) and he has scaled the Matterhorn twice. His manners captivate. At dinner on board he sweeps Captain and crew, First Lord and (perhaps more than anyone) the diarist clean off their feet. I ask him if he knows the Dalmatian coast. "Like my pocket," he says, and asks for charts to show our captain how to navigate the inlet of Sibenik. I hope so much he liked me in my baroque dress made for King Edward's party at Blenheim, with all the peonies and amethysts. I did my best, but I can't really *see* anything in my cabin.

The Dalmatian inlet proves a flop and the next stop is Athens, where we can't land, as we're too grand and cumbersome to do anything not prearranged with deputations and opposite numbers and the rest of it. So we anchor off Sunium and dine on deck, and throw our searchlight on Poseidon's temple. Greek mariners returning from trading loved to see it, and Byron carved his name there. Perhaps it was the first sight of Attica for those returning from Troy—no, it wasn't built then, but they saw the headland and the white foam and thought of their wives.

The romantic girls want to sleep on deck, and so really do I.

They drag their beds up secretly and Duff catches them and isn't pleased. I drag mine up when he's gone to bed and he catches me and is cross and frightens the girls, who punish him by treating him as a dragon. We all wake up black as sweeps with coal-dust and that pleases Duff, and tempers are tempered for the long voyage. Every day we stop the ship and bathe and the 150 crew jump over the other side.

It's all wonderful, and excitement sends up a spark in the shape of an aggressive Greek gunboat that turns on itself and seems to be about to grapple, but after an exchange of silent coloured courtesies like two suspicious dogs, we both sail away, we into the British (why British?) lee of Skyros. While Duff inspects we are left to explore the little white town and breathe the aromatic smells of the island, dried by summer and graced with olives to save it from aridity, and to criticise the huge nude that commemorates Rupert Brooke and immortal poetry. After a visit to the *Malaya* and being shaken to pieces by the firing of the biggest gun, we sail away to the strains of *Rule Britannia* from each ship.

"Flags," "Sparks," "the Chief," "the Sub" and "the snotties" are weaving in and out of the story, with books read and letters written, as we cut through the blue sea to Rhodes, where I ask in the huge modern State-run hotel for a postcard to send to my dearest farmer, and there isn't one. But when I come out of the cool sea, wet as a seal, there on the beach is a proper writing-table with rulers, spare nibs, sealing-wax, calendars, a bust of Mussolini and a dozen postcards for my convenience. Banquets and drives with officials, shopping for Turkish coats and net to make curtains for our windows against the wide eyes of sailors, and always the joy of returning to our ship and our delightful company.

In Cyprus, where the heat is tropical, we land at Kyrenia and find in the courts of Bella Pais two strange Englishmen, highly-informed and amusing. They show us the glories of the troubadour-haunted St Hilarion and tell us of the Kings of Cyprus and Jerusalem. We dine with Sir Richmond and Lady Palmer at Government House, newly built on the ashes of Ronald Storrs's library, while the orchestra plays the expected *Iolanthe* in the stifling garden. I talk to a respected Turk who had been to the Coronation and who says that "he is hand in blouse with Lady L." and that he has "a corn in the flesh" and (best of all) that "he kicked up a rump." Three malaprops in ten minutes is good going.

Then there are the Lusignan-built churches, now mosques, French-Gothic, soaring out of palms, with confusing interiors. Two angles of East and Mecca make an extraordinary warring design. The naves take your eyes East, the Mohammedan pulpits and lamps and the laying of the rugs drag them diagonally to Mecca.

We are away that night from Famagusta, Alexandria-bound, and after Alexandria, where we leave *Enchantress*, we come to Cairo, which is not at all to my liking—loud and crude and common, and just saved from damning by the Citadel and a twelfth-century mosque and a monastery in a Biblical cave high above the city, where we smoke and drink tea with an old abbot. The pyramids, as seen from the Mena House Hotel, are in place and no surprise, though going inside Cheops's I find gruesome, without interest, merely appalling discomfort of crouched progress and claustrophobia, and an asphyxiating smell of elephants (which I am told is really batstench). Beautifully-caparisoned white donkeys are a happy surprise, and they run willingly and smoothly like bicycles, but their riders deform them. Darkness falls and obliterates tourist-traces by the time we get to the Sphinx, so I deign to be impressed and am impressed too by Tutankhamen's glitter, though Egyptologists think it common and (worse) vulgar. Sakkara passes muster, as does its archaeologist Mr Emery. In fact he reconciles me to a lot, as do the hook-wormed natives at their agricultural tasks and the brown nudes bathing in brown Nile-water seen through scarlet trees. I am homesick for *Enchantress*, the only spellbinder, so back to Alexandria.

Beautifying next at a hairdresser's, but even the Egyptian *coiffeur* fails me, and emerging into the sunlight after a cool hour in his transformatory, I find my hair violet (a porphyry renaissance). I look a fright, but what does it matter? There is so much worse to come, because now my handbag (my "face") has been lost in transit, for all the zealous efficiency of secretaries, and without my face I can't see how I am to envisage the party on *Barham* thrown by the Commander-in-Chief, Sir Dudley Pound, tonight at 8.30. In my bag lies all my treasure—the silver ear-snails, the funny pearl ear-rings, the *eau-de-nil* aquamarines (in this country so appropriate), the half-mourning amethysts, the important diamond dolphins, the trembler (all Conrad's presents, in fact). Still I keep my purple hair on, acting under splendid control and rewarded by news that the Air Force was bringing my bag on wings. The familiar ship's faces make up for petty disasters, and so does the light springing deck, until Flags comes in to say that the bag won't arrive until morning and I know again that I shall lose face, and that my skin-disease will begin again if I use other people's unguents. I get encouraged when a sharp signal is sent to say that it must be here before 8 p.m., and discouraged by the answer saying: "Only if a private plane costing £14 is chartered." Our signal replies "No" and the next message reads: "Casket sent by RAF due 7.15." The poor culprit who lost it is sent to the airfield, only to hear: "Airplane delayed will reach Aboukir (forty miles away!) 7.50." Dinner 8.30, so I leave the ship in the old red-and-white dress and am piped on to *Barham* plastered in Liz's brunette muck and fit to cry. Still we dance on deck until midnight, when national anthems play us off.

Tomorrow the big ship goes out to shoot the biggest guns at a target, and the three cruisers shoot also and exercise in other ways. I say to the Commander-in-Chief that I should love to see it, and he is delighted with the idea and orders *Enchantress* to follow along and watch the fun. It never strikes me how unpopular it will be to have the anchor weighed, the ship stoked, taken out and made to go full speed ahead for half a day, thereby keeping the officers from tennis and rest. The Commander-in-Chief has got all the blame, thank God! So now we are at sea (Liz, me, Mogs and Flags only—the others are on the flagship) and it's pitchy and some of us feel sick. Liz and I are so sleepy from last night's debauchery that as soon as the guns are fired and the depth-charges exploded, the multiple pom-poms aimed and the air-targets missed, we return to our beds and sleep for two hours. O, I'm ashamed to think of the cost and the energy and the work of 150 men, robbing the taxpayer to amuse two women who could hardly keep awake.

The next evening the barometer-chart shows a horrible V. They say that the thing has gone wrong, but I am sure it is a typhoon-warning. This gloomy augury produces a laugh, but I laugh last. Chaos and Cape Wrath have come again! Conrad can never never know what it was like. No John Julius to fear for, thank God, and my only duty is to Liz, whom I visit twice on all fours and find pretty well, drugged with sea-sickness remedies and resigned. Nothing can be done about Mogs, who is a prisoner in her cabin, all its furniture (cupboards and bureau) having broken loose and piled itself into a barricade. Even Duff is past his usual storm-crossness and will send word to the Captain that there is no need to stick to schedule-time, little realising that we hove to long before. The little ship's beams can't take the battering, I know that. Water is everywhere, tearing down the passages, bearing the ship's treasure to and fro—silver candlesticks and (O! bad omen) the bugle. I look like a Dalmatian dog because my bureau has also broken loose and covered me with ink. I am on my knees as usual, praying without knowing how to make myself heard. The ship seems without a crew. No sailor or steward is seen or heard above the roar of waves and shivering of timbers. I look through the porthole once, and see mad milk boiling over and no sky. I bang the shutter with a vow not to look again. *Lead, Kindly Light* (written in a storm) brought the ship in. I try to say it.

At noon it eases imperceptibly and allows George Gage to put his endearing face through my open door. He is like a star, smiling and with the terrifying story (that he thinks funny) of our Admiral sitting forlorn but taut in his cabin, while laid out on his bed, like a boiled shirt before dinner, is his life-jacket. Of our escorting cruisers only one remains. The other is standing by a ship in distress miles back. At 4 the Captain sends word that the storm is over. Prayers are answered. From death to life for me, but the ship is still cavorting maniacally.

Valetta in view, the most beautiful town in the Mediterranean after Venice. They cheer us into port. We (or rather I) have not exaggerated the dangers, and they tell us that the anemometer broke in a 105 m.p.h. gale. *London* and *Devonshire* both lost their aircraft.

The diary ends on this sensational note, and there is no record of our disembarkation at Naples, nor of how Mussolini put his private railway-coach, made up with bedrooms, baths, kitchen and staff, at Duff's disposal to take his party to the English Channel, nor is there any description of its saloon, emblazoned with a sheep-and-goat list of pro- and anti-sanctioners, Great Britain being the leading goat.

CHAPTER TEN

The Fog of Peace

Duff's nostalgia for the Army and its frustrations was being swept away by ocean and enthusiasm for the Senior Service. The Royal Navy, the pride of the Island and England's spoilt darling, was at this time (with black war looming) having its expansion thwarted by insane economies. Since the Coronation Mr Chamberlain had been in office. His relationship with Duff, never too happy, had not prevented the Prime Minister from promoting him to the Admiralty, and never was there a First Lord more determined to make a success of his appointment and to wipe out the impression of failure that his bare eighteen months at the War Office might have given. Duff's ambition for the highest office having faded, his desire now was to give all he had of imagination, strength and fight to the Navy's glory and aggrandisement, and after fulfilment to retire, aged hardly more than fifty, to an untrammelled life of writing and other activities. Leisure too he yearned for. This happy calculation had not reckoned with Mr Chamberlain and the drama of Munich.

There was patient and persevering work to be done, and for me a lot of entertaining of friends and foes. The German foe Ribbentrop was the Ambassador in London. We saw him too often. He was a suave man who had learnt a few languages to smooth his way. He had a certain elegance and a considerable power of irritating everyone by punctuating his platitudes with references to the Führer. Emerald Cunard was the best of his baiters. "Tell me, dear Ambassador," she would. say, "what does Herr Hitler truly think about *God*?" The Führer had not yet determined what teaching was best for his people; it was one of the many subjects under consideration. Or again she would ask: "We all want to know, dearest Excellency, why does Herr Hitler dislike the *Jews*?" He was greatly at a loss for replies. I remember his leaving one particular luncheon, kissing the shrinking hands of the ladies, and as the door shut out his departure Winston and Duff and some other patriots dancing and shouting with glee at having been sent so despicable a German Ambassador. He entertained all London at a reception at his atrociously decorated Embassy in Carlton House Terrace. I took my mother, who, pointing at an heroic-sized bust of Hitler, whispered to Ribbentrop as he bade her goodbye: "You know I can't help rather admiring him. *Please* don't tell Diana."

Ribbentrop's post was next filled by a dear old career-diplomat called Dirksen. I engaged a conjuror to amuse him and his wife when they dined with us. It was an enormous success. Conjurors always are with Germans, as indeed they are with me. I remember that before the first war the Lichnowskys hired a really clumsy conjuror from Harrods to divert the Dukes and Ministers after a banquet. The English yawned, while the Germans gaped at the wonder of it. Princess Lichnowsky was much loved in England. She was a Bavarian and an artist. Once she asked me to pose for her in the nude. I was very young and thought that it would be frumpish to refuse, so I stripped. She took a reel of photographs and never got to the easel. When the war came and the Ambassador left in tears, surrounded by the tearful, I wondered to what use that reel might be put. None, I resolved.

Dirksen had something innocent and likeable, with no ray of humour to light him through the diplomatic morass designed by Hitler and tangled by Ribbentrop. I told him how much his predecessor had been disliked and why, and what not to do. He thanked me profusely for the information and advice. He was impressed by Admiralty House and its dolphins, and with the scallop-shell Wedgwood dinner-service that I had bought. "I collect fish these days," I babbled, "shells and Neptunes and mermaids on dolphins' backs. I am developing a fish complex." Lightly said, but his poor face looked heavy with anxiety and sympathy: "Zo, you say you have a feesh-complex?" I shuddered at what I was heading for, and hoped that he would not report my failing to the Wilhelmstrasse.

This winter was to bring me and my family anxiety, death and sorrow. My mother since her widowhood had been living happily enough, pleased with the rebuilding of Chapel Street. In the big rooms she was able to give exhibitions of her drawings and of the pictures of others. For the first time she showed to the public her monument of Haddon, my little brother. Severe critics were moved to write eulogies about her academic *chef-d'œuvre*. T. W. Earp wrote: "In its tender gravity the modelling of the recumbent figure takes a foremost place among the statues of children in European art." She showed me an old letter from Cecil Rhodes. I have it still. On seeing the effigy, he wrote: "I thought no man could suffer as I did about the Raid. I thought it was the biggest suffering ever meted out to man, but this beats it all."

The news that her son's monument had been accepted by the Tate Gallery sustained and fortified her against injurious age. For ten years she had been victim to attacks never precisely diagnosed. She resigned herself courageously enough to a yearly bout of pain, fever and sickness that would possess her for a few days only. She had no wish to die. Her faith was childlike but very individual. The thought of death she tried to banish. There was still so much to be drawn and painted and built and put in order before she left us all. She feared too for the lame ducks (queues of them) that would fall without her, and she sighed for two of her grandchildren whose unborn children she could not hope to see. We never knew her age. I only once heard her refer to being old as "the time when one has a sentence hanging over one." She found comfort in being almost sure that, dead, she would command greater power and judgment and capacity for helping her favourites, and that her lost son would rejoice at her return.

Her last attack was severe and she seemed too weakened to survive. My sisters were away, but my brother John was a help as the sad days dragged on, getting new opinions and accustoming me to the inevitable. She was operated on, and never again was she her sensible self. She lay singing snatches of old songs like Ophelia, and describing in some new-given idiom, strange and beautiful, the things that passed before her half-blind eyes. She died three days before Christmas 1937. My brother and I were with her at 34 Chapel Street, the house that she had re-created for me, while at Belvoir the whole family were assembling for their yearly jubilation. John was sure of what he meant to do. That her death should cast clouds over the Castle Christmas would have enraged her, so she must be alive in all hearts until the festivities ended.

I stayed with her who had once been my all-in-all, through this macabre holiday, warding off the inquisitive press, lying to anxious enquirers, trying to calm and silence the faithful maid and the rest of her people. She was buried at Belvoir. I did not follow her so far, but remained in London, greatly dejected. The press later excavated and exposed this story and hoped to scandalise its readers, but I think sincerely that the deceit was inspired by my mother, and that thus she would have ordered her end.

To escape I took John Julius to the snows of Savoy, whence I wrote to Duff:

Mégève 11 January 1938

The Victor Rothschilds are here to help me. Victor set Barbara, John Julius and me an examination paper (prepared with pains earlier) on mathematics. I had to leave out two subjects (multiplication in double-numbered sums, and all division), ten items in all, but I won! Barbara and John Julius tied! The Rothschildren seem fond of me. I grow on people, given time.

I hope that a fortnight's rest will put me into a calmer state—rest and hitching my star to "the wagon." If I'm no better I'll have to consult a doctor. It can't go on like this. I'm not happy. How can I be happy? My poor Mummy, my poor Mummy! I shall get serener about it later. I'm more unhappy because I'm without you. You don't know yourself how good you've been to me these sad days. None like you, none.

And to Kaetchen:

I have put off writing and thanking you for your sweet telegram and verse until I got free of England, so that I might have time and solitude to tell you a lot, and now I am so exhausted with letters that my pencil and mind both drag and stick. One is overwhelmed with condolence and the letters smother. I like it when people say the right things about my mother herself, but I can't bear them inflicting me with my own grief. It sounds ungrateful, and curiously enough I go on answering them—strangers, friends, Mother's friends, Mother's crocks and crooks—and something forces me to write them all long letters. I would not see any of them although they went on clamouring, but I had and have my own way about sorrow—a way of effort not to groan and cry and do all the things that would have made her so frantically unhappy to be the cause of, but the friends who gather round the bereaved have a different idea.

I think that my mother had a wonderful life. *Death* must be terrible, but she had a short illness, half of it semi-conscious and the other half unconscious. She had great fortune in life—energy, art, love, adored children and grandchildren and undiminished love from them to the end. Best of all she died before she saw them decay and die or meet with tragedies or break their hearts. The same applies to her grandchildren. What better future can one ask God to bestow on one's child? I was there when she died, but she knew nothing and I felt calm and was surprised at my lack of hysteria. I saw her put in her coffin and I stayed in the house alone with her until they took her to Belvoir, and nothing seemed to shake me. But I would not go to Belvoir, and once all was finished and time told me that the grave's door was closed, I got sad, sad, sad, and had to crush surging memories and heart-rending sentiment. There are great terrors when one starts to think too. Her loneliness (perhaps) worries me.

Meanwhile Kaetchen has his work cut out. So much must be settled. I have no decisive power for the moment. Chapel Street is mine, so is Gower Street, so is the Admiralty. No more money. In fact I do not think that there will be enough to cover the small bequests that she has made. I have not seen the Will but I know all this. Duff and I keep howling: "If only Kaetchen were here!" I think you'll have to hurry and come home a little sooner this year. I feel a naked and lost child. I also feel as if I'd lost a child.

Kaetchen returned, and his nervous hands re-arranged chaos into order. Gower Street must go to the highest bidder, and with it what I cherished most in bricks and mortar. The buyers dealt reverently with Rex Whistler's decorations. The cracked Roman vase in its niche, the Roman plaques and prints of classical nymphs, hanging casually and not too flatly on the walls in *trompe l'œil*, are boarded over and can be salvaged yet.* The Chinese walls painted by my mother and me, with

* They were carefully removed and, under the supervision of the Slade School, re-erected round the walls of a small circular dining-room in University College, London.

their birds and ghostly white trees, were obliterated by an hour's whitewashing. They had served their purpose. The books had already come to Admiralty House. The pictures and furniture were all moved to Chapel Street, and to make room for them a sad sale of half my mother's curious chattels was held in the orangery room and garden. She had herself organised a sale at Arlington Street before it closed its private doors, and now part of what she could not bear to sell must be bartered and forgotten. Rex Whistler must make the longest room, with its two galleries and six high windows, into a library. The design was drawn of globes and obelisks and draperies that were to surmount the high glazed lining of shelves, each section with a tablet announcing its literary subjects. All were cast and stood waiting. I wonder where they still wait.

In the early spring Austria was ravished by Germany. Duff had had serious influenza that kept him from his work for nearly three weeks. The beasts being fought by him at the Treasury could pause and disarm for peace. A £6,000,000 reduction on ships was their aim, and Duff fretted in his fever-bed, fretted for the Navy, for Anthony Eden's resignation and for the country's probable defeat in war, while I fretted for his lungs and his relapses, and for the most perfect early spring crocuses and blackbirds in the Park and the pale sunshine that I had no heart to enjoy. I had grown very fond of Duff's successor in the War Office, Leslie Hore-Belisha, and I would pester him with instructions to see that Duff was not in a draught during Cabinet hours (did he realise how feverish he still was?) and to remind him on leaving to put his muffler over his mouth. Leslie was sweetly patient with my hen-clucking. He lived with anxiety, as I did. Night and day the war-dread encompassed me.

ROYAL VISIT TO PARIS

Duff could not absent himself from his work, so, when the King and Queen went to France in July 1938, I went alone with Liz Paget to revel in the triumphs of Paris. Our *Enchantress* took the King and Queen over the Channel. Liz and I, on the newish ferry-boat, were four hours late. At noon on 19 July I was writing:

At the port

We had a merry dinner with the Rothschilden and Winston and Venetia, Winston packed for the Ferry with bezique-cards in hand for plucking me. But a message came from the Chief Whip that trouble would be debated next day. Too disappointed to believe it, Winston tore round to the House, only to meet us again at Victoria with the news endorsed. He'll start tomorrow night instead.

Liz and I babbled until Folkestone, where the grinding and honking and pounding started. Half-sleep, for the desultory foghorn moaned all night, and wide awake at 6 to a sense of utter stillness and a sad absence of vibration. The fog had been so impenetrable that we hove-to twice. Will it lift for Majesty? What a fever our Peter Frend and his company will be in! Perhaps they'll stop the other traffic and go all-out-blind.

In the train

The line has a soldier, armed cap-à-pie, my lord, from head to foot, posted every hundred yards. They stand in blood-red pools of poppies and seem to be advertising a second world war. It's very exciting and I'm enjoying it immensely. If only my dear were with me.

Paris

We saw the King and Queen from a window, coming down the Champs Elysées with roofs, windows and pavements roaring exultantly, the Queen, a radiant Winterhalter, guarded by too many security measures. The Minister who was responsible for their safety told me that their fears and safeguards were such as to put a plain-clothes policeman in every window on the route and to have hefty citizens lean in a ring against the suspect trees lest they should fall on the procession.

Each night's flourish outdid the last. At the Opera we leant over the balustrade to see the Royal couple, shining with stars and diadem and the Légion d'Honneur proudly worn, walk up the marble stairs preceded by *les chandeliers*—two valets bearing twenty-branched candelabra of tall white candles. This custom seems to have died, for in 1957 no candles lit Queen Elizabeth to her Royal Box.

The Elysée and the Quai d'Orsay outshone each other in splendour and *divertissement*. Malmaison, decked doubly with roses, received the Queen. It was here that I talked to two crying old ladies who begged for my place on the Royal path. "*Vous la voyez toujours*," one said. "*Si seulement nous avions un roi*," said the other. Monarchy dies slow in many French hearts. A cook-general at a friend's house, serving a *blanquette de veau*, had said to me when the King was acclaimed earlier in the year: "*Enfin, nous avons un roi!*"

The most beautiful of the fêtes was given at Versailles on a radiant summer's day. The mist had not lifted when we arrived in the early morning to watch the review of troops and machines of war, so the fly-past of aeroplanes was postponed. We lunched in the Galerie des Glaces, with thirteen glasses apiece for the thirteen precious wines, all bottled on the birthdays of presidents and kings. The servants, in livery of the date with powdered hair (another ceremonial custom since shed), served the company feather-light delicacies in a single hour. Grace said, we walked in procession to the chapel galleries to look down on the members of the Comédie Française in clothes of the Great Century, sitting on ornate chairs, while some heavenly choir sang Monteverdi, and the Roi Soleil flooded the scene with dazzling shafts of light through the top-less windows.

A sinister reminder of reality clutched at all hearts, like a deathly hand, when the fog of peace dispersed. The aeroplanes of war shot noisily past, casting menacing shadows across the serenity of the service. Later, by the Bassin d'Apollon, we watched, from a grassy dell where shepherdesses tended their lambs beneath tall trees garlanded with roses, living nymphs dance round the stone horses of the Sun. Hysterical security measures faded away as day succeeded day, and on the last night the dancing people were allowed near and everywhere. Many times the King and Queen were summoned to the balconies by insistent clamouring. No one shouted quite as loud as Henry Bernstein and our group, who had left the great halls of the Quai d'Orsay in favour of the crowds below. I can never forget it. To the French the Royal Visit seemed a safeguard against the dreaded war. That at least is what they told me but I could see nothing to allay fears.

CHAPTER ELEVEN

Enchantress *in the Baltic*

EARLY in August 1938 we set out on another cruise in the *Enchantress*, this time to the Baltic, taking Brendan Bracken with us. The rest of the party was unchanged. George and Imogen Gage and Liz Paget had proved themselves the perfect shipmates. We met at Portsmouth in the festivities of Navy Week. We watched from a green Admiralty lawn a sham battle of appalling ferocity and thunder carried on overhead and all around, with planes falling, shrapnel bursting, anti-aircraft guns banging away, and conversation with Lord and Lady Cork and Orrery therefore quite impossible. I remember tedium and lots of tears for Nelson's *Victory* and a few for the *Queen Mary* shimmering past like a ghost.

Spirits were very high (Duff's the highest) because of everything, plus the new superstructure Duff Cot. I wrote:

Today most of us have slept half the day, some from liver, some from exhaustion. The ship is full of the Royal crossing to France. The Queen had nobbled everyone, naturally, from the Commander-in-Chief to the marine who always occupies on all fours the bathroom. The First Lieutenant, Mr Costobadie, is like the ailing Knight at Arms. I doubt his being able to cast it off. The King forgot his hotwater bottle and a frenzied message preceded their arrival telling the ship to provide one. A child was despatched to Boot's Cash Chemists on a bicycle before it was realised that he would never edge his way back through the crowds and the guards, but the clever Puck got back in forty seconds. He should get a

medal, and so should our smashing Captain who only got two
photographs.

Next day I was woken by the crashing, pounding, dragging,
shouting, grinding and gnashing which precedes picking up
one shabby little pilot, and by guns firing from ship and shore.
We found ourselves in a peaceful sleepy lock, the entrance to
the Kiel Canal. There a suspiciously-looked-at German
officer came aboard, with epaulettes and a suitcase that terrified
us with its long-stay look. I wrote to Conrad:

His conversation ran entirely on how much percentage of ground
is covered in London with buildings from a bombing point of view.
He was surprised and no doubt disappointed to hear only seven per
cent. He was on the *Deutschland* when it was bombed the other day
by the Government in Spain and he gave a good description in
technical English. He is quite nice, but I never forget for a minute
the dead and those to die.

At Kiel two Admirals came to pay their respects in pidgin English
and we respected them back in pigdin German. Also came the English Naval Attaché, Admiral Troubridge, whose beat is the Baltic.
His father was the Admiral who wasn't (I repeat *wasn't*) to blame
for the *Goeben* evading us. He looks all I like—light in spite of bulk,
beautiful and smiling. He will add a lot to our cruise.

We all got into three shut motorcars, together with the Liaison
Officer and his unilingual Frau, and drove for an hour to an inn
where we were warned that the "midgets" might be troublesome.
They stayed their stings, but we weren't warned that the choice of
food was jellied eels or smoked eels, or of the drink—a much-
extolled *spécialité*, "light, very light beer *mit etwas darin*." They
would not divulge the *etwas*. I guessed optimistically (being in
Baltic waters) that it was *aquavit* but it proved to be raspberry
syrup. We sat and sat over our eels until the "midgets" came in
force, while Tommy Troubridge talked loudly about the procession
down the Champs Elysées. I could hear it, and so of course could
my Hun neighbour, so I paused to listen, thinking it referred to the

Royal visit. Not at all! It was soon clear that it was the Victory Parade of 1919 that he was describing. The Boche guns, he said, had been stacked up in a heap like so many matches.

"You scribe in your day-book, *ja?*" the Frau-Liaison has just said to me. I'm on a particularly unattractive beach. Some are trying to sleep it off (the ones who were not in on the eels and rasp-berry beer) and Liz is having a kümmel with the *Enchantress* boys. The day started early. We went (the Quality, some new nobs and an impressive wreath of English roses and oak leaves) to the local Admiral's minute yacht. Five old German wives came along. We were in smart rig, stockings, hats, gloves, badges, caps, etc. We came to a magnificent War Memorial on the sea's verge. I was moved by it, but even more by seeing my poor Duff looking for all the world like a man on his way to execution. He was walking in front of us, head down, the picture of dejection, in "civvies," two strong uniformed giants on each side and his wreath borne by two others in front of him. A band played a dirge and muffled drums shuddered as we walked down the dimly-lit tunnel that led to the mortuary. There the wreath was laid while the strains of *"Ich hat einen Kamerad"* came from the upper sunlit air. Why do French and Germans like introducing sinister morbidity into their memorials? The Romans didn't, did they? Our cemeteries are like gardens, brilliant and serious. I remember in a French war *ossuaire* seeing notices that read: "Silence. Do not disturb the dead."

Well, we came out of the tomb and found a fascinating working model of the Battle of Jutland, which we all studied. Does anything like what goes on in my head go on in theirs at such moments? I doubt it. They love the subject of war and talk of casualties with the pride that "sides" have in "scores."

Lunch was at their Admiralty House between Admiral Albrecht and Admiral Carl. I did my best and so did they with our maimed tongues. I shall face the same flanking tonight at *Enchantress*'s dinner. After the Admirals had shown us their pictures, all of them subjects of defeat (the sinking of the *Breslau* etc.) they drove us for an hour and a half very fast to this ghastly beach, rather like Pagham, although there appeared to be many charming deserted bays quite near Kiel. Germans are bunglers *au fond*, thank God.

HIGH JINKS AT GDYNIA

Enchantress's dinner went all right. I found that my untaught German couldn't explain the Gents and Ladies situation. I took the ladies one by one, but they each said: "*Schön, sehr schön*" instead of "Thanks" or "No thanks." The Chief Admiral spoke for his colleagues the decisive words "We don't want . . ."

No doubt our ideas about foreign countries are as naive as foreigners' are about ours, but this seems very surprising. The Admiral, praising what Hitler has done and wishing for my sympathy in his plight, said: "It is difficult for you Engleesh to understand the straits of a country that must rely on its harvest. In a bad year our people starve." I told him that we never had a good year. Our people would be dead if we relied on a harvest. "*Ach*, but you have Canada." I said that we had to pay for Canadian corn, and that meat was cheaper to buy from the Argentine than from Australia, and often corn too (for all I know this may be true), but I could see that his view was unshaken. If one had colonies one took free what was needed. Another said to Duff: "I suppose you always take your vacation in your colonies?" Duff had to propose the health of Hitler. It all but choked him. The German proposed the King. I drank one in water, one in wine.

Brendan is the life and soul of all decks. He and I insisted on going to Lübeck for its beauty's sake. Liz and he are great German-baiters. At a restaurant they asked the band to play "*Wien, Wien,*" a tune that they had heard was forbidden on account of Jewish composership, but it was willingly struck up. Nettled by this, they asked for "The Red Flag" disguised as "*O Tannenbaum.*" Again the band was nothing loath, played it with verve and condescendingly laughed at us poor mutts.

It was high jinks last night and no heelers, and tziganes and bonnets high over the windmills of Gdynia. We trooped out to dine with Colonel Beck [Foreign Minister of Poland] at a Government House suite of rooms. Scrumptious fare of bortsch and crayfish and vodka. I sat next Beck. There must be more to the Colonel than I can see, for I saw nothing but an Ancient Pistol and a weak tipsy Pistol at that. He repeated himself with the persistence of a cuckoo and waved his tail with peacock vanity. Still he is a colourful freak and enjoys everything in life, I should think. He has told me so often that he is "the only Colonel Beck" that I'm beginning to think that he protests too much. The ribbons he wears, he says, are equivalent to V.C.s. He has fought fifteen wars, and he says that Hitler has power and charm and flair, but he is not "a Colonel Beck," that the man in the street is his friend, *"parce que je ne suis pas méchant,"* and that if the man in the street smiles at you it shows the splendid kind of man you are.

Duff went back after dinner to write all these things home, but we went on to be stifled and delighted in a little night-club. The Poles dance like reeds in the breeze, and the Colonel pinched all our thighs and tangled our toes and became less articulate in his sketchy French, and repetitions followed more quickly as the champagne slopped over. One lady not practised in English said to our Captain that she had seen *Enchantress* and that it had looked *"awful"*—no, she meant *"funny."* The Captain hardly spoke again until we got to the quay at 3 a.m. where we taught him and Flags and Tommy Troubridge to dance the Lambeth Walk and the Palais Glide, all laughter and voices suppressed so that Duff shouldn't wake and look out of his porthole and have a stroke. The curtain fell on the three girls carrying Flags like Hamlet onto the ship. He's not so big as Nelson. The sailors on the gangway never smiled.

9 August

We've had an all-Beck day. The fellow is so intense and concentrated a bore that we took him on in shifts. The demon alcohol must be the trouble. I don't believe that he was once sober. In the morning he took us round all the interstices of this gigantic new port (Gdynia). It was very hot, and feigning interest for two hours non-stop exhausts.

Then it was lunch on board for Beck and all his polliwogs, and off again afterwards *en masse* to a peninsula called Hell, where there is a fashionable bathing resort called Jorata. We went there by battleship, improbably enough (a small destroyer, it looked). Rather archaic boats circled round us, packed with Poles, looking like something from the Bayeux Tapestry. They wave and shout "We lofe you!" in a most engaging way.

THE ONLY COLONEL BECK

After a perfunctory bathe and the whole picnic generally missing fire, we sat down in a "Dancing" with a band to make one scream, and a lot of cakes and whisky. This meal was my lowest hour of the trip. Beck had become completely unintelligible. The brag record was still on. I would hear the same old phrase occasionally: "*Il n'y a qu'un Colonel Beck.*" Duff, to my horror, was dancing (with dignity, thank God). It seemed likely to last until bedtime.

The wars of Troy came to an end one day, and so did this Chinese torture, and 8 o'clock saw us shot of the lot. Dinner *en famille* and *en ville*. Three delicious courses we ate, which by some confusion of language or thought turned out all three to be crayfish, but none the worse for that.

To these letters Conrad replied:

Let me speak only of your second instalment descriptive of Colonel Beck—a literary gem, an intellectual treat. You are a great letter-writer, Diana. You scribble in forty words—punctuation, spelling, syntax, grammar and construction all faulty, I strongly suspect—but the result is: Colonel Beck in his habit as he lived is before me. I might read his life in three volumes but it would only be stuffing and padding and would not tell me anything more essential about him.

The papers announcing the list of dinner parties and balls make it sound like the Congress of Vienna wherever you go. I have wondered many times whether I should enjoy being with you. That your company is dear to me I mention formally. I should not mind ordinary roughness at sea as I could lie quietly in my bunk. "Catting" has no terrors for me. But the awful ceremonial, the Admirals and worse still their wives, dinners, picnics, speeches and healths! It all sounds to me a nightmare. Then the night-club life, champagne and lurching home round 5 a.m. Imagine what a wet blanket I'd be! The kill-joy and no mistake.

My letters continued:

Danzig   *10 August*

This morning it was like waking up in the middle of the Battle of Aboukir—a bombardment of guns from Germans, Poles, Free

Citizens and our own muzzles. We were in the mouth of the Vistula. Duff had a morning of calls and suchlike duties, so Liz and I and Mogs and George and Troubridge paid our first visit to the old town. Have you been to Danzig? It's too beautiful, I think—a baroque Amsterdam, with trees and public buildings like Hatfield and Blickling. Streets and trees and sun and gables and cobbles and inns and steps are what I like best to see—better than a picture or a museum or a waterfall. A street in Venice or Peking, a group of yurts in the Gobi or igloos with squalling Lapps give me more fun than seeing Dante's angel, had he painted it, or reading the volume that Guido Reni treasured.

Lunch on board, while the ship, that had lain all morning in the river mouth, steamed into the middle of the town. A dull afternoon at Zoppot, the *ville d'eau* eight miles out.

Liz receives orchids at every stop from London.

In the evening work began again. Dinner in the Rathaus. Wonderfully rich and beautiful and candle-lit. I sat next Herr President Greiser (unilingual Freeman) and Herr Something-Else (also without French or English). Delicious food and an atmosphere of rich merchants (Venetians, Holbein, velvet coats, orders and Hanseatic League) which maybe I only imagined. Another magnificent candle-lit room for a whoopee with Goltwasser and Kurfürstens. Carl Burckhardt, who is the League-of-Nations-elected Commissioner of Danzig, and whom I have met through Raimund, was not present, but tomorrow will be his day. Herr Blume, a little Dickens character with a bigger English vocabulary than ours and far more jokes and energy, is to be our guide tomorrow.

11 August

I made Duff walk round the old town at 9 this morning. He didn't like doing it much, but was kind. The Frauengasse and Langegasse and the Heiligegeistgasse are so great a delight to me. At 11 Herr Blume and Frau Huth and a nameless Fräulein marched us off for some serious sightseeing—the Marienkirche with an *erste Klasse* Memling in the sacristy representing the Day of Judgment. Herr Blume is one who is not content that the subject of a picture is Jacob and Esau. He likes to tell you the story of Jacob and his father as well, so of course it takes longer. We were fairly whacked by 1 o'clock, but without a breather off we toiled to lunch with Swiss Carl Burckhardt, the League of Nations Commissioner. This was our first civilised meal. He was a great friend of Hugo von Hofmannsthal and talked like him, and his voice and French were so unlike what we have been hearing, and his wife was attractive in a dress painted with all the birds and their names. He was a trifle highbrow for me (you and I once said how often in conversation we felt ourselves to be well out of our depth). I was treading water a bit, he very serious and unsmiling.

George and Duff had a *chasse* with him and the Président du Sénat afterwards, while foolishly we others went to a ghastly castle, four times the size of Windsor, built by the Ritter of the Empire after the Crusades. It was eighty kilometres away, all restored roughly in 1860 and looking exactly like St Pancras. We had Herr Blume with us to lengthen out the tedium, whereas the *chasse* was a splendid turn. A great deal of whisky and *gâteaux* between the flights of duck, a chorus of horns *mit Dirigent*, a speech from the President to beaters and foresters, more corning and horning, while the shooters stood to attention over the bodies of eight melancholy duck.

In the evening we returned hospitality to twenty-four Freemen and women. I had the Commissioner (still unsmiling, intense and interesting) and the President (utterly German-speaking and square). It was as these *Enchantress* dinners always are (dreadful!), but "I think that they enjoyed themselves."

To my surprise when all the guests had gone the glorious Swiss and his wife lingered with the *idée fixe* that the night should not end, and that we must find fun at Zoppot where there was a *soirée de gala*, so off we went minus Duff and spent a few hideous hours in a boiling scrum of monstrous Germans, unpowdered, unbanted and unhaired (it is their own gross tastelessness that makes them so disgustingly ugly and one can with justice blame *them* more than nature), with a band blaring into one's ears. Burckhardt carried on undaunted with his smileless highbrowism, while I trod water and sipped warm champagne. Liz was there and Mrs Burckhardt and her girl-friend, a Pole called Potowski, and George Gage.

At 2 a.m. the host asked us to go shooting with him. "Now?" "Yes, we often shoot at night." "All right." This disconcerted him a little, and finally it was settled to return to his house and discuss possibilities etc. The *chasse* scheme was dismissed, as I had feared it would be. Instead the gramophone was turned on and a little desultory dancing was performed, while his wife and her friend disappeared, I hoped to cook eggs. The wintry talk flowered while dancing from room to room, and I feel that Carl is to be a friend at least. Now it's Friday and we're at sea, thank God, for twenty-eight hours. We need a rest.

Helsingfors   *13 August*

Everything progresses well. It's a life of extremes—ghastly moments and enchanting ones. The one-and-three-quarter days at sea came under "enchanting"—rest after effort, smoothest waters, purest sky, the full moon rising over the starboard side and the sun sinking on the port side. We walked round the rather nice watery town with Russian traces left, and then there was the usual scramble to dress for dinner with the British Minister, Mr Snow. Mrs Snow is everything that is best in British womanhood, long-legged, good, unaffected and serene. He told me that they sit down with Finns at 6 p.m. to a crayfish feast and stay until 2 or 3 a.m. with scarcely a word spoken.

The Air Attaché West, V.C., with a wife and wooden leg, chucked a luncheon party to picnic with us. They told their host that as they could not be back until 4 and as lunch was for 1.30, they'd be too late. "Not a bit," said he. We saw them off at 3.45. They told me later that they'd really got down to it at 5 and I saw them come home at 10.30.

Tonight at the Snows' well-run house I sat between the host and the Finnish Foreign Minister, named Holsti, a darling English-speaking *douce-viveur*. The great Field-Marshal Mannerheim was there. He made Finland and is treated half-royal, half-Godhead. He looks fifty and is said to dye his hair (and Brendan swore that he had rouged lips) and he is only seventy-two. He's old Russian Imperialist (that I find irresistible) and says in French "*Pardon.*" I had never heard of him, had you? Field-Marshal Mannerheim.

FINNS ARE LIKE BEAVERS

We (Snows, Wests and Holsti, our party, the Sub and the Doc) all went on a picnic. Four motorcars. It took place on a high flat rock. The day, as always, was perfect and a large lovely lake shimmered at our feet. Some of us scrambled down a long rocky steep to get a bathe, not so successful as it was quite a shallow lake and grounded with very yielding black slime. I said to my sweet old Holsti: "Do you like picnics?" "Better than anything else in the world," he said, with the sincerity of a saint professing his faith. Everything practical is done by the Cabinet in this country. George wanted a canoe for the sake of exercise. The Minister for Defence was consulted and the Minister of Agriculture for worms and rods. The Foreign Minister is always opening the car-door, and is ready for any odd jobs.

Finns are like beavers. They work in a violent unceasing way for themselves, cutting and building and quarrying silently, and are delighted with the results. They've done a good job in their Parliament House. It's a modern Versailles with a dash of Solon about it. The Members do their lobby-strolling in a really fairy-like *galerie des glaces* of marble and crystal. I suppose that, with all their achievements and pride of independence, they can be chewed up by one of several countries in a jiffy.

The Prime Minister took us over his Senate and his stadium and then it was aboard again to dress for Mannerheim's blow-out. Wonderful house, marvellous food and wines, all of which he arranges, the right flowers, china objects and the right lighting, and after dinner a first-class budding she-pianist. She played everything I liked best and so beautifully that I gave her a handsome jewel off my person. A man said to me at dinner: "In England you have very good cow and pig races." I wish we had!

15 August

Do you know about a Finn-bath? It's world-famous. They steam you up Russian-fashion and then flog you within an inch of your life with birch-rods, and so hurl you into cold water. George and I started the day by walking to the town in quest of this sensation, but when we arrived it was not yet open, so we had to content ourselves with a bit of shopping without words. Trying to get a dish of yoghourt was very funny. I acted milking the cow and cutting a lemon, licking it and putting on a wry face. It worked.

Our dinner tonight on board was rock-bottom. I had Field-Marshal Mannerheim and the Prime Minister. I worked my hardest and so did Troubridge, but it was like working stickjaw; and the food tasted to me filthy because of Mannerheim's epicureanism.

Stockholm *18 August*

Alas, alas! the weather has broken on us—thunder, lightning, torrents, and all the anticipated beauties of land and water in the Swedish approach frustrated. The heavens opened as we actually arrived and it looked very glamorous and Northern Capital, Vasa, Christina, Gustavus Adolphus, Venice of the North. There are many French, Italian and German warships in the harbour, so there was a world-war bombardment.

20 August

Sherry with the Belgian Military Attaché, who is alongside in a tonless yacht. Tom Troubridge said to a guest, pointing at it from our deck during a cocktail party: "These yachts have had a baby. Isn't nature wonderful?" The Swede said: "Please?"

Now we've sailed and it's blowing a gale, but we are in the islands most of the way.

21 August

Duff is poring over *Brighton Rock*. The others don't read at all. Occasionally they pick up *Denmark On £10*, lay it down again and stroll on deck. Flags only looks at an old *Daily Sketch*.

We had the Doc to dinner. He's an Arctic and Antarctic explorer, but hadn't a great deal to say about the poles. Afterwards we played "the game" and I gave them "pemmican" to act and no one except the Doc had heard of it. Don't you think that's surprising? It's household to me.

Copenhagen *22 August*

Arrived in this darling Copenhagen today with weather much improved and aneroid rising. The usual guns and consuls and liaison men, plus the King's yacht and the King on it. He's called the Kong in Danish.

Those boring old Polish destroyers *Thunder* and *Lightning* (British-built) are moored on top of us and play "The Lambeth Walk" on their loudspeakers for the benefit of all hands without any "stand easy." This makes it difficult to concentrate on reading or writing. Back to the ship to pick up Duff and go to that royal little square Amalienborg to write our names on the Kong and then gobble the freshest of shrimps laid on a dairy-bed of butter and white bread, outside the Grand Hotel. Duff likes it better than any capital. What is there that makes it so enchanting? Next came the Rosenborg Museum, where there are life-size lions in silver, and crowns for the Kongs wrought beyond Cellini's art, that disappear into the ground at the first touch of a burglar's thumb.

28 August

Tomorrow will be my last day at sea, and what comes after? Is it war? Or is it Geneva for me?

CHAPTER TWELVE

Days of Dread

IT was Geneva. John Julius's school was over and, armed
with the address of a small hotel on the Lake, recommended
by my delightful new friends the Burckhardts, we packed into
the car, picked up Mademoiselle in Paris and headed for the
city that had always attracted me. There, I knew, the war
skeleton would recede and we should hear good stupefying
peace-talk. I wrote to Conrad:

Geneva   *September 1938*

This is certainly the place for a lady who needs her confidence and
her desirability bolstering up (not that these are the worst of my
worries, but it's a flattering place during an Assembly of the League
of Nations). I haven't seen one woman under sixty and the intellectual boys are just spoiling for diversion.

The whole of my first week was one of complete detachment from
the world. In a half-house by the lake *plage* John Julius, our acrobatic Mademoiselle and I fit in a treat. Our own door and morning
maid (all in the new-age streamline), our own bread, milk, cakes
and Evian to buy in the morning, our own jams and jellies. Flowers
smother us and everything is "Sir Hollywood." Reading, teaching,
rowing, poring over newspapers trying to keep abreast, eat up the
time. After two days Men were let loose into my drowsy sex-numb
life, since when I have never eaten with fewer than five delegates.
Chips is here and Mr R. A. Butler, Mr Peter Locksley (F.O.) and
Mr Hayter there, and another wild charmer (who looks after the
press) called Charles Peake everywhere. MM. Foster and Steven-

son and an Unknown are due tonight. Over and above all this lustre, who should I run into, and needless to say cut until they forced themselves on my dense eyes with "*Ah! elle ne nous reconnait pas*," but my dear beautiful Carl Burckhardt from Danzig and his wife. The Captain [Euan Wallace], alias "The Plunger," arrives tomorrow.

And to Duff:

10 September

Men still grow up from the ground as though dragons' teeth had been sown. Roger Makins (F.O.) today, and the bigwig Halifax on Sunday. Our little boy has a "snivelly cold" but not a "nasty snivelly cold," and he's very gay and good and very like you in many ways, preferring the bar of the Carlton with billiards and drinks and other chaps to exploratory wanderings through old streets and dappled woods.

I'm dreadfully unchic. My equipment was for beach-baking twenty miles away. My car is a disgrace, full of crumbs and silver paper and little pools of old rain. I cut no figure at all, but *there are no other women!*

11 September

We all thirteen of us went into France for lunch outside Divonne (Restaurant Marquis), the party romping-gay on a snow-panorama-ed terrace, Mademoiselle and John Julius at a separate table. On the way back I insisted on us all stopping at Coppet, assuring them that it was a museum. Far from it! The house is privately owned by three *gratin* French sisters, who were today giving a party *de circonstance*, into which the whole motley crowd of us, hatless, in old slacks, open collars, golf-jackets and rather flushed faces, found ourselves hurled before we could collect ourselves into a retreat. A bearded young man said: "We last met in Cairo" and introduced me to the hostesses. I then had to present my crew to fifty people, all over sixty, dressed for a reception or a *goûter*. Agonising it was. The sisters three took us round the entrancing house themselves, and as they are great-granddaughters of Madame de Staël they knew a lot.

DAYS OF DREAD

Two new dragon's teeth were incarnated in Bob Bernays and Buck De La Warr (now head of the Mission in Halifax's place), who joined our dinner throng. Carl told the story of your shoot at Danzig and they all rocked and appreciated him very much. I bridled. I must ask Holsti to a meal and anyone else who entertained us on the Baltic cruise. I half-think of giving a fork-supper in Byron's house, the Villa Diodati, above the Eaux Vives. Carl showed it me. I could have the lovely *salle* lit with candles and get a local restaurant to provide food. It's a scheme that needs courage. What do you think? I must repay. They've all carried me and handled and dandled me like their precious "Luck" and I might, but for doom ahead, have been unusually happy. I've just read Saturday's *Times* from cover to cover and think it looks ink-black, and instead of the fête it's more likely to be the aeroplane or trooptrain.

13 September

The rumour and panic in the Carlton are not quite what you would expect. Only Charles Peake acts with melodramatic activity. He tears in with typewritten bits and pieces that seem to say nothing new (but always equally bad).

Tomorrow I am to be hostess to the British Empire banquet. I wanted to go on a Swiss treat, but Chips is very firm with me.

Just come from visiting Maurice de Rothschild, who used to swim with me in Venice covered with blubber. He still had some on his nose and chin today to cure a fast-generating cold. He was quite unselfconscious about it and snatched kisses as he showed me his monstrous château stacked with Boldini pictures of fine ladies with feet like submarines. I have to lunch with him and his blood-brother Litvinov tomorrow, in exchange for which *supplice* he will give all my boys dinner and Château Yquem.

On Friday I am throwing my Byronic fête in the empty Villa. The room was decorated by Jean Jaquet in *boiserie* and busts. The chairs are covered with chintz that Byron himself chose. John Julius and I have collected sixty candelabra from various *antiquaires*. I've ordered the collation—*consommé chaud, langoustes, pâté de canard de Périgord, entremets, friandises et fruits.*

HIDING THE SKELETON

I must leave this pleasant lea and go and dress for Litvinov, red in tooth and claw. John Julius refuses to lunch up at the Villa. He prefers it down in the Town, so I've had to lie for him. Maurice wanted us three to move into his forbidding mansion for the rest of our days here. I had to explain as best I could that I'd rather die, though I'm really devoted to Maurice—always was and always will be.

A lovely sight-seeing evening last night with Carl in first twilight, then lunatic moonlight, then total darkness, ending up at Lausanne and all that you like in bar and restaurant—an exquisite *truite flambée* for Madame, a *châteaubriand saignant pour Monsieur*. Hanging over this fantastic evening were the spectre words *état de siège* and "ultimatum." We heard them over the strains of "The Lambeth Walk." My Byron festa tomorrow threatens to be another Brussels Ball.

O God! tonight I'm hostess. Buck De La Warr is host. Halifax never came. "Hiding the Skeleton" shall be the name of this party. As neighbour I shall get Mr Bruce of Australia and who else?

Later. No less than President de Valera, who sat on my right. The fussers of the party felt nervous that he might not rise to his feet for the Royal Anthem. I guaranteed to have him standing if I had to take a pin to him. It was a dramatic evening—Charles Peake shuttling in and out with paper messages and whispers, his floating hair and flashing eyes adding to our tension. I remember talking to de Valera about God, and how people pray, and getting on rather happily with him. Too much to say and too tired.

Talking to you on the telephone breaks the diary rhythm. As you know, Geneva is far from being the hub of the world and its crises. It's now an utterly detached *pièce de musée* side-show, like a Quaker society in the Hebrides carrying on its good works alone and unknown. There are serious committees for Disarmament Now and for protection of minorities, and wet blankets for white slaves. Newspapers rarely arrive, but last night when Euan, looking exactly like a dear big schoolboy (which he is), prompted by maniacal-looking Charles Peake, stood up and said that "the Coroner has got his flying-boots on"—in other words the Prime Minister was going to have tea with the Führer—we all felt and smelt Whitehall. For good or bad, we were in touch.

I remember my heart stopping at Euan's pronouncement and the immediate reaction of "This can't be right. Where is Duff to explain and guide?" followed by trying to trust in de Valera's sincere and vehement approval. "The best thing England's ever done," he said. Fears of his slighting the King's health and anthem were forgotten and he stood up with the best of us loyalists.

16 September

Lunch *chez* Maurice was gloomy. Litvinov looked as if he had just drunk blood. Maurice thinks Lord Winterton, when all is said and done, "*un peu coco.*" What could it mean? He couldn't explain, no more could Litvinov, who smelt of garlic so strongly that he couldn't have explained anything to anybody without asphyxiating them.

My party is tonight. I quail. I spent the day transporting candelabra from Town up to Villa and winding rose-wreaths for the busts. Maurice is to supply Montrachet, red Burgundy, Château Yquem, Champagne and Cognac. It's to be a surprise. No one knows but Carl, who is ordered to produce six Swiss Venuses for the delegates' delectation. I remembered suddenly and sadly the need of women. I'll write results tomorrow.

17 September

It was glorious! We even illuminated the big chandelier with redundant candles. Four tables, two waiters, a chef in cap, a barman and a radio for the dance (this last a near-impossibility because of no electricity). The six *indigènes* were breath-taking—Elisabeth Burckhardt in a red Watteau coat—all *hochgeboren* and dressed in Paris with flowers in their hair and a tiger lily round one of their wrists. We were thirty-two strong and I'm sorry to say that forty-two bottles of wine were drunk, excluding the cocktails and *apéritifs* and thirty Armagnacs. It cost a fortune and was worth it. They danced until about 1 (it began at 7.30) and then they moved on to somebody's ball, which is all rather blurry. "I can't remember how I went to bed." I can really. I was deposited relatively intact by a favourite at 2 a.m. Enclosed are two Collinses. Rab's is very winning:

> I write to thank you very much for a delightful party. I thought it was going to be the Eve of Waterloo, only the other way round, and now it's over I'm sure it will be a prelude to preserving "*notre civilisation*," as the Radio and M. Bonnet say.
>
> In one of my most exalted moments I asked an apocryphal figure in white, *la femme du Vice-Consul*, to come with me onto the *balcon* to see the view. I started a verse of Lamartine's "*Le Lac*" but when I looked round, the *balcon* was bare and my partner had ratted. So I went round the garden and down the avenue alone, and thought of the history of the house and wondered where Claire Clairmont's slipper was found, and thought how nice it would be to live there with no Committees of the Assembly.
>
> Yours gratefully,
R. A. BUTLER

> It was the most enjoyable party that members of the Delegation have had within their collective memory. It's unlikely they will ever see its like again or feel as cheerful as they did this morning.
>
> Yours, R. MAKINS.

What was my surprise, on returning to London, to find trenches being dug in parks and gardens. Memory, ever heedless, must now take over this long saga. We were clinging tensely together, so I wrote no letters. All classes of men, collared and uncollared, were excavating, delving and scooping out shelters like so many grave-diggers. The fool's paradise, Geneva, faded with memories of carefree days and blessed sleep at night. How could I have danced and been so gay while Duff was struggling to mobilise the Fleet? In Switzerland we had had no idea of the situation's gravity.

Admiralty House had become a central whorl, the navel of anti-appeasement. Many were suspicious of dealings with the fiend Hitler. The outcome might well be shameful. Anti-Government subversion was knocking at the door. "The country's honour"—was it safe? Mr Chamberlain must not betray it. He must be gingered, he must be gainsaid, he must GO! Where was Winston? Why, stamping to and fro amongst the Admiralty's dolphin furniture, flaming his soul out with his impotence to flout the aggressor in his own way. Duff was the hard core of the bold. Members of Parliament, newspaper allies and old friends darted in and out for meals and through the night—the Oliver Stanleys, Cranbornes, Walter Elliots, Wallaces, Hore-Belisha, Buck De La Warr, Eddie Winterton, Brendan Bracken and Shakes Morrison. They all seemed to hold the same resistant views. "Sound" was the word adopted during the crisis. The unsound, I suppose, kept away from our house, and the waverers talked soundly enough until nearly the end. The King was "sound," Duff opined, after seeing him at a Privy Council meeting. Had he not bought a revolver for practice in Buckingham Palace gardens? Lord Halifax, the Foreign Secretary, was said to be sound, so was France (in spite of the jitters of M. Bonnet, the Foreign Minister), the Vatican, the United States, the Commonwealth and the majority of the rank and file. The press was stout-hearted enough save for the timid *Times* and the *Daily Express*'s persistent prophecies of peace. Why, then, was the situation deteriorating, Sir Eric Phipps panicking in Paris, Sir Nevile Henderson hysterical in Berlin, and appeasement gaining ground in 10 Downing Street?

My own condition was deteriorating fast. Fear did more harm to my physique than to my morale. Sleep was murdered for ever. My heart quaked, yet I must appear valiant. My hands shook, so work must be found to steady them. Always a pessimist, I could imagine nothing worse than what must happen perhaps tomorrow—war, death, London utterly demolished, frantic crowds stampeding, famine and disease. That sadistic scientist Victor Rothschild took pleasure in watching me writhe at his calculations of blast and his reasoned prophecies of annihilation by gas and germ-warfare. (It is surprising that I still delight in him.) The Prime Minister had gone to Godesberg. The sands were running out. More trenches were appearing. An expert, naturally without experience, came to prescribe measures of safety for Admiralty House— more hoses, sandbags, emergency measures of all kinds. We knew that precautions were of no avail. Victor had said so, but we took them all the same, in the way that one touches wood or crosses fingers.

I had found daytime occupation at the W.V.S., a body some years old, of voluntary women who gave their services to a wide number of causes. Lady Reading, its begetter, had organised her helpers to assemble gas-masks for civilians, so Venetia Montagu and I sat in the Tothill Street workrooms clamping snouts and schnozzles on to rubber masks, parcelling them and distributing them to queues of men and women. Mothers would ask me for small ones for children. There were none as yet. I felt sick all the time, like many others, no doubt. It was a grisly job for a neurotic but better than inaction.

Duff kept a firm lid on his boiling indignation, but I could hear it singing and spitting. It gave him sleepless nights. He must have been a barbed thorn in the tangle of Cabinet meetings, obstructing and clamouring, and an exasperation to his leader, who had never liked him. The Prime Minister, still in Godesberg, had left no authority for the mobilisation of the Army or of the Fleet, which preparation for sudden war required. Without it Duff took much upon himself, recalling sailors from leave and dispatching them to man the Suez defences. On Mr Chamberlain's return, bearing worse terms for Czechoslovakia, Duff told me that it was time he left the Government. This seed of resignation was sown after the first visit to Hitler. The political soil generated it fast. He told the Prime Minister, after a Cabinet meeting, of his intention. Mr Chamberlain was, he said, not surprised and probably relieved, but asked for no precipitate action. He struck Duff as a man bewitched and bound by Hitler's magnetic spell.

That same day the scene was changed. It was planned to send the Grey Eminence, Horace Wilson, on another visit to Hitler with an ultimatum. If the demands were not accepted, he must be told that France would fight for the Czechs and so would we. Duff came back from Downing Street elated and scarcely able to believe his ears. On hearing that the Prime Minister had gone to confer with the Opposition, he hastened to offer his resignation in another shape. He was, he said, should his office be required, prepared to serve Mr Chamberlain in a lesser position or as a private Member of Parliament. I was elated too, although I did not like the thought of Duff resigning from the Navy that he loved, or of leaving the beautiful house that I felt should last longer as our home. It was wonderfully fortunate for me and my peace of mind that, having absolute faith in Duff and his acts and motives, any questioning of them was unthinkable and exerting influence upon them not to be dreamt of.

An account of these dread days is clearly and excitingly set down in *Old Men Forget*, so I will tell only of my own part and emotions at this time. Calm old friends came and went among the distracted politicians, or sat to hold my hand and to praise Duff. Conrad was there, and Venetia, Hutchie, George Gage and others. An unreasoned optimism lasted for a short spell. Leslie Hore-Belisha bet Duff £2 to £1 that there would be no war. Brendan Bracken bet him an even fiver. Hitler had made a speech that Winston thought was a retreat. This pronouncement was seized upon, and "He's on the run!" was the cry, but Horace Wilson somehow muffed the strong line and the flash of hope died out.

Duff was fighting as never before to get the Fleet mobilised, so that Germany should have proof of our intentions. The Prime Minister reluctantly promised to announce it on the radio on 27 September. We listened to the broadcast—Duff, George Gage, Venetia and I—sprawled over my dolphined bed. There was no word of mobilisation. Winston telephoned almost inarticulate with rage. The speech, he said, was a preparation to "scuttle."

Many talked of resignation next day, but I felt that only Duff would act. The Fleet, however, *was* mobilised, with our anticipated reaction from Germany—Munich. On the afternoon of 28 September Lady Reading flung open the door of the snout-and-schnozzle assembling room and announced that the agony was over. The Prime Minister was to fly next morning for his third meeting with Hitler, which could only mean settlement and peace. Many of us burst into tears, and then laughed hilariously—the laughter that follows narrow escape from death. We finished our shift, nevertheless, and I ran the short distance to the Horse Guards Parade on winged feet. At dinner that night were Winston, Walter Elliot, the Cranbornes, Barbie Wallace and Hutchie. It was the first cheerful evening since I had returned from Geneva. At dawn next day the Cabinet and their wives drove down to Heston air-field to cheer the Prime Minister out of port. Our spirits soared in the half-light. He carried our prayers and wishful trust.

On the 30th the Munich terms were in the papers. Duff read them and decided to resign. In the evening the thunder of cheering, that I longed to be part of, filled our ears from White-hall. The Prime Minister called at the Palace to announce his so-called triumph to the King and Queen. They were photo-graphed on the balcony on each side of him (a photograph that I saw next day torn and burnt in the fireplace by a man of principle). The Mall and Whitehall, I could imagine from the noise, held millions of joy-mad people, swarming up the lamp-posts and railings, singing and crying with relief and belief that it was peace and never another war. Duff and I sat on my bed holding hands and staring at the monstrous-faced radio. That evening he resigned and next morning took leave of his leader. "I think he was as glad to be rid of me," Duff wrote afterwards, "as I was determined to go."

I telephoned the news to Winston, whose voice broke with emotion. I could hear him crying. Many people felt bitterly about Duff's action. He had stained a perfectly radiant day and made some feel outraged and others conscience-struck. My pride in him glowed brightly, but there was much to be faced and much to be lost. A friend in Paris wrote to Lord Louis Mountbatten:

I did not think that one solitary statesman of the four Powers who sold Czechoslovakia could possibly emerge with honour from the crisis, but yesterday your First Lord emerged with great honour.

Captain Frend of the *Enchantress* wrote to Duff:

If you had been on board when the news came through, you would have appreciated how much you are respected and liked by all on board by the gloom that descended on the "little ship."

DUFF RESIGNS

I was in the House of Commons to hear Duff's speech of resignation. Such speeches come before any other business, and the House was impatient to get it over and listen to Mr Chamberlain, the hero of the day. What Duff said was masterly and moving. A note from Winston was handed to him as soon as he sat down: "Your speech was one of the finest Parliamentary performances I have ever heard. It was admirable in form, massive in argument and shone with courage and public spirit." From the Left Josiah Wedgwood wrote: "Love and admiration more than you have dreamt of will I hope compensate for loss of office and salary. Anyhow this old colleague from better days is proud of you. Also I think it is a good spot on a bad page of English history. I do dislike belonging to a race of clucking old hens and damned cowards." *The Times* Lobby Correspondent, a dear friend called Anthony Winn, reported Duff's speech and what had been thought of it. His account did not accord with the policy of the paper. It was therefore suppressed and a piece by the Editor inserted instead, headed "From our Lobby Correspondent," describing the speech as "a damp squib." Anthony Winn resigned next day.

I am truthful when I say that what sadness I felt for the loss of Duff's position, the beautiful house and the yacht that went with it, and all its many splendours and advantages, was immediately comforted by my relief and pride—relief that at last was laid the spectre often with me of ambivalence, a spectre laden with doubts and fear of borrowed judgment. Many of the political wives with wavering husbands were sure and unbending as steel. Should I have been so trusty without Duff's fiery lead? This haunting bogey was forgotten anyway for a while. Lord and Lady Stanhope succeeded to the dolphins and the improvements, Captain Cook's paintings, the

Nelson bust and relics. The mermaid came with me. Duff's name was added to the graven tablet of First Lords and his picture hung in the passage. After a few weeks of answering, with my help and five secretaries, the many thousand letters from Czechoslovakia and all parts of the world, we left the Admiralty for ever and spent a quiet week at Trianon. I remember being very happy, proud and calm. The lovely autumn days healed and strengthened us. The statues and groves were half-buried in dead leaves. There was a refreshing melancholy in the past glories. Daisy Fellowes lent us her motor-car. We read aloud and went occasionally to Paris for a play. The Aga Khan, a true friend for twenty-five years, took us to dinner at a famous country restaurant and stayed arguing about Munich at our hotel until 4 a.m. "Why did you do it, dear boy?" he reiterated, "Why did you do it?" As an avowed admirer of Hitler he could not see the case against appeasement.

Our honeymoon over, we moved into the house that my mother had built for me with loving thought and ingenuity. 34 Chapel Street was a little too elaborate and above the capacity of our straitened fortunes. Duff on his resignation had been offered a lucrative engagement to lecture in the United States, but had refused it, as he had already agreed to write for a year a weekly article in the *Evening Standard*. He had suggested the autumn of 1939 as an alternative date for the lecture-tour. These contracts should help us to realise Rex Whistler's design for our library. The work was started, but nine months was not enough to give it birth, and for reasons of war it was never finished.

The New Year took me and John Julius to the snows, to Mont Genève, where Hannibal crossed into Italy goading his elephants before him. Across the frontier in blatant letters was written: *"Mussolini a sempre ragione."* I told John Julius never to forget the idiocy of the words.

I wrote to Duff:

My nerve has gone. It's the humiliation of not being able to pick myself up which is so mortifying. Whether my muscles are degenerating or whether the snow is in too engulfing a condition to allow my anyway diseased limbs (Herb's disease) and doubly-broken leg to fight it I don't know. I do know that I'm the picture of Humpty Dumpty and often too in-pieces to rise. If people are passing I have to be dealt with as Sir John Falstaff would have been. Two helpers pulling, others excavating the snow beneath and levering me up, and then crash! I go down again as I'm saying *"Merci."*

I feel better. I could not forbear flying at Mademoiselle for telling me how tired I looked, *"et beaucoup, beaucoup changée."* Is it drink and rich food? Is it escapism? Is it climate? How can I be acutely and absurdly miserable in England? And so conscious of the weight of misery falling from me like Christian's burden when away? It's perplexing and despairing, for I want to love my life as it deserves to be loved. I can be utterly thankful for my condition and above all things for you. Age doesn't worry me, or deterioration, loss of lovers, death of friends. It's introspection, disease of apprehension, lack of interest. Try and guide me, my darling.

Ideal snow conditions. John Julius and I have not gone back since last year. That isn't to say that we are not disastrously bad and quite uncontrolled. It's the air and *light* above everything that make prowess always within one's grasp, and then never being tired surprises. You can wake in the morning or after a rest quite battered, feeling that you can't ever move again and don't want to. Then as soon as your eyes see and your feet touch the snow you are whole and light and jubilantly active. Perhaps the snow's a witch like the sea or a South Sea island and takes you from all you love and all stability, and finally smothers you and keeps you for centuries in regions of thick ribbed ice, and sends you imperceptibly back to the dust of the earth.

No letter from you. Two from Conrad, but he writes ahead as Mother always did.

John Julius plays a game of geography with all the French children. It's just what I want for his language. They gabble and scream. I have to invent questions for the places on the map. The booklet that goes with the game is too advanced. Edmond (a boy of eleven) has never heard of Chicago. His father didn't know Mecca. John Julius always knows Port au Prince and Banff and Antananarivo.

It's going to snow. As I opened my window, which is the whole of one end of the room, it was fog that bulged in instead of the light of immense stars.

Later. It snowed and snowed and now the sun is breaking through and all my room is full of sun and cloud. Clouds are racing across, sometimes over my bed. It's like a fairy dream or even a stage effect portraying the River of Life or Eternity or delirium.

The snows melted and brought us back to the last year of uneasy peace. An optimistic calm lay upon England to the casual observer, but behind many doors anxiety was waxing. We waited for war. Duff was writing his weekly articles for the *Evening Standard* and, according to one of the many letters fulminating with abuse that he received, "keeping his fellow-countrymen in a constant state of jittery anticipation, and endlessly fanning the flames of prejudice and hatred against the wicked Nazis on account of their supposed acts of aggression." He received too a remarkable letter from his brother-in-law, Herbert Hindenburg, nephew of the Marshal (to me "Uncle Paul"). Duff's half-sister, Marie Hay, had been married to this German for forty amicable years, and had just died. His letter berated Duff for his outrageous attitude towards the Führer and asked him on the same page to do all he could to advertise his (Herbert's) newly published memoirs. His dead wife he did not mention. Staunch Tommy Bouch was meanwhile writing a stinging letter to our constituency agent, repudiating the Conservative Party and withdrawing his subscription.

March brought us the occupation of Prague by the Germans and soon after, on Good Friday, the Italians crashed into Albania. Cassandra's prophecies come true were infuriating our opponents and inexplicably solidifying their heads. We waited in our new house in Chapel Street and at our Bognor cottage. There was a general rather sinister tendency not to make summer plans. I see that we went to Paris in April for a meeting of Pan-Europa. Coudenhove-Kalergi (the movement's mainspring) was one of my heroes—good news from Tartary. In him East and West met most felicitously, both physically and spiritually. A big Paris theatre had been taken and hung with Utopian flags. I sat in a box with Madame Kalergi, who blacked out my senses by telling me she felt sure that either my husband or hers (or both) would at any moment be killed on the platform by a bomb.

In June I must have felt a flash of hope, or the need for a flutter, so I visited the school at Le Rosay where only very tentative arrangements could be made for John Julius's year abroad. I wrote to Conrad:

In the train   *June 1939*

It's Geneva ho! I'm off to see about John Julius's school and to look at the Velasquezes still cowering in some gallery, safe from their Civil War.

I'm enjoying ecstatically the fun and bustle of the journey which I've arranged in a flash to my individual taste, i.e. the most uncomfortable way possible and the cheapest. I've left Victoria with very little money (banks were shut) and I board the Dieppe boat at 9.45 p.m. (second class). At 2 a.m. I get on the Paris train which I get out of at 6.30 a.m. I cross Paris and catch the 7.30 a.m. to Geneva, arriving 3ish p.m. I go straight to the Exhibition and on to the school, dine with Carl, perhaps do some sightseeing by night, and at dawn catch the train back to Paris, take in Anthony Eden's lecture and dine with ultra-"sound" Mr Michael Wright, catch the first train next morning to the Newhaven boat, stop off to tell Maurice the news at Rottingdean, have my car driven by the egregious Holbrook to meet me there, and roll up at Bognor at 6.30. Not everyone's idea of fun, but perfect for me!

I've got no French language, which makes me fearful, embarrassed, tongue-tied and befogged with Carl. That's the fly in my ointment. Then I have two books about Byron ("*Ne crede Byron*"), the crossword, and I sure feel larky. How will the farmer take it? Admiringly, I hope, with only a *soupçon* of jealousy. I wouldn't want you to spur me on as a husband does—and did.

I began to write to you as I would to a foreign lover (or as I mean you to think that I do), starting "*Mon cher amour*," but truth to tell I couldn't get on with it, because I can't write a love-letter in French or English or any language. I can only "say it" in loving looks, in ways and service, in sacrifice and fortitude, and sometimes on the telephone. The "Captain" can say it in masculine cries, and Lord Adare says it (to me) in Limerick sausages. Carl says it in conundrums. You say it best in letters, in words, in desire to please, in butter and eggs, Easter eggs and jimmy o' goblins, my sweet farmer. Heaven! I hear the tinkling tongue of ten. Lovers, to bed!

Now were the days numbered and we were counting them by the shore of the sea that no longer served us as a wall. Near by in the Sussex Downs lived Euan with his wife and five sons. The days were long and, as I see them now, particularly radiant. I remember feeling that all they lit had the poignancy of a child that has to die. At Horsham was Hilaire Belloc, wonderfully detached from events of dread, still singing and discoursing and rollicking and concealing his Christ-like attributes. Maurice Baring at Rottingdean was enduring with saintly fortitude a slow and merciless overthrow. Weekly I went to see him sitting in his garden and later bedridden by his painful paralysis. He did not yearn for death, though every day was racking and his nights were without rest. His valiance was never daunted. He could no longer write, and to hold a book was all but impossible. Two little triolets I must record:

My body is a broken toy
Which nobody can mend.
Unfit for either play or ploy,
My body is a broken toy,
But all things end.
The siege of Troy
Came one day to an end.
My body is a broken toy
Which nobody can mend.

My soul is an immortal toy
Which nobody can mar.
An instrument of praise and joy,
My soul is an immortal toy
Which nobody can mar.
Though rusted from the world's alloy
It glitters like a star.
My soul is an immortal toy
Which nobody can mar.

(These poems may be misquoted. Lord Ribblesdale, the "Picturesque Peer" painted in Sargent's best manner at the Tate Gallery, told me, when I was too young to believe him, that it was gentlemanly to get one's quotations very slightly wrong. In that way one unprigged oneself and allowed the company to correct one.)

These visits, which had continued for years, used to make me dreadfully sad. I would dress my best to please him (for he had high standards of a grander epoch) and gather a load of gossip and jokes and secrets and plans for better days (he never gave up hope), but for all his laughter and good spirits I felt my offerings insufficient and beggarly, and myself a shadow of what I wanted to be. He had a nurse who devoted her life to him at the expense of her family happiness, and a blue budgerigar called Dempsey who sat on his head or shoulder night and day, chattering unintelligibly into his ear, making to Maurice perfect sense that he communicated to me—often whole lines in the Chinese tradition: "The pear-blossom floats on the sad waters where alone I sit."

During these last two months of summer the apocalypse was shadowed ahead as certainly as the twilight signals the night. I do not suppose that the people who came to laugh and bathe and drink and picnic at Bognor can have felt quite as despondent, quite so near yielding to despair, as I did, but they too were doubtless in disguise. I was lucky in that my son was still so young, and my husband too old for the Army, but I counted myself no happier than my sister Letty or Barbie Wallace, each with five sons, for death I knew was to take the lot of us without discrimination like the peoples of Sodom and Gomorrah, suddenly by fire and cataclysm, without quarter, without dignity. Many of our circle had already died. Edwin Montagu, then Michael Herbert and his brother Sidney, had been pressed into untimely graves. Others had joined our company—the Ronald Trees, Rothschilds, Cranbornes and Walter Elliots. My nephews and nieces were growing up. Liz Paget, by marrying Raimund von Hofmannsthal, had made him legally one of our closest. The colours of our private society flew bravely enough. Our last picnic on Ha'nacker Hill betrayed no faint hearts. There on the green Sussex Down stood the old mill, its sweepers gone, its clapper still:

Ha'nacker Hill is in Desolation:
   Ruin a-top and a field unploughed.
And Spirits that call on a fallen nation
   Spirits that loved her calling aloud:
   Spirits abroad in a windy cloud.

MY CONTEMPTIBLE IDEA

Spirits that call and no one answers;
  Ha'nacker's down and England's done.
Wind and Thistle for pipe and dancers
  And never a ploughman under the Sun.
  Never a ploughman. Never a one.

A favourite Belloc poem, often recited by him and by us, had
come true, I felt.

On that day in August I saw the picture of desolation as
clear as truth and, as I thought, for the last time. A contemptible idea kept tapping in my mind, hard to accept and impossible to banish, an idea that I could not share with Duff until
it forced me to confess. It was possessing every part of me as
I stared at the old mill and as we opened our hampers and
grabbed merrily for food and Austrian white wine with which
to toast the future.

The next day, 1st September, found John Julius and me
bustling down Bognor High Street buying sweets, my Idea
and presaging voices muted by the lively crowd and the
laughing boy when, out of the emptiness of a parked motor-
car, I heard the radio's smug and soulless announcement
that Germany had invaded Poland.

There was no doubt whatever in my mind that this meant
the Second War. Duff would be killed in a trench in France,
so would all the mothers' sons. It would be 1914 repeated,
ending with total obliteration. Yet the dread and anticipation
of despair armed me for the first assault. The news meant little
enough to John Julius, bent on the thrills of the Fun Fair,
and truth to tell a resigned calm fell upon me. Before so world-
shaking a catastrophe time stops, the stormed mind reels and
lags, waiting for pain to penetrate. The communiqué's words
turning repeatedly and almost meaninglessly in my head, we

bought lobsters for Duff's dinner, somehow dodged the Fun Fair and returned home to await worse alarms—to wait for the declaration of war, for Duff to put on his old khaki and march off, followed by my seven nephews and Rex Whistler, to an obscure and muddy death, while the rest of us, frantic with terror, jammed and static in a narrow exodus, were bombed to extermination beneath our razed towns. I had forgotten that Duff was nearly fifty and no longer svelte. So apparently had he, for already a month before he had been to his tailor and ordered a Second Lieutenant's first-war Brigade of Guards uniform, puttees, Sam Browne, tin hat, water-bottle and all. His touching preparations for war had wrung my heart and bowels as completely as thoughts of a million casualties.

And there he was at the cottage door, looking for all the world relieved. He had spent the morning at Goodwood playing golf very badly and without power to concentrate. In the club-house after the round he had found two men, one of whom he knew, discussing future race-meetings. As he left the bar, one man had said, "Hitler started on Poland this morning." Duff asked him his meaning. He replied that the Germans had invaded Poland and bombed several cities. He then turned back to his friend and went on talking about the St Leger. "That was how I heard," wrote Duff in his diary, "that the second World War had begun. As we drove back to Bognor my heart felt lighter than it had felt for a year."

That afternoon we returned to London. The black-out had extinguished any demonstration of patriotism or pacifism. We dined with Winston Churchill, his daughter Diana and her husband, Duncan Sandys. Winston told us confidentially that he had already been invited to join Mr Chamberlain's Government. On leaving the Savoy Grill, lost in the unfamiliar and total darkness, we were nearly run down and kindly succoured

by an outsize car in which sat the Duke of Westminster, the
"Bendor" I had once loved. It was an uncomfortable salvation.
He started by abusing the Jewish race, a red-rag subject where
Duff was concerned. When from this dangerous ground he
plunged confidently on through some defences into praise of
the Germans, rejoicing that we were not yet at war, and when
he added that Hitler knew after all that we were his best friends,
he set off the powder-magazine. "I hope," Duff spat, "that by
tomorrow he will know that we are his most implacable and
remorseless enemies." Next day "Bendor," telephoning to a
friend, said that if there were a war it would be entirely due to
the Jews and Duff Cooper.

The next day to me was confusion. Duff, greatly disturbed
by another "scuttle" speech of the Prime Minister's, had again
lost all serenity. While he hurried from the House of Commons to Winston's and to his own "group" meeting, which
included Anthony Eden, Bob Boothby, Brendan Bracken and
Duncan Sandys, a dramatic thunderstorm broke over London.
Conspiracy was in the air. Winston, and only Winston, can
save the country! The heavens themselves were blazing forth
the death of something, while Brutus and the rest plotted
through the night.

I, meanwhile, was saying goodbye to my new house, wondering what precautions were worth taking, whether to buy
reels of sticky tape to criss-cross over the window-panes, what
to leave to brimstone and what to try to preserve by evacua-
tion. The American tour had been quite forgotten. War (an
act of God) annuls contracts, and preparations had never really
begun.

On Sunday the 3rd, war was declared. Duff was not with
me to hear the Prime Minister's announcement, and at noon I
heard the unmistakable banshee-wail of the Alert. I knew

that the first bomb would kill Duff, but it did not fall on the Members as they walked to the House of Commons (faster than usual), and the All Clear caught them at Prayers. We returned that day to Bognor. Duff's reaction, I knew, would be fierce, frustrated and difficult to soothe. My Idea would resolve everything. A moment must be chosen during the ensuing days when I must tell him my solution. That week he expressed his dejection and zest in a moving poem, which he published in *Old Men Forget*. It ended:

> More gladly though would we give all
> That yet we have to give.
> Oh, let the old men man the wall,
> And let the young men live.
>
> It may not be. Not ours to fight,
> Not unto us, O Lord,
> Shall twice in life be given the right
> To serve thee with the sword.
>
> Yet our deep love and fierce desire
> Must aid our country still—
> The steadfast faith, the quenchless fire,
> Th'unconquerable will.

While these sentiments in his heart and head ordered themselves into metre, I could only think of Death. Death was the Idea, and solemnly, in complete sincerity, I proposed a suicide pact. I should be more ashamed of my dastardly poltroonery if Duff with his love and his laugh and his poem had not cleared my brain of its disorder and fortified my unsound mind in the twinkling of his eye. So, banging my doors against Death, his scythe and his hourglass, Death whom I had summoned, we slept on new plans and more lively ideas.